Hinduism Today

Continuum *Religion Today*

These useful guides aim to introduce religions through the lens of contemporary issues, illustrated throughout with examples and case studies taken from lived religion. The perfect companion for the student of religion, each guide interprets the teachings of the religion in question in a modern context and applies them to modern-day scenarios.

Available now:
Judaism Today, Dan Cohn-Sherbok

Forthcoming:
Christianity Today, George D. Chryssides
Islam Today, Ron Geaves
Sikhism Today, Jagbir Jhutti-Johal

Hinduism Today

Stephen Jacobs

continuum

Continuum International Publishing Group
The Tower Building
11 York Road
London SE1 7NX

80 Maiden Lane
Suite 704
New York NY 10038

www.continuumbooks.com

British Library Cataloguing-in-Publication Data
A catalogue record for this book is available from the British Library.

ISBN: HB: 978-0-8264-4027-3
PB: 978-0-8264-3065-6

Library of Congress Cataloging-in-Publication Data
Jacobs, Stephen.
Hinduism today / Stephen Jacobs.
p. cm.
Includes bibliographical references and index.
ISBN 978-0-8264-3065-6 — ISBN 978-0-8264-4027-3 1. Hinduism—Social aspects. 2. Globalization—Religious aspects—Hinduism. I. Title.

BL1215.S64J33 2010
294.5—dc22

2009050326

Typeset by Free Range Book Design & Production
Printed and bound in Great Britain by CPI Antony Rowe Ltd, Chippenham, Wiltshire

Contents

Acknowledgements

Many people have helped and supported me in the writing of this book. First and foremost is my wife Judith Wester, without whose patience and support I would not have been able to complete it. I would like to thank everyone at Sivananda Ashram for all their gracious hospitality, and their willingness to answer questions from someone who is not a *sadhāka*. Particular thanks must go to Swami Gurupriyananda for allowing me to participate in the *abhiṣeka*, and for his wonderful explanation of this ritual. Thank you to Manoj and all his family for welcoming me into their home and including me in their evening *pūjā*. Thanks also go to my good friends Swami Prasadji and Amit Bhatnagar for long conversations and being expert guides. I must also acknowledge everyone at the Madras Café, not only for the excellent sustenance, but also for their friendly welcome, useful advice and allowing me to use the premises as my office during my time in Rishikesh. In Delhi, I thank Sanjay and Neeta Deewan for their warm welcome into their home. Thank you to everyone at the Shri Venkateswara (Balaji) Temple at Tividale, and in particular Dr Rao and Ram Aithal. Everyone at the Shree Krishan Mandir in Wolverhampton has also always made me very welcome; in particular I must acknowledge Mr Bhardwaj (who very tragically and suddenly died whilst I was working on this book), Mr D. L. Chadha and Pandit Madhu Shastri. I also have to thank George Chyssides, Ron Geaves and Annie Conder for conversations and very helpful suggestions. Thank you to Fi Rowe for her meticulous and thorough proofreading. Also thank you to Tom Crick and Kirsty Schaper at Continuum and Nick Fawcett for all his work editing the manuscript.

For Brendan and Jean

Hinduism Today

Image courtesy of Mohan Ayer (2009)
www.hindugallery.com

Hail to thee of auspicious form, whose
head is crowned with a garland of stars ...
I adore thy trunk flung up straight in the
joy of the dance, so as to sweep away the clouds.
Destroyer of obstacles, I worship thy snake-
adorned body ... the treasure house of all success.
(Cited in Grewal, 2001, p. 101)

Introduction

The central concern of this book is to identify what Hinduism is as a lived religious tradition, and to give a sense of what it means to be a Hindu in today's world. This is clearly a very ambitious task, as Hinduism is such a diverse and complex religious tradition. There is no doubt that those people who identify themselves as Hindus and belonging to a religious tradition called Hinduism understand and practise this in a startling diversity of ways. The ascetics who spend their lives wandering from pilgrimage place to pilgrimage place, the austere philosopher monks pondering the nature of reality, the followers of transnational *gurus* such as Satya Sai Baba, the shopkeepers who always offer incense to an image of a deity before opening their shops, the priests who perform complex rituals in temple; all regard themselves as Hindus, yet their religious practices appear to be totally different and their conceptions of what it means to be a Hindu seem to be radically divergent.

Yet underlying this mélange is what the cultural commentator Raymond Williams calls, 'a structure of feeling'. Williams (1988, p. 90) suggests that culture can be understood to indicate 'a way of life'. Interestingly, many Hindus refer to their tradition as being 'a way of life' rather than a religion. Williams, in his seminal work *The Long Revolution* (1980), argues that any formal description can never fully capture the sense of a culture as the lived reality of a people. This lived reality that evades formal description is best understood as a structure of feeling, which Williams (1980, p. 64) maintains 'is as firm and definite as 'structure' suggests, yet it operates in the most delicate and least tangible parts of our activity'. Short of giving you directions to the nearest Hindu temple or including a plane ticket to India, I hope that this book, which is of course a formal description, will convey some idea of the structure of feeling of the kaleidoscopic phenomenon that is known as Hinduism.

I have attempted to convey a sense of this structure of feeling, not only by describing certain aspects of Hinduism, but also by relating a number of the stories that are so integral to the Hindu world. I have also referred to some of the rich visual imagery that is also fundamental to gaining any understanding of Hinduism. I would totally endorse Diana Eck's (1985, p. 17) statement: 'Since India has "written" prolifically in its images, learning to read its mythology and iconography is a primary task for the student of Hinduism.'

While the primary focus of this book is about Hinduism as a lived and vibrant religious tradition in today's world, it is not possible to gain a sense of Hinduism today without some sense of the past. Consequently, I have also on occasion provided some historical contextual material. A book like this is also necessarily a selective account. The selection is primarily based on my own personal encounters with Hinduism, both in India and in Britain. However, this is supplemented by other specific ethnographic studies.

Chapter 1 introduces you to some of the basic aspects that any student of Hinduism will have to know. This chapter outlines some of the historical context and indicates the ways in which Hinduism has developed and changed over the millennia, making it what it is today. It introduces you to some of textual sources, beliefs and practices of Hinduism. Chapter 2 develops some of the themes raised in the first chapter, primarily through a case study. The case study is based in a small town in northern India called Rishikesh, which can be thought of as a window into the Hindu world. Rishikesh is a vibrant town of temples, shrines, pilgrims, ashrams, monks and ascetics, located in the foothills of the holy Himalayas and on the banks of the sacred river Ganges.

The third chapter looks at some more specific issues for Hinduism today. The focus of this chapter is on caste, gender and politics. The major theme that unifies these three important issues is the concept of *dharma*. In many ways, this chapter explores relationships, both within the Hindu community and between Hindus and others. The next two chapters look at what might be called the expansion of the Hindu world. In particular, these chapters explore how Hinduism today might be considered to be both a product and an agent of what is sometimes referred to as globalization. Chapter 4 specifically considers the impact that changes in the media context has had on the ways in which Hinduism is understood and practised. It raises questions about the influence that new technologies such as television and the internet have had on what is often regarded as primarily being an oral tradition. This chapter also looks at some of the groups that now have a global following.

Chapter 5 examines Hindu communities that are based outside of India. This chapter is again a case study, focused on the Hindu community in Wolverhampton in the West Midlands. The wider question raised in this chapter is what impact, if any, the move from the original context to a totally new cultural context has had on the ways in which Hinduism is understood and practised. Finally, the last chapter will try to give some indication of how current trajectories are likely to continue into the future.

A Note on Terminology

Hindu texts are composed in a variety of languages; however, Sanskrit (*sanskṛtam*) – literally 'polished, refined' – retains a special place in Hinduism. The *Vedas* and other important texts are composed in Sanskrit. Sanskrit is a member of the Indo-European family of languages to which most European and many of the Indian languages belong. These languages derive from a single language, which no longer exists, known as 'Proto-Indo European'. Apart from Hittite, Sanskrit is the oldest surviving language of this family. Sanskrit was the language of the people known as the Ārya, and is no longer used in everyday conversation. Only a few people actually study Sanskrit any more, and most Hindus do not know any Sanskrit. However, it is still used in many rituals, and there are many important Sanskrit terms that are widely used to indicate particular religious ideas. Some of these terms, such as *karma*, have even been incorporated into the English language. Translation inevitably entails a degree of interpretation that does not do justice either to the term in its original language or to the term in its translated form. For example, the Sanskrit term *Brahman* cannot be adequately translated as God without distorting the deeper meaning of both terms. I have tried to keep the terminology to a minimum, and where possible introduce these terms with a roughly equivalent English translation followed by the Sanskrit term in brackets. I have also provided a glossary of terms at the end of the book.

Furthermore, Sanskrit is written in a script known as *Devanāgarī*, which has 50 letters. There is now an accepted convention of diacritical marks when transliterating *Devanāgarī* into Roman letters. For example 'a' is pronounced as in the word b*u*t, and ā is pronounced as in the word f*a*ther. For the most part I have utilized the diacritic conventions and not anglicized the spelling. For example, I have indicated the spelling Kṛṣṇa, not Krishna as it is often written.

The image at the front of this book is of the deity Ganesh. He is perhaps the most popular of all the deities in the Hindu pantheon. As the verse below the image indicates, he is regarded as the remover of obstacles and the bringer of success. He is often propitiated before embarking on any new venture. I hope that he will remove any obstacles in your venture of trying to gain an understanding of Hinduism today.

Chapter 1

Hinduism: The Basics

Hinduism can be said to be the oldest and at the same time the youngest of the so-called world religions. It can be argued that it is the oldest surviving religion in the world as its roots can possibly be traced back to the third millennium BCE.[1] The claim that Hinduism might be thought of as being the youngest world religion is based on the observation made by many scholars that the nineteenth century was the first time when the term Hinduism was used to signify a single religious tradition. In order to understand the idea that Hinduism is both young and old at the same time, it is necessary to explore the etymology of the term and the diversity that is subsumed under the umbrella of Hinduism.

Etymology

The term Hindu derives from the Indo-Aryan term *sindhu*, which is generally translated as 'river'. In Persian this term became 'hindu', and this was used as a designation for the river that is now known as the Indus, which flows through the northwest of the subcontinent, in present-day Pakistan. The term then came to be used to indicate the land through which the Indus flowed and the people living in that area. In other words the term 'Hindu' was in origin a term that was coined by outsiders to designate a territory and the population of that territory, and had no cultural or religious significance.

In the eighth century CE Muslims began to make their presence felt on the subcontinent, and some of the indigenous population converted to Islam. Consequently, the term Hindu came to indicate those who lived in the region who were not Muslims. In this period, the term Hindu was not used to indicate either a self-designated identity or a unified religious community. The term Hindu gradually began to acquire a more narrow definition signifying Indians who were clearly not Muslims, Christians, Sikhs, Parsis or Buddhists. Eventually, in the nineteenth century, the term Hindu acquired the suffix 'ism' and it came to be considered as being a single unified religious tradition.

It can be argued that to represent Hinduism as a religion is also a misconception. There is no word in any of the Indian languages that is directly equivalent to the English word 'religion'. There are a number of terms that have religious connotations, but these are not precisely captured by the term 'religion' either. Consequently, to label Hinduism as a religion misconstrues the actual beliefs and practices of Hindus. Indeed it is not uncommon for Hindus both to deny that Hinduism is a religion as such, and to suggest that Hinduism is itself a misnomer. It is frequently suggested that Hinduism is not a religion, but 'a way of life'. It is also common to hear Hindus suggest that the term *Sanātana Dharma*, which can be roughly translated as the eternal truth, is a much more appropriate term than Hinduism.

Nonetheless, there is a sense in which many people in the world today identify themselves, and/or are identified by others, as being Hindu. For example, in the 2001 British census 558,000 people identified themselves as being Hindu. In 2001 there were over 800 million Hindus in India and figures of up to 900 million Hindus worldwide (Adherents.com). There are numerous places of worship, both in India and other parts of the world that are clearly identifiable as being Hindu. There are also many organizations that identify themselves as being Hindu. Hinduism is taught as a subject in both schools and universities. So, clearly, there is a strong sense, among both insiders and outsiders, that Hindus constitute a religious community.

Diversity

Like all religious traditions, Hinduism is very diverse. However, it can be said that the diversity of Hinduism is of a completely different order to the diversity found in other religious traditions. The reason for this claim of radical diversity is that Hinduism has no founder figure or foundational event, no universally accepted canon of texts, no credal statement and no overarching institutional structure. There is no single source of authority that universally applies to all Hindus for all times. There is nothing that you can say about Hindus or Hinduism without some form of qualification. This has led some commentators like

Heinrich von Stietencron (2001, p. 33) to suggest 'our problems would vanish if we took "Hinduism" to denote a socio-cultural unit or civilization that contains a plurality of distinct religions'.

Historical Developments

In order to understand the diversity of the Hindu tradition(s) today, it is necessary to have some idea of some of the major historical developments. Rather than give an extended historical account, I have highlighted four particular periods, which in many ways can be seen as representing different aspects of the religious culture found on the subcontinent. These periods are: the Indus Valley Civilization, the Vedic period, the classic medieval period, and the Hindu Renaissance.

The Indus Valley Civilization

The earliest evidence of religious activity on the subcontinent are some archaeological finds that were made in the 1920s at two sites near to the river Indus, called Mohenjo-Daro and Harappa.[2] Consequently, the culture has been named as the Indus Valley Civilization. There have since been more than a thousand related sites discovered by archaeologists. The Indus Valley Civilization (IVC) covered an area of roughly a million square miles. It probably began to develop around 2500 BCE and fell into decline some time around 1800 BCE. There is considerable conjecture about the religious life of the IVC and whether certain aspects of Hinduism today can be traced back to this culture. Speculation focuses on three particular finds. First, a number of terracotta figurines were found, some of which might represent a Mother Earth goddess and hence could possibly be the antecedent of goddess worship. Second, a large number of soapstone seals, one of which depicts a figure seated in what some commentators have suggested is a yoga posture, and might possibly represent an early form of the god Śiva. Third, a large bitumen-lined tank, which could possibly be the precursor to the tanks used for ritual purification still found in the temples in South India.

The Vedic Period

While there is speculation regarding a continuity between the Indus Valley Civilization and Hinduism today, the next historical evidence is more clear. However, this evidence also raises a number of issues that still have resonance for many Hindus today. By about the middle of the second millennium BCE a group of people calling themselves Ārya, literally 'Noble Ones', began to make their presence felt on the subcontinent. We know about these peoples through an extensive corpus of compositions that are collectively known as the Vedas. What is less clear is where the original homeland of these people was, and this continues to be a sometimes highly emotive issue for certain sectors of the Hindu community.

The most widely accepted thesis is that the Ārya probably originated somewhere in the region of the Caspian Sea, then migrated West into what is currently Iran, and then split, some continuing West into Europe, and others migrating south into the subcontinent. However, this migration thesis, which implies that the foundations of Indian culture lie outside the Indian subcontinent, has been challenged. There is some archaeological evidence, albeit rather tenuous, that the IVC was an Indo-Aryan culture, and this would suggest that the Aryan homeland was in fact the northwest region of the subcontinent, which would mean that the foundations of Hindu culture could be traced to the subcontinent itself. While there is no substantive evidence as yet to fully support the thesis that the Ārya were originally from the subcontinent, at the same time the migration thesis is also highly speculative. It is important to stress that this is not just a dry intellectual issue confined to academics, but a deeply political and contentious debate alive within the Hindu community. Many Hindus perceive the thesis that the Ārya originated outside of India as a continuation of a colonialist discourse that suggests the inferiority of Indian culture.

We know about the religious life of the Ārya through the compositions known as the Vedas. The Vedas were primarily communicated orally, and were not written down for at least a thousand years, and this makes it very difficult to date them. Most scholars date the earliest portion to between 1500 and 1200 BCE, and the later compositions as late as between 500 and 300 BCE. The Vedas must be regarded as a corpus, rather than a single unified work. The Vedic corpus reflects substantial changes in beliefs and practices. While much of the Vedas remains obscure and the majority of Hindus know very little of the actual content, the Vedas still retain a hugely important place in contemporary Hinduism.

The central ritual of the Ārya was a fire ritual known as *yajña*. This ritual tended to be an immensely complicated rite that involved constructing a special site according to very precise geometric configurations and orientation, and involved different types of priests. The ritual would be sponsored by an individual to obtain a specific end, such as health or wealth. The focus of the ritual would have been on a number of invisible entities known as the *devas*. The *devas* were mostly associated with natural phenomena such as thunder, fire, the dawn, and so on. Many of these *devas* also displayed human qualities. Over a thousand different names of these *devas* can be discerned in the Vedic corpus, though only a handful of them seem to have played any significant role in the religious life of the early Indo-Aryans. While most Hindus today would recognize the names of the most important of the Vedic *devas*, they have largely become marginalized in favour of a quite different pantheon of deities that became increasingly significant in the medieval period.

The Medieval Period

There is no archaeological evidence from the Vedic period of any visual representations of the *devas* or any permanent places of worship. This greatly contrasts with the rich visual culture of the medieval period. The Gupta Period (4th–7th century CE) is often referred to as The Golden Age of Hindu Art. Images continue to play a central role in the religious life of most Hindus.

The Brihadishwara Temple, Thanjavur (Tanjore) This beautiful temple was built in 1010 by Raja Raja, in the Chola style.

Alongside the growing salience of images, permanent places of worship also came to be significant features of religious life. The most common term for a temple is *mandir*, which means dwelling. In other words temples are regarded as dwelling places for the *devas* in the form of images. In the medieval period, temple building came to be closely allied with political power. The large and magnificent temples, particularly those in South India, were clearly very costly to construct. These temples represented not only the genuine devotion of rulers, but also their political and economic status. While it is frequently suggested that it is perfectly possible to be a good Hindu without ever going to a temple, temples are still being built and continue to be an important part of the Hindu religious life.

It is also in this period that the *devas* of the Vedic pantheon recede in importance, and what might be referred to as the classic pantheon of deities becomes prominent. In particular there are three clusters of deities that came to be of particular significance. These are various manifestations and deities associated with Śiva, the various manifestations and deities associated with Viṣṇu, and various manifestations of the goddess.

Linked to the increasing salience of images, temples and the growing prominence of this different pantheon of deities is a new form of worship, known as *pūjā*, which involves the sequenced offerings of various items to an image of a deity. *Pūjā* remains as the core ritual practice of most forms of Hindu devotionalism.

The Hindu Renaissance

Between the late eighteenth and early twentieth centuries there were a number of significant reinterpretations of the Hindu tradition. While there is no absolute accord as to the precise dates, this period is frequently referred to as the Hindu Rennaissance. Indeed, it is possible to argue that it was only in this period that the very idea of Hinduism as a religion coalesced. From the late eighteenth century onwards there was increasing contact between India and Europe, and this led to what Wilhelm Halbfass (1988) has termed a new hermeneutic situation. This hermeneutic situation is exemplified by a Bengali intellectual called Rammohun Roy (1772–1833).[3] Roy is sometimes referred to as 'The Father of Modern India', and he is often attributed with being the first Indian to use the term 'Hinduism'.

Paul Hacker (1995) argues that Rammohun Roy is the precursor of what he terms 'neo-Hinduism'. He suggests that this began around 1870 and continued through to the middle of the twentieth century. As Hacker's terminology suggests, this was a novel form of Hinduism, which can also be understood in terms of modernity. The apologetic discourses of 'neo-Hinduism' have added another stratum to Hinduism, which is still prevalent today. While it is important to acknowledge that neo-Hinduism is itself a very diverse phenomenon, there are a number of important themes that run through most of the new forms of Hinduism that emerged between the end of the nineteenth century and middle of the twentieth. The most significant of these themes posits that Hinduism is a religion and that Hindus constitute a religious community. While there was no absolute agreement on what Hinduism is or on the precise boundaries of the Hindu community, the debates about them were instrumental in reifying these concepts.

Linked to these overarching themes was the necessity to provide a history. In the discourses of neo-Hinduism, as is still the case, the Hindu community is said to have had an unbroken history that can be traced back to the Vedic period. In particular, the experiences of the ancient Vedic seers, known as the *ṛṣis*, are given a foundational role in the formation of the Hindu community. Linked to this understanding of the foundation of Hinduism, neo-Hindu discourses often suggested that the religion had degenerated from its Vedic roots, and that it was necessary to return to those ancient roots. Further, they suggested that these roots had been misinterpreted, and that if they are understood properly they are entirely compatible with modernity. Indeed, this discourse suggests that the truth expounded in the Vedas, if interpreted correctly, is scientific and rational.

For many Hindus as well as academics, Swami Vivekananda (1863–1902) has come to epitomize neo-Hinduism. However, it is important to stress that although Vivekananda is regarded as having a seminal role, he is not the only figure of importance in this period.[4] Swami Vivekananda was a disciple of the Bengali mystic Ramakrishna. After Ramakrishna's death in 1886 Vivekananda became the leader of the small band of Ramakrishna's devotees, and his reinterpretation of Ramakrishna's teaching as having a universal salience has become central to many forms of contemporary Hinduism. Bharati (1970, p. 278) suggests that 'Modern Hindus derive their knowledge of Hinduism from Vivekananda, directly or indirectly.'

This very brief historical overview highlights some of the developments of the religious tradition that we now know as Hinduism. All of these developments are important in understanding some of the basic beliefs and practices that can be identified in Hinduism today. As I have indicated, the first substantial evidence of the religious life on the subcontinent are the compositions known as the Vedas. While many Hindus today know little of the content of the Vedas, they are still regarded by many Hindus as foundational texts.

Texts

There are literally thousands of different Hindu texts, of diverse types. These texts are classified into two types: those that have primary authority, referred to as 'that which is heard' (*śruti*); and secondary texts, referred to as 'that which is remembered' (*smṛti*). There is no universal or absolute agreement on which texts fall into which category; however it is generally agreed that the Vedas belong in the primary category of *śruti*.

The Vedas

The Vedas are generally regarded as not being of human origin, but as containing an eternal truth that was revealed to the Vedic seers (*ṛṣis*). The structure of the Vedas is highly complex. There are four different Vedas and four different strata to each of these Vedas. This can be diagrammatically represented as in Table 1.

Table 1: *The structure of the Vedas*

	Ṛg Veda	Sāma Veda	Yajur Veda	Atharva Veda
Saṃhitās				
Brāhmaṇas				
Āraṇyakas				
Upaniṣads				

It is possible to fill in all of the empty cells with names of particular compositions; however for our purposes it is not necessary.[5] The earliest portions of the Vedas are the *Saṃhitās* of the Ṛg Veda. These, for the most part, are extravagant hymns of praise to the various *devas*. The *Saṃhitās* of the Ṛg Veda only record the hymns and give no indication as to how they were sung or incorporated into ritual practice. The majority of the Sāma Veda comprises hymns taken from the Ṛg Veda and arranged in a form for use in a ritual context with notations as to how they were to be chanted in the ritual (*yajña*). The Yajur Veda also derives much of its content from the Ṛg Veda *Saṃhitās*. It also contains a collection of prose formulae, known as *yajus*, which were muttered by a priest during the ritual. The style and content of the Atharva Veda is quite different to that of the other three Vedas, as it is much less concerned with the ritual and mostly contains spells and charms to ward off problems of everyday living, such as ill health, snake bite and so on.

There is a rough chronological development through the strata or genres of the Vedic corpus. However, it is important to note that the boundary between these different genres is not always clear-cut. The *Saṃhitās* are verse compositions and are the earliest portion of the Vedas. They are primarily focused on the *devas*. The *Saṃhitās* also contain the *mantras*, which Fritz Staal identifies as 'bits and pieces from the Vedas put to ritual use' (cited in Alper, 1991, p. 10). These *mantras* are still incorporated in numerous Hindu rituals, even though many people may no longer understand their meaning. The *Brāhmaṇas* are later prose compositions and may be considered as appendices to the *Saṃhitās*. The *Brāhamaṇas* primarily focus on the correct performance of the ritual itself. Clearly identifiable in the *Brāhmaṇas* is the concept that creation is governed by an inherent order and is not merely the subject of the capricious intervention of greater powers. This concept of an inherent order is referred to as *dharma*, which becomes a dominant theme in much Hindu thought. The *Āraṇyakas* develop some of the ideas in the *Brāhmaṇas*. *Āraṇyaka* roughly translates as 'forest or wilderness treatise', which suggests that this portion of the Vedas contained esoteric knowledge.

The term *Upaniṣad* more or less translates as 'to sit near'. This suggests a group of students sitting near to a teacher (*guru*), and again seems to imply that the teachings were regarded as esoteric. The focus of the *Upaniṣads* is on the meaning of ritual performance. There are 108 canonical *Upaniṣads*, and 14 of these are considered particularly significant. As with all Hindu texts, it is extremely difficult to date the *Upaniṣads* accurately. The earliest were probably composed about the eighth century BCE, and the latest were probably composed towards the beginning of the Common Era. Consequently, even when looking just at the *Upaniṣads*, it is not possible to identify a consistent doctrine. Nonetheless, it is clear that a number of new interrelated ideas emerged in this period, ideas that became central to most subsequent forms of Hinduism. These are: there is a continuous cycle of life, death and rebirth (*saṃsāra*); that activity (*karma*) is the driving force of *saṃsāra*; and that it is possible to escape the wheel of transmigration (*mokṣa*).

Vedānta

The *Upaniṣads* are sometimes referred to collectively as *Vedānta*, which literally means 'the end of the Veda'. The implication is not just that the

Upaniṣads appear as the last portion of the Vedic corpus, but also that they represent the culmination of the thought that has preceded them in the other strata of the Vedas.

Vedānta is also the term used for philosophical schools of thought[6] that base their metaphysical speculation on ideas found in the *Upaniṣads*. Arguably the most influential school of thought is the monistic school of *Vedānta* known as *Advaita* (literally 'non-dual').[7] The most famous exponent of this school of thought was Śankara[8] (8th–9th century CE). *Advaita Vedānta* is based on ideas found in the *Upaniṣads* that are encapsulated in a number of aphorisms referred to as the 'great sayings' (*mahāvākyas*). The most famous of these sayings is found in the *Chāndogya Upaniṣad*, which states '*tat tvam asi*'. This literally translates as 'thou art that'. The implication of this is that there is only one fundamental reality that pervades existence, which is referred to as *Brahman*, which for lack of a better translation I will refer to as Absolute Reality. We mistake this Absolute Reality for the phenomenal world of names and forms. The phenomenal world is regarded as a misperception (*māyā*)[9] of the underlying and pervading reality of *Brahman*. There are a number of analogies and metaphors used to describe this misperception. So Śankara suggests:

> All modifications of clay, such as jar, which are always accepted by the mind as real, are (in reality) nothing but clay. Similarly this entire universe which is produced from the real Brahman, is Brahman Itself and nothing but That. (Śankara's *Vivekacūḍāmani* 251, Mādhavānanda translation, 1978)

Underlying our individual self is also a true Self, which is called *ātman*. However, we also mistakenly identify our selves with our bodies and minds. Once we really know that our true Self is the *ātman*, we will also know that *ātman* (thou) is in reality nothing other than *Brahman* (that). The metaphor that is commonly used to illustrate this idea is that the drop (that is the sense of ourselves as discrete individuals) will realize that we are in reality nothing other than the ocean (*Brahman*). Once we achieve this state of knowledge – that in reality we are nothing other than *Brahman* – we will become liberated from the wheel of transmigration.

'That which is Remembered'

While most Hindus know of the Vedas, many know very little about the actual contents of this extensive corpus of compositions. Most Hindus are far more aware of the secondary literature. The secondary class of texts are referred to as *smṛti*, which means 'that which is remembered'. These relate to compositions that are said to be of human origin, and are regarded as retelling and elucidations of the revealed texts. There are a vast number of texts that fall into this category, some of which have continued to play a very significant role in the lives of Hindus. Within the broad category of *smṛti* are a number of different types of texts, the most important types being the *dharma* texts (*Dharmaśāstras & Dharmasūtras*), the Epics (*Itihāsa*) and the Ancient Tales (*Purāṇas*).

Dharma *Texts*

These texts are very difficult to date, and were also composed over a considerable period of time. Ludo Rocher (2005, p. 110) tentatively suggests between 500 BCE to 500 CE for the composition of the most important *dharma* texts. *Dharma* is a very important concept that still informs Hinduism today. It is a complex concept for which there is no direct translation into English. In different contexts, *dharma* can have connotations of righteousness, law, duty, justice, morality and religion. The term derives from the root word *dhṛ*, which means 'to uphold', and literally translates as 'that which holds together'. *Dharma* indicates all the things that sustain and hold together creation at cosmological, social and individual levels. Its opposite is *adharma*, which implies chaos.

Perhaps the most important of the *dharma* texts is the *Laws of Manu*, which was probably composed sometime around the beginning of the Common Era. *The Laws of Manu* systematizes orthodox conceptions of *dharma*, and deals not only with the duties of caste, but also with cosmology, how to choose a wife, forbidden foods, the correct demeanour for a king, how to treat guests, how to clean various objects and so on. While many Hindus are not necessarily familiar with the text itself, *The Laws of Manu* still informs many Hindus conceptions of social relations.

The Epics: the Mahābhārata *and the* Rāmāyaṇa

The Epics are perhaps the most well known of all the Hindu texts. The Sanskrit term for these texts is *itihāsa*, which means 'so it was'. The implication is that these texts are histories. These texts are narratives interspersed with sub-plots and didactic passages. The stories have been told and retold and have become what Chris Rojek (2007) has called myths of genealogy, which he identifies as stories 'that dramatise the culture or world-view of a people' (p. 68). There are two texts that fall into this category – the *Mahābhārata* and the *Rāmāyaṇa*.

The *Mahābhārata* is fundamentally a story of a civil war, in which two sets of cousins, the Pāṇḍavas and the Kauravas, are in dispute about the line of succession to the throne of the land. It could also be said to be a story of *dharma*, in that the Pāṇḍavas could be considered to represent *dharma* and the Kauravas *adharma*. It is also sometimes referred to as the Fifth Veda, as it is suggested that the truth revealed in the Vedas is retold in narrative form. It is the longest narrative poem in the world, having in the region of a hundred thousand verses. There is considerable debate as to when it was actually composed, but it is clear that it grew through a process of telling, retelling and accretion.

The *Bhagavad Gītā* is located in the narrative of the *Mahābhārata*. The Pāṇḍavas have done all that they could do in order to resolve the dispute with their cousins, but all negotiations have failed to shift the Kauravas' intransigence, and consequently war has been declared. The *Bhagavad Gītā* begins with the two armies, which are lined up facing one another, ready for the battle to be unleashed. Arjuna, who leads the Pāṇḍavas' army, takes advantage of this brief pause, prior to the charge, to get his charioteer to take him between the opposing armies. Arjuna's charioteer is in fact the god Kṛṣṇa. Arjuna looks across the field at the two armies, and sees that brothers, friends, sons and fathers are on opposing sides, and knows that there will be a terrible slaughter with death, bereavement and injury on both sides. Arjuna breaks down and says to Kṛṣṇa that he can see no good coming from the battle and that even the Kauravas are his own kin and that this battle will bring nothing but chaos (*adharma*). Arjuna then declares that he will not fight. The *Bhagavad Gītā* is basically Kṛṣṇa's explanation to Arjuna as to why he must lead his army into battle. For many modern Hindus the *Bhagavad Gītā* has become the most important religious text and source for doctrinal ideas.

Kṛṣṇa employs three basic arguments, which can be found in summary in the second chapter. In the first argument Kṛṣṇa indicates that Arjuna has made a basic misidentification by confusing the Self (*ātman*) with the body. One's true Self is not born and cannot die. Kṛṣṇa states that just as we cast off old clothes 'so the embodied self, casting off its worn-out bodies, goes to other, new ones' (*Bhagavad Gītā* 2.22, W. J. Johnson translation). Therefore there is no need to grieve, as ultimately no one is killed. Clearly this is a reference to the doctrine of transmigration. The second argument that Kṛṣṇa utilizes is that death is ineluctable. Finally, Kṛṣṇa indicates that Arjuna has not fully understood the nature of *dharma*. His duty as a warrior supersedes all other aspects of *dharma*.

The rest of the *Bhagavad Gītā* can be seen as an exposition of three paths to liberation from the wheel of transmigration (*mokṣa*): the yoga of action (*karma yoga*), the yoga of devotion (*bhakti yoga*) and the yoga of knowledge (*jñāna yoga*). The yoga of action suggests that while one has to act, one should become detached from the consequences of action, and that this attitude will lead the aspirant to liberation. The yoga of devotion (*bhakti yoga*) suggests that the path of personal devotion to Kṛṣṇa will liberate the devotee. The yoga of knowledge (*jñāna yoga*) suggests that the knowledge of the true nature of the Self (*ātman*) leads to liberation.

The *Rāmāyaṇa* is possibly the most loved of all Hindu texts. It tells the story of Rāma, who is commonly regarded as an incarnation (*avatār*) of the deity Viṣṇu. He is the eldest and most loved son of Daśaratha, King of Ayodhya. When Daśaratha appoints Rāma as his successor, his youngest queen, Kaikeyī, is concerned that she and her son Bharata will become completely marginalized. Kaikeyī had saved the life of the king, and had obtained Daśaratha's promise that he would grant her any two wishes that she cared to ask for. Recalling this, she requests that her son Bharata be crowned king and that Rāma be forced to go into exile in the forest for 14 years. The king has to keep his promise, and Rāma accepts his fate and retires to the forest with his beautiful wife Sītā and his half-brother Lakṣmaṇa. In this period the 10-headed demon Rāvaṇa becomes enamoured with Sītā's beauty, abducts her and takes her to his island kingdom of Lanka. Rāma enlists the help of the monkey kingdom, and in particular the monkey god Hanumān, to rescue Sītā. Rāvaṇa and his demon allies are defeated, and Sītā is rescued. Rāma returns triumphantly to Ayodhya where he assumes his rightful place as king and he reigns over a golden era. In many ways this narrative is also about *dharma*. Rāma represents the dutiful son and the ideal ruler who fulfils all of his duties to his people. Sītā represents the ideal wife, the embodiment of wifely duty (*strīdharma*). The relationship between Hanumān and Rāma represents the ideal relationship between the devotee and god.

The Rāmāyaṇa was originally composed in Sanskrit and is attributed to the sage Vālmīki. There is also a version composed in Hindi by the poet Tulsīdās at the end of the sixteenth century known as the *Lake of the Deeds of Rāma* (*Rāmacaritmānas*). Although Tulsīdās' Hindi retelling of the narrative is probably the most popular rendition, there is no single authoritative version of the Rāmāyaṇa. Ramanujan (1994) argues that the Vālmīki version must not be seen as an original telling from which all other tellings diverge. He suggests (p. 46) that there is 'a pool of signifiers (like a gene pool), signifiers that include plots, characters, names, geography incidents and relationships'. Each narrator, including Vālmīki, draws on this symbolic pool in order to construct their own particular narrative. In other words, the narrative has both structure and a fluidity that ensures the telling of the story can be both familiar and new at the same time. It is this dual nature that has entailed that the story retains vitality, and therefore a special place amongst the vast array of Hindu texts.

The Ancient Tales: The Purāṇas

Traditionally there are said to be 18 *Purāṇas*. However, as with all genres of Hindu religious texts there are no clear criteria for determining what defines the *Purāṇas*, and Ludo Rocher suggests a list of 82 (cited in Matchett, 2005, p. 129).

A number of important themes can be identified in the Purāṇic literature, which continue to significantly inform the Hindu worldview. These themes constitute what Madeleine Biardeau (1994) has called 'a universe of *bhakti*'. This is a context in which devotion to a personalized form of the deity, who is also considered as an all-pervading reality, is considered as the religious practice *par excellence*. The deities of what might be called the classic pantheon come into prominence in this universe, and deities like Śiva, Viṣṇu and the goddess come to take precedence over the earlier Vedic *devas*.

This mythic universe is informed by a very complex understanding of time and space. Just as the individual Self (*ātman*) undergoes a continuous cycle of life, death and rebirth, so too does the universe. The universe is considered as alternating between manifestation and dissolution. The metaphor that is often used is that creation is like a spider that alternates between spinning a web and then reabsorbing it back into its body. This period is envisaged as a day and night of Brahmā. The day of Brahmā is the period when the universe is manifest and lasts for 4,320,000,000 years. The night of Brahmā is the period when the universe resolves back into its undifferentiated form, and lasts a similar length of time.

As well as developing a highly elaborate conception of time, the Purāṇic cosmos also has a very complex notion of space. The *Purāṇas* suggest that there are many thousands of parallel universes. Furthermore, the *Purāṇas* propose that there are different worlds or realms (*loka*) inhabited by different beings. In particular, the *Purāṇas* suggest three worlds: the world of the gods (*devas*), the world of humans, and the world of demons (*asuras*). Although these are regarded hierarchically it would be wrong to think of the realm of the *asuras* as equivalent to the Western concept of hell. In some places in the *Purāṇas* seven or even fourteen different *lokas* are indicated.

Gods and Goddesses

The *Purāṇas* are the source of many of the narratives of the gods and goddesses that might be thought of as belonging to the classic pantheon. Anyone arriving in India cannot but be overwhelmed by the diverse and colourful images of an extraordinary pantheon of gods and goddesses with multiple arms, animal heads or festooned with a garland of skulls. These images are not only found in temples and shrines, but can be found in virtually all Hindu shops, offices and homes. These deities are, for the most part, different to the earlier Vedic pantheon. However, before looking at some of these gods and goddesses, it is necessary to have some idea of how this amazing and colourful pantheon should be understood, and for this we need to look at some terminology.

Terminology

The presence of many gods and goddesses seems to suggest that Hinduism is a polytheistic tradition. While many Hindus might well believe in a multiplicity of gods and goddesses, this term really distorts the nature of belief of many other Hindus. The reformer Rammohun Roy suggested that the belief in a multiplicity of gods and goddesses was a misinterpretation of the allegorical nature of the Vedas, and that the many deities actually represent aspects of one deity. Rammohun Roy (Roy and Ghose, 1978, p. 90), for example, argued that 'the real spirit of the Hindoo scriptures ... is but the declaration of the unity of God'. Rammohun was clearly advocating that Hinduism, if understood correctly, must be considered as being a monotheistic tradition. This interpretation that the many gods and goddesses reflect different aspects or characteristics of one supreme deity is widely accepted amongst certain sectors of Hindu society, particularly the well educated.

Hinduism cannot really be understood only in terms of monotheism, as this misrepresents the actual beliefs of many Hindus. This conundrum led the famous Sanskrit scholar Friedrich Müller to coin the term henotheism, meaning the belief in a single deity while not denying the existence of other gods and goddesses. While this term perhaps captures the important concept that many Hindus have of a chosen deity (*iṣṭa deva*) as the main focus for their devotion, it still fails to exhaust all the ways in which Hindus understand the sacred. Almost all types of 'ism' – animism, pantheism, monism, monotheism, polytheism, henotheism and so on – can be found within Hinduism. Indeed it could be questioned as to whether these distinctions make much sense in relation to Hinduism.

The *Trimūrti*: Creator, Preserver and Destroyer

It is often suggested that there are three main gods in the Hindu pantheon, each having a different role. These are Brahmā the creator deity, Viṣṇu the preserver, and Śiva the destroyer. These three deities are referred to as the three forms (*trimūrti*). While there are references to the *trimūrti* in the Purāṇic literature, they are not normally represented together, and they do not play a significant role as a group. Śiva and Viṣṇu are important deities in their own right. However, Brahmā, while he plays a significant role in the Purāṇic narratives, is not regarded as a significant focus for devotional practice. Iconographically, Brahmā is most commonly portrayed as seated in a lotus that is emerging from Viṣṇu's navel. In other words, he is represented as secondary to Viṣṇu, and this might be considered as a visual representation of henotheism. Furthermore, there are many references to Śiva and Viṣṇu performing all three functions of creation, maintenance and destruction as individual deities. A clearer way of trying to comprehend the diverse multiplicity of Hindu deities is to think of them in terms of three broad devotional strands. There are the devotees of various forms of Śiva known as Śaivites, devotees of various forms of Viṣṇu referred to as Vaiṣṇavas, and devotees of various forms of the goddess who go under the generic name of Śāktas.

Brahmā seated in a lotus, emerging from Viṣṇu's navel. The goddess Lakṣmī is seated at his feet.

Śaivism, Vaiṣṇavism and Śāktism

Heinrich von Stietencron (2001) argues that we should understand Śaivism, Vaiṣṇavism and Śāktism as distinct religions. However, two arguments contradict this thesis. First, although these three devotional branches tend to refer to different mythic narratives, they all involve very similar ritual practices, such as the performance of *pūjā* and the practice of pilgrimage. Second, the dividing line between these three groups is not as distinct as von Stietencron supposes. It is not unusual to find Śaivite images in a Vaiṣṇava temple and vice versa. In fact there is a general movement towards a more ecumenical form of devotionalism apparent in some contemporary forms of Hinduism. In her study of contemporary temples, Joanne Waghorne describes a temple in the outskirts of Chennai, established about thirty years ago, called the Sri Sankara Narayan Mandir – Sankara is an epithet of Śiva and Narayan an epithet of Viṣṇu. In this temple there is an image (*mūrti*) in which half the body is Viṣṇu and half is Śiva. 'A superb stone image of Vishnu still waits with a linga, Shiva's iconic form, to be installed together in the central sanctum' (Waghorne, 2004, p. 6).

Forms of Śiva

Śiva, literally 'Auspicious One', like all the Hindu gods, has many different forms and names. Traditionally, Śiva is said to have 108 different names,[10] and the *Śiva Purāṇa* lists 1,008 names. There are also numerous different Śaivite sects, all of which conceptualize Śiva in a variety of ways. For the purposes of this brief introduction, I will only indicate some of Śiva's most popular iconographical forms. One of the most popular representations is as Lord of Yoga. In this depiction Śiva is shown seated in a meditational posture on a tiger skin. He has long matted locks, which are adorned with the crescent moon, and also the Goddess Gangā is seen emerging from his hair. He is generally depicted as wearing an animal pelt around his waist, he has a snake wrapped around his neck and he is festooned with beads known as Rudrakshas. There is a third eye on his forehead, which is also marked by three horizontal stripes. To one side his trident (*triśula*) is embedded, points up, in the ground. Draped over this trident is an hour-glass-shaped drum (*ḍamaru*). Each of these elements of the image has a particular meaning.[11] For example, it is sometimes suggested that the three prongs of the trident represent creation, maintenance and destruction. Overall, this image represents Śiva as the ideal ascetic.

The most common representation of Śiva in temples is his aniconic form – the *liṅga*. This is normally a smooth stone column with a rounded top that stands on a plinth called a *yoni*. While the *liṅga* and *yoni* suggest the male and female genitalia, and much is made of this in the academic literature (see, for example, Flood, 1996, p. 151; Smith, 2008 p. 800), most Hindus themselves do not relate to the sexual connotations of this image, but perceive the *liṅga* simply as a form of Śiva. Nonetheless, there is a sexual element in some narratives of Śiva. Wendy O'Flaherty (1973) nicely captures the ambivalent character of Śiva by referring to him as the 'erotic ascetic'.

Śiva, as well as being characterized as both ascetic and erotic, is also represented as a happily married family man. One of the most popular representations of Śiva in contemporary iconography pictures him with his consort Pārvatī and two sons in their mountain abode. Consequently, Śiva appears as a very ambivalent figure: he is not only a householder, but also an ascetic, he is both sexual and renunciant. He is depicted as being wild, frenzied and uncontrolled, yet also represented as the epitome of restraint. For an outsider these contradictions, which are implicit in the representations of Śiva, can appear to be very confusing, but for the majority of Hindus such apparent oppositions are not antagonistic, but complementary.

Śiva has a constellation of other deities that are associated with him; the most important are his consort Pārvatī, and his two sons Skanda and Gaṇeśa. Skanda, like many Hindu deities, has a number of different names: he is also known as Kārttikeya and in South India he is called Murugan or Subrahmanya. Skanda is often depicted with six heads and riding a peacock. The worship of Skanda as an independent deity is primarily found in South India, generally under the name of Murugan, and in the Punjab as Baba Balaknath, where he is often iconographically represented as a young ascetic (see Geaves, 2007). Gaṇeśa, also known as Gaṇapati, is perhaps the most popular deity in all of India. He is easily recognizable because of his elephant head. He is regarded as the remover of obstacles, and consequently you often find images of him above doorways. It is common practice to propitiate Gaṇeśa before embarking on a journey or beginning any new venture.

Forms of Viṣṇu

Viṣṇu is not such an ambiguous figure as Śiva, but like Śiva appears in many different forms. References to Viṣṇu can be found in the Ṛg Veda, but he was probably a relatively minor deity. However, by the time of the *Viṣṇu Purāṇa* in the early centuries of the Common Era, Viṣṇu had become an important focus of devotional activity and was regarded as the supreme deity. Various manifestations of Viṣṇu remain central to Hinduism today.

One of the most important forms of Viṣṇu is that of Nārāyaṇa. This form can be easily recognized, Viṣṇu being represented iconographically as holding the four main objects associated with him: the conch, the discus, the club and the lotus. Nārāyaṇa is often represented as reclining on the serpent Śeṣa afloat on the cosmic ocean. When Viṣṇu sleeps, the cosmos is un-manifest, but when he awakes the cosmos once again becomes manifest.

However, perhaps the most important conceptualizations of Viṣṇu are his divine descents (*avatāras*). The term *avatāra* derives from the root word *tṛ*, which means 'to cross', and *avatāra* translates as 'to cross down'. The implication is that the sacred 'crosses down' into the mundane world. The reason for this is to restore *dharma* to the world. Kṛṣṇa explains to Arjuna that: 'Whenever dharma decays and adharma prevails, I manifest myself. For the protection of the good, for the destruction of the evil, and for the establishment of dharma I take birth from age to age' (*Bhagavad Gītā* 4: 7–8).

While there are a variety of different lists, 10 *avatāras* are most commonly accepted today:

1. *Matsya* – the Fish.
2. *Kūrma* – the Tortoise.
3. *Varāha* – the Boar.
4. *Narasimha* – the Man-lion.
5. *Vāmana* – the Dwarf.
5. *Paraśurāma* – Rāma with the Axe.
7. *Rāma* – the hero of the *Rāmāyaṇa*.
8. *Kṛṣṇa* – mentor to the Pāṇdavas and destroyer of the demon Kaṃsa.
9. *Buddha* – leader of the unorthodox astray.
10. *Kalkī* – the avatār yet to come, who will announce the end of the current cycle of time.

The tales of these *avatāras* are primarily to be found in the *Purāṇas*, and are familiar to most Hindus. The two most significant and well-known *avatāras* for Hindus today are Rāma and Kṛṣṇa.

Rāma is of course familiar through the various tellings of the *Rāmāyaṇa*, and most Hindus know the basic story. Iconographically, Rāma is easy to identify: he invariably carries a bow, and is often depicted with his brother Lakṣmana on one side, his consort Sītā on his other side, and his devotee the monkey god Hanumān kneeling at his feet. In many ways Hanumān has eclipsed Rāma in popularity. In northern India numerous shrines have emerged dedicated to him. In Delhi there is a 50-metre-high image (*mūrti*) of Hanumān that towers over the newly built metro line. Every day, but particularly on Tuesday which is Hanumān's special day, hundreds of people flock to this *mūrti*.

Non-Hindus are probably more familiar with Kṛṣṇa than any other of the Hindu deities. The reason for this is that the International Society for Krishna Consciousness (ISKCON)[12] has become relatively popular, and has a significant profile in the West. There are three main sources for tales about Kṛṣṇa – the *Bhāgavata Purāṇa*, the *Mahābhārata* and a text called the *Harivaṃśa*, which was conceived as a supplement to the *Mahābhārata*. Although there seem to be two different Kṛṣṇas, the pastoral Kṛṣṇa and the warrior Kṛṣṇa, Hindus only perceive one Kṛṣṇa. Episodes from Kṛṣṇa's life are very popular themes in both tribal art and brightly coloured poster art. Representations of Kṛṣṇa as a child (*Bāla Kṛṣṇa*) are very common. Kṛṣṇa is represented as having been a very mischievous child, who was inordinately fond of butter. The conceptualization of deity as child relates to the notion of divine play (*līlā*). The concept of *līlā* suggests that creation is a joyful, self-determined activity that has no goal beyond itself.

The most popular representation of Kṛṣṇa portrays him as a youthful cowherd playing a flute. All the milkmaids (*gopīs*) are totally enamoured of this beautiful youth in their midst. In the devotional poetry of the medieval period there are descriptions of Kṛṣṇa's radiant beauty. There are many rich narratives that relate to the pastoral Kṛṣṇa's play with the *gopīs*. For example, Kṛṣṇa is said to have stolen the clothes of the *gopīs* when they were bathing in the river. Another episode relates how Kṛṣṇa multiplied himself so that all of the *gopīs* believed that they were dancing with him. In particular, the *gopī* Rādhā is regarded as having a special relationship with Kṛṣṇa, and they are often portrayed together. There is clearly a great deal of sexual imagery in the narratives of Kṛṣṇa and the *gopīs*, but most Hindus do not relate to the erotic aspects. The relationship between Rādhā and Kṛṣṇa is regarded as a metaphor for the 'pure love' (*prema*) that the devotee should have for the Lord (Flood, 1996, p. 139).

This pastoral and erotic Kṛṣṇa seems to be quite different to the warrior Kṛṣṇa of the *Mahābhārata*. In the *Mahābhārata* Kṛṣṇa is the ruler of the kingdom of Dvarka, and is called by the epithet Vasudeva. He is represented as the advisor to the Pāṇḍavas and Arjuna's charioteer. Images of Arjuna with Kṛṣṇa either in or alongside the chariot before the commencement of battle are also very popular. In Chapter 10 of the *Bhagavad Gītā* Kṛṣṇa tells Arjuna his real nature; that he is: the Vedas (10:22); Śiva (10:23); the beginning, middle and end of creation (10:32), and so on. At the beginning of Chapter 11, Arjuna indicates that he now knows Kṛṣṇa's true nature and asks him to reveal his supreme form. Kṛṣṇa bestows Arjuna with divine sight, and in a very famous passage Arjuna describes what he sees.

> O God, I see in your body the gods and all kinds of beings come together, Lord Brahma on his lotus seat, all the seers and divine serpents.
> I see you everywhere, many-armed, many-stomached, many-eyed, infinite in form; I cannot find out your end, your middle or your beginning – Lord of the universe, form of everything. (*Bhagavad Gītā* 11:15–16)

This form of Kṛṣṇa is known as Svarūpa Virāt, and can be found iconographically depicted with multiple heads, many of them clearly recognizable to Hindus as various other deities and sages. The various arms of Svarūpa Virāt hold objects associated with the other deities, such as Śiva's trident and Viṣṇu's conch. Normally, a comparatively smaller Kṛṣṇa and Arjuna are depicted to one side. This iconographic representation of Kṛṣṇa clearly indicates that the other deities are somehow incorporated within the cosmic form of Kṛṣṇa, and are therefore subsequent and lesser powers. It also is a visible representation that Kṛṣṇa is both the material and efficient cause of creation, and is therefore both immanent and transcendent.

Forms of Devi

The goddess has an important place in Hinduism. On one level there are many different goddesses, but on another level there is only one Goddess often referred to as Mahādevī (Great Goddess). In this account all the various goddesses are actually different manifestations of the supreme Goddess who is equated with Ultimate Reality. As we have seen, there is some, although equivocal, evidence to suggest goddess worship in the Indus Valley Civilization, but it is impossible to substantiate a continuous tradition of goddess worship from this time. The goddesses of the Vedas, like Uma the goddess of dawn, play a very minor role in relation to the masculine *devas*. However, by the time of the Epics and the *Purāṇas* the goddess had an important place in the religious life. In Hinduism today, various aspects of the goddess are a clearly visible and vibrant aspect of religious life for many Hindus.

There are two different ways of trying to comprehend the various different goddesses. The first typology suggests that there are three types of goddess: goddesses that are subservient consorts to male deities;

goddesses that are equal to or dominate a male deity; and independent goddesses. The second typology, suggested by Wendy O'Flaherty (1980, p. 91), indicates that there are two types of goddesses. The first type are dangerous, ambivalent and erotic, which O'Flaherty calls 'goddesses of the tooth'. The second are the more benevolent goddesses that O'Flaherty terms 'goddesses of the breast'. There is some overlap between these typologies in that, in general, goddesses of the breast tend to fall into the subservient consort category.

We have already encountered one of the most benevolent consorts – namely Pārvatī. Pārvatī's sole purpose is to lure Śiva away from his extreme asceticism and she 'extends Śiva's circle of activity into the realm of the householder' (Kinsley, 1987, p. 35). She is almost invariably depicted with Śiva and represents the ideal Hindu wife and mother.

However, perhaps Śri, more commonly referred to as Lakṣmī, is the most significant of the consort 'goddesses of the breast'. Lakṣmī is portrayed in the image of Viṣṇu reclining on the serpent massaging the god's feet, clearly indicating her subservient role. However Lakṣmī is often depicted standing alongside Viṣṇu in a form referred to by the composite name Lakṣmīnārāyan. Lakṣmī is also often depicted on her own. Iconographically she is depicted either standing or seated in a lotus, with elephants showering her with water, and gold coins spilling from her hands. In this form Lakṣmī is associated with wealth and prosperity. The lotus is a very popular motif in Hindu iconography. The lotus is a flower of great beauty that seems to float free on the surface of the water, yet it is rooted in mud. The mud, as it were, represents the material world, and the ability to float above the mire clearly suggests transcendence. Consequently Lakṣmī is often perceived as the mediator *par excellence* between the mundane and the sacred. Lakṣmī *pūjā* is regarded by many as the most important day in the festival of Dīvālī. Clay lamps are lit in order to invite Lakṣmī into the home to ensure prosperity for the coming year. In Northern India, many businesses begin the new financial year on this day, and account books are sometimes bought to the temple to be blessed.

There are two most common representations of the more fearsome goddesses, namely Durgā and Kālī; however it is equivocal whether or not these can be regarded as separate goddesses. There are a number of narratives that give different accounts of Durgā's origin. The best-known account relates how the demon (*asura*) Mahiṣa, through his intense austerity, wins a boon from Brahmā that he cannot be killed by a man. Consequently, he conquers both the human world and heaven (*svarga*). The gods, seemingly unable to defeat Mahiṣa, gather together, and in their anger and frustration, each emits a ray of energy that coalesce together to form the Goddess Durgā. The gods each provide Durgā with the weapon particularly associated with them, so Śiva gives her a trident, Viṣṇu gives her a discus, and so on. Durgā then mounts her lion, and sets off to defeat Mahiṣa, who often takes the form of a bull. On one level Durgā is the product of the male gods, yet she is also independent and defeats the *asura* and his armies without the assistance of the male deities.

Another tale relates how two powerful *asuras*, Sumbha and Nisumbha, defeat the *devas*, who then have to petition Durgā to come to their rescue. At one point in the narrative Durgā faces the two generals of the *asura* army, and in her anger Kālī springs from her brow. Kālī is clearly the personification of Durgā's wrath. She is described as dark skinned, emaciated with lolling tongue, armed with a sword and noose, and festooned with a garland of skulls. Kālī cuts a terrifying swathe through the demon's army. Clearly the goddess of the margins, she seems to be the antithesis of benign consorts like Sītā.

Although fearsome and independent, Kālī is also closely associated with Śiva. This, of course, makes sense, as Śiva is also wild and associated with the margins. Kinsley (1998, p. 74) observes that, while Pārvatī brings Śiva into the realm of domesticity, Kālī encourages his wild behaviour. In some mythic narratives Śiva is represented as dominating Kālī; however one of the most commonly found representations of Kālī depicts her standing over the inert form of Śiva. This seems to suggest that the goddess has the dominant role. In this image Kālī represents the animating principle of creation known as *śakti*, which literally means 'power, energy'. *Śakti* is therefore conceived as the power to create, and is envisaged in feminine terms. Creation, or more accurately the manifestation of the cosmos, is contingent upon the interplay of the pair of primordial binary opposites represented in terms of gender. In other words, the image of Kālī standing over the inert form of Śiva can be seen as a visual representation of a very complex metaphysical worldview.

The rich visual culture of Hinduism and its colourful iconography is central to any understanding. As we have seen, these images can give a good insight into the complex Hindu worldview. Although many Hindus might have some comprehension of the metaphysical intricacy of these images, most Hindus see them in a very different way. I use the word 'see' very deliberately here, as sight is central to the way in which most Hindus approach images of the deities.

Ritual Practice

Perhaps the most important concept in the religious practice of Hinduism is *darśan*. This term means 'to see' and has the connotation of 'auspicious sight'. When they go to a temple Hindus do not say they are going to worship or to pray but that they are going for *darśan*. Similarly, when a Hindu goes on a pilgrimage they conceive of going for *darśan* of the particular deity associated with the place of pilgrimage. When a Hindu goes to see their spiritual preceptor (*guru*) they also use the term *darśan*. Often simply to sit in the sight of and see the *guru* is considered more beneficial than any formal teaching. *Darśan* is a two-way process. That is, the worshipper both sees and is seen by the deity. The deity or the *guru* is said to give *darśan* and the devotee is said to receive *darśan*.

There are numerous examples of eyes in Hindu imagery, which emphasize the belief that it is not only the devotee who sees the deity, but also the deity who sees the worshipper. Some village shrines, for example, are little more than roughly hewn rocks with large stylized eyes painted on them; the famous image of Jagannāth, a form of Kṛṣṇa, is depicted with huge saucer eyes, and Śiva is often portrayed as having a third eye. When the devotee goes to the temple the most important thing is to be 'seen' by the deity.

The image of the deity in the temple is known as *mūrti*, which means form. This suggests that the infinite, which transcends all form, takes on a defined and limited shape. The images are 'brought to life' or imbued with the deity through a special ritual of establishment, which transforms it from something mundane into something sacred. For many Hindu devotees the deity is perceived in some fundamental way to reside in the image; the latter is not simply a symbol. In Vaiṣṇava theology in particular, the *mūrti* is regarded as an especially accessible form of the sacred.

Pūjā

The most important ritual activity in contemporary Hinduism is called *pūjā*. *Pūjā* is practised in both homes and temples, by both priests and ordinary people. *Pūjā* is a daily ritual, but it is also incorporated into annual festivals. In the temple, *pūjā* is generally performed by the priests (*pūjārī*) on behalf of the devotees. However it is not a congregational form of ritual, and will be performed regardless of whether or not there are devotees present. In some wealthy households a priest might be employed to conduct the *pūjā*. *Pūjā* can also be performed without the intermediary of a ritual specialist. It is performed before an image. In a home or shop this may well simply be a brightly coloured picture from the bazaar. In the temples these images might be carved out of stone or wood, or cast in bronze.

Pūjā involves making ritual offerings to an image. This may be very simple – such as lighting some incense and waving it before an image in a domestic shrine – or immensely complex and involved, with the offering of a wide range of different objects to the accompaniment of chanting. Shortened forms do not mean that the *pūjā* is considered as being incomplete in any way. In fact it is common practice to shorten and simplify the ritual. For example, at dawn or dusk the ritual may be reduced even more. A tray with burning camphor or an oil light is waved before the image of the deity while the devotees chant a *mantra*. This simplified ceremony is termed *āratī*. As Fuller (1992, p. 68) observes, 'ritual abbreviation and simplification are ubiquitous procedures' and this simple waving of a flame before the image is considered to be effectively performing the complete ritual. At the end of the *pūjā* or *āratī*, the priest will present the oil lamp or burning camphor, and the devotee will cup their hands around the flame and then bring their hands up to their forehead. A red powder made from turmeric (*kumkum*) or the ash from the burning incense will also be offered. The devotee will then mark the centre of their forehead with this.

Offering of food to the deity is also a common feature of daily worship. This might involve simply some sweets or it might be an elaborate meal. This food is then distributed amongst the priests and the devotees. The Sanskrit term *bhoga* literally means enjoyment of the sense objects; more specifically, it means food. By offering food to the deity, it becomes transformed into *prasād*, literally 'grace'. In other words, the food becomes a symbol of the grace of the deity instead of being simply an enjoyable indulgence. The flame, the red powder or incense ash, and the *prasād* have all been in contact with the deity in the form of the image. So cupping the hands in the flame, marking the forehead and eating the *prasād* all symbolize the transfer of divine grace to the devotee.

Although *pūjā* is not the only form of ritual found in Hinduism, it is incorporated into most forms of ritual activity, such as pilgrimage. We will discuss this more fully in the following chapter, which will use the small town of Rishikesh as a case study to explore in more depth some of the facets of Hinduism raised thus far.

Chapter 2

Hinduism in India

Rishikesh: A Place of Pilgrimage

Rishikesh, in many ways, can be considered a microcosm of the Hindu world. It is a small town about 200 kilometres north of Delhi, on the banks of the sacred river Gangā (anglicized as the Ganges), in the state of Uttarakhand. The area around Rishikesh is sometimes referred to *Dev Bhoomi* – the 'Land of the Gods', as there are a number of important pilgrimage places (*tīrthas*) that are located in the region. Rishikesh is regarded as the gateway to four sacred places, known collectively as the four abodes (*cār dhām*).[1] These are Badrinath, Kedarnath, Yamnotri and Gangotri. The significance of these places of pilgrimage, and of Rishikesh itself, is indicated by the fact that during the pilgrimage season (May to October) the population of Rishikesh increases tenfold (Keemattam, 1997, p. 22).

As well as being a necessary place en route to the *cār dhām*, Rishikesh itself is regarded as a *tīrtha*. There are three main reasons for this. First, there are references to Rishikesh in both the Purāṇic and Epic literature. In the *Skanda Purāṇa*, it is mentioned that Viṣṇu, pleased with his austerities, appeared to the sage Raibhya Muni. Viṣṇu consented to the sage's request to remain. The place then became known as Hṛṣikeśa, which roughly translates as 'one who has conquered the senses', indicating that the sacred can be readily accessed at this place because of the ascetic practices of Raibhya Muni. This name, over time, became Rishikesh.

Second, Rishikesh is associated with the religious practices of many holy men. Rishikesh itself is also sometimes referred to as the city of saints, as it traditionally has been a place where individuals have come to practise austerities. According to the devotees, some of these ascetics have had a direct experience of the sacred, and consequently have achieved liberation (*mokṣa*). Perhaps the most influential of these individuals was Swami Sivananda (1916–63), who arrived in 1924 in Rishikesh, which he himself describes as a 'holy place with many Mahatmas'[2] (Sivananda, 1995, p. 21). Sivananda settled in a spot about two miles north of the town of Rishikesh, where he began a period of intense spiritual practice (*sādhana*) and service to others. In 1934, responding to increasing numbers of people who were attracted to his teaching, Sivananda established his own ashram, to accommodate these followers. The Sivananda Ashram is now a thriving institution with about two hundred permanent residents. There are now several dozen ashrams in the area, which are home to various monastic communities that offer a variety of services such as providing accommodation to devotees, classes in yoga, and various charitable activities.

The *ghāts* at Rishikesh.

Third, and perhaps most importantly, Rishikesh is located on the banks of the sacred river Gangā. Pilgrims and locals all flock to the banks of the Gangā, and every day one can see Hindus making ritual ablutions (*snān*) in Gangā's sacred water. Much of the banks around Rishikesh is lined with steps (*ghāts*), to allow relatively easy access to

Gangā's swiftly flowing current. In the bazaars, pilgrims can buy plastic containers in order to take Ganges water (*Gangā jal*) back home. They add this to water from their normal supply, which transforms it into a ritually pure form that can then be used in domestic worship. Many local shopkeepers and café owners will sprinkle their premises with *Gangā jal*, to purify them before opening for custom in the morning.

Pilgrimage: *Tīrthayātrā*

For many Hindus pilgrimages to holy places (*tīrthayātrā*) is still an important aspect of their religious life, the sacred being regarded as particularly accessible at places like Rishikesh. *Tīrtha* literally translates as 'to cross over',[3] and is often understood as meaning a ford. The connotation is that a *tīrtha* is a place where it is possible to cross from mundane space to sacred space. Furthermore, many pilgrimage places, like Rishikesh, are also located on the banks of rivers.

Alan Morinis (1984, p. 2) observes that pilgrimage is 'both an individual's behaviour and a socio-cultural institution'. The social-cultural institutions that support the process of pilgrimage, like other aspects of the Hindu tradition that have their roots in the mists of time, have also undergone transformation in the context of the contemporary world. In the numerous pilgrimage places scattered throughout the sacred geography of India, the ritual specialists are the prime factor in the perpetuation of pilgrimage as a socio-cultural institution. Furthermore, the priests at the places of pilgrimage (*tīrtha purohit*) play a significant role in the maintenance and transmission of Hinduism as a religious tradition. Pilgrims return home with the sacred knowledge obtained at the *tīrtha*, and disseminate it amongst friends and family. Pilgrims must be familiar with the ritual practices at the *tīrtha*, and yet at the same time recognize the special and distinctive nature of the place. In many ways, the ritual network that constitutes the sacred geography of Hindu India can be thought of as a spatial manifestation of the philosophical idea that pervades much of contemporary Hindu thought: namely, unity in multiplicity.

Pilgrims visit sacred places for particular benefits that are supposed to accrue from visiting them. Although in the normative discourses religious practice is intended to achieve final liberation from the cycle of life, death and rebirth, in practice most pilgrims suggest the reasons for pilgrimage are the acquisition of karmic merit or more mundane goals such as good health, prosperity, successful marriage and so on.

There are a number of reasons why pilgrimage not only remains a very popular religious practice in the contemporary context, but is arguably more widely practised than ever before. First, it is achievable by the vast majority of Hindus. It does not necessarily entail elaborate ritual performance or rigorous ascetic practice. Second, a pilgrimage entails a clearly defined break from the routines of daily life and consequently can be an enjoyable undertaking. Many pilgrimage places, like Rishikesh, are located in places of great natural beauty. Furthermore, these places cater not only for the religious needs of the pilgrims, but also for more mundane requirements. In most pilgrimage places, there are bazaars where pilgrims can buy religious paraphernalia – such as coloured lithographs or framed photos of the images (*mūrti*) of the deity or deities associated with the particular *tīrtha* – as well as jewellery, new clothes, and toys for the children, etc. Eating out has for many also become an enjoyable part of the pilgrimage experience. Third, widening access to new media, in particular television and the Internet, means that growing numbers of people know about various pilgrimage places. This, coupled with modern modes of transport, means that many *tīrthas* are far more accessible than ever, and pilgrimage has become a less arduous and hazardous activity.

Religious Tourism

The combination of increased mobility and a growing middle-class sector with a disposable income has led to a new phenomenon that has been labelled 'religious tourism'. Pilgrimage and tourism are normally thought of as being two distinct forms of travelling. However, 'these two forms of travel increasingly overlap, because many people travel with the objective of achieving both the recreational and the religious need, and there are immense difficulties in distinguishing between the two' (Shinde, 2007, p. 24).

The local economy of many *tīrthas* has become reliant on the influx of pilgrims, and the concept of religious tourism has now been recognized by many regional and local governments, which are developing the infrastructure to cater for this potentially lucrative market. Religious tourists require more modern conveniences than the traditional pilgrim. In the Rishikesh area, this is reflected in several recently opened luxury hotels, and a large number of new businesses offering leisure activities such as rafting and trekking, as well as jeep rides up to one or more of the *cār dhāms*. A trip to Rishikesh is regarded as much as a holiday as a chance to visit sacred places. Rishikesh is only 250 kilometres north of Delhi and many people visit from the urban capital for a weekend, or even a single day, mostly by car.[4] Although many of these urban visitors might briefly visit a temple or ashram, and possibly even take a ritual dip in the Gangā, the primary impetus is leisure, and the characteristic structure is more akin to tourism than pilgrimage.

A Middle-class Religious Disposition

Religious tourism is primarily a phenomenon associated with the middle class. Class as a social category has largely been overlooked, primarily because scholars have typically seen it as an alien concept that cannot be imposed on the Indian context. However, many Indians do identify themselves as being middle class. The middle class in India is not a clearly defined category, but can be understood as primarily being an urban phenomenon where meritocracy is regarded as taking precedence over, although not totally replacing, ascriptive social categories.

It is clear that the middle class is an economic category defined by a certain level of disposable income. However, it is also a cultural category characterized through discourses that pertain to lifestyle choice, and in which identity is expressed through specific cultural practices. The middle classes are not only located between the rich and the poor, but also locate themselves between the superstitious practices of rural India, and the godless West. This has led to what might be considered a distinctive form of middle-class religious disposition, which is articulated in terms of both authenticity and modernity.

Though still appealing to a perceived authentic tradition, this middle-class religious disposition is not only expressed in terms of lifestyle choice, but also tends to support the belief that there is a natural progress from less to more rational forms of religiousness. This view suggests that the majority of people are incapable of perceiving that *Brahman* pervades and transcends all of creation and is beyond name and form. Consequently, most people require some sort of tangible focal point in order to understand the sacred. This is not wrong, as such, but the veneration of the sacred with a name and form is a very partial understanding of the sacred reality. Ultimately, this view suggests that we will all come to an understanding of the sacred without the necessity of an intervening object of worship. Swami Sivananda (2007, p. 115) suggests that 'an idol is a support for the neophyte. It is a prop of his spiritual childhood. A form or image is necessary for worship in the beginning.'

For the middle classes, this account legitimizes various religious practices, as these are perceived in terms of leading to spiritual achievement. This notion of spiritual progress is a direct corollary of the sense held by the middle classes that achievement in the mundane world is something that has to be earned. In other words, there is a rational explanation for ritual performance. This rationalization not only legitimizes their own ritual practices, but also enables the middle classes to suggest that Hinduism is an all-inclusive tradition. The discourse is not so much about right and wrong as about a progression from rudimentary to more evolved religious practices.

As choice is a defining characteristic of middle-class religious disposition, it is of no surprise that middle-class religiosity manifests in a number of different, albeit overlapping, arenas. These include the sponsorship of and participation in a new style of temple worship. Joanne Waghorne (2004) argues that in many ways the middle classes have taken the place of royalty as the primary patrons of temples. One of Waghorne's (2004, p. 9) informants observed: 'Once only kings could build temples, but now we middle-class people are able to do this.' The building of large temples in the medieval period was symbolic not only of the devotion, but also of the political and economic might, of ruling dynasties. In the contemporary period, the patronage of temples by groups from the middle classes is similarly indicative not only of their piety, but also of their social, economic and political significance. The middle classes also are drawn to transnational *gurus* such as Satya Sai Baba (see Babb, 1991), Mata Amritanandamayi (see Warrier, 2005) and Sri Sri Ravi Shankar. Many of the middle classes are also active in various ashrams, and practise yoga and meditation.

Choice is considered to be commensurate with the ethos of modernity and being authentically Hindu. The middle-class Hindu is making a choice as a reflexive and autonomous individual, yet paradoxically at the same time appealing to a reconstructed tradition in order to anchor and legitimize that choice. This narrative of choice is often articulated in terms of the famous verse in the Ṛg Veda, 'That which exists is One; sages call It by various names.' The middle-class religious disposition accepts that the sacred, although 'One', manifests, and is therefore approachable, in an infinite number of ways. The appropriate mode of religious expression and practice is thus determined by personal predilection, rather than imposed tradition.

An Exuberant Popular Disposition

Modern transport has also had a dramatic impact on the way in which less economically successful Indians undertake pilgrimages. The disposition of these pilgrims is quite different to that of the middle-class religious tourist. It is less restrained and more exuberant. While there is an opportunity for making small purchases, the impetus and focus of the journey remains primarily religious. For these pilgrims, this style of journey to a sacred place is less about a personal individual choice and more embedded in senses of collective identity.

In the month of Śrāvana (July/August),[5] thousands of relatively poor villagers, mostly small-scale farmers, descend on Rishikesh in order to go to the small temple dedicated to Śiva in the form of Neelkanth in the hills about 12 kilometres from Rishikesh. The month of Śrāvana is believed to be particularly sacred to Śiva, and in particular the last three Mondays are regarded as especially sacred. This is a period in the agricultural year when the needs of tending the land are minimal, and it is possible to get away. Modern transport, even for the less affluent, enables people to travel much further afield. Many villagers club together and hire a bus to take them to various sacred places. This is a relatively new phenomenon, which enables pilgrims to visit a number of different religious sites across India, and is sometimes referred to as a *darśan* tour.[6]

The temple at Neelkanth. The myth of the churning of the ocean is depicted in stucco work.

Neelkanth is associated with the famous myth, the churning of the ocean (*samudra manthan*), which is found in various recensions in the *Purāṇas* and Epics. The narrative tells of how the gods (*devas*) and the demons (*asuras*) have to cooperate in order to produce the nectar of immortality (*amrit*). Mount Mandaranchal is placed on the back of Kurma, the incarnation (*avatār*) of Viṣṇu in the form of a tortoise. The king of the serpents wraps himself around the mountain, the *asuras* take hold of his head, and the *devas* grab his tail in order to churn the ocean. In the process of the churning a number of treasures, for example the moon, emerge from the ocean. However, the churning also produces a poison that threatens to destroy everything. Śiva swallows the poison in order to protect creation and holds it in his throat, which consequently turns blue. One of the epithets of Śiva is Nīlkaṇṭha, which literally means 'Blue Throated'. Like many temples, the small temple at Neelkanth also has a visual representation of the mythic narrative realized in stucco work. These visual representations are significant in perpetuating the mythic narratives. The vast majority of Hindus do not read the *Purāṇas*, but the encounter with visual images often provides the occasion for the retelling of the narratives.

The Sacred River Ganges (Gangā)

By far the most important feature of the area around Rishikesh is the River Ganges, better known as Mahā Gangā (Great Gangā) or Mātā Gangā (Mother Gangā). Diana Eck (1983, p. 214) suggests that 'the Ganges carries an immense cultural and religious meaning for Hindus of every region and cultural persuasion'. One of the most significant ritual activities for many pilgrims to Rishikesh and many of the other *tīrthas* located on the banks of Gangā is to take a ritual dip (*snān*) in her sacred water. The ritual purificatory power of water has long been, and remains to this day, an important aspect of Hindu religiousness, and Ganges water (*Gangā jal*) is regarded as the purifying substance *par excellence*.

There are numerous mythological narratives about Gangā. The most widely known tale tells of King Bhagiratha, who is informed by the sages (*ṛṣis*) that he must invoke the cleansing presence of Gangā in order to lift a curse on his ancestors, which prevents them from entering heaven. Since Gangā's descent from the heavens would completely submerge the earth, Śiva agrees to break her force, and she flows harmlessly through his matted locks and frees Bhagaritha's ancestors from the curse. One of Śiva's many epithets is Gangādhara – the bearer of Gangā – and in most iconographical representations of Śiva it is possible to identify Gangā emerging from his locks.

Gangā is frequently associated with death rituals. In particular, there are four *tīrthas* – Hardwar, Banaras, Prayag (Allahabad), and Gaya – that are regarded as being particularly auspicious places to die or be cremated (see Parry, 1994 and Justice, 1997). For Hindus, cremation should take place as soon as possible after death. If it is not possible to arrange either the moment of death or the cremation at one of these *tīrthas* located on the banks of Gangā, some ritual performance at one of these crossing places is regarded as particularly desirable. This might involve the offering of the flowers used during the funerary rituals, or consigning bone fragments that are retrieved after the cremation to the Gangā.

Male relatives, in particular the eldest son, will endeavour to make the journey to the *tīrtha* associated with their family and perform a ritual known as *śrāddha* on the thirteenth day[7] after death. In this thirteen-day period, the immediate family, and especially the eldest son, should not participate in any activity other than the rituals associated with death; they should eat frugally and avoid leaving the house as much as possible. However, in the modern world, this period is often curtailed to three or four days. Nonetheless, the ritual requirements of the death of an immediate family member can be very disruptive to the household for upwards of a year. For example, no marriages are supposed to be arranged or celebrated until the first anniversary after the death.

In places like Hardwar and Banaras, the ritual specialists (*paṇḍas*) are also the record keepers. The relationship between a particular family and a specific family of *paṇḍas* in many instances goes back for generations. Lining the banks of Gangā, at places like Banaras and Hardwar, these *paṇḍas* set up wooden platforms for their consultations, and they will record details of births, marriages and so on, when family members make a special journey in order to perform *śrāddha*. *Śrāddha* might also be performed on the anniversary of the death, or during the fortnight of the ancestors.

Gangā is regarded as both the archetypal sacred waters and a goddess who can wash away one's sins. As a goddess, she is most often iconographically represented as emerging from Śiva's locks. She is also portrayed as a benign goddess riding a crocodile with a lotus saddle, and holding a pot in one hand and a lotus in the other. However, the river itself might also be considered as a form of the divine (*mūrti*). Every evening, just before dusk at a number of places along the *ghāts* at Rishikesh, *Gangā Āratī* is performed. This normally begins with *kīrtan* (literally 'to repeat'), a form of congregational devotional singing and chanting. Many of the sacred songs, often referred to as *bhajans*, derive from the development of the medieval devotional (*bhakti*) traditions, but remain very popular today. A number of these popular *bhajans* also find their way into the soundtrack of Bollywood films.

These devotional songs have catchy tunes, sometimes derived from the film versions. They are sung out by an individual, frequently to the accompaniment of harmonium and percussion, with the refrain being repeated by a chorus or more commonly by the entire congregation. The *Gaṅgā Āratī* will also include chanting of some of the widely known *mantras*. The ritual ends with the waving of lamps over Gaṅgā, which are then passed around all who are gathered. Many of the gathered devotees will also buy small boats made from stitched-together leaves, which contain flowers, a small cube of camphor, and a stick of incense. The camphor and incense are lit, and this offering is then released into the swirl of the fast-flowing current.

Renouncing the World

Pilgrims come to places like Rishikesh and other sacred places (*tīrthas*), not only because of the association with the mythic narratives of the *Purāṇas* and Epics, but also because of the association with holy men (and occasionally women). Just as the sacred can take form in an image (*mūrti*) and in nature as in Ma Gaṅgā, the sacred can also manifest in specific individuals. For the most part, although there are important exceptions, the sacred manifests in particular individuals because of their ascetic practices. Renouncing the world is a very significant aspect of the Hindu worldview, as it is commonly believed that it is not possible to achieve liberation while actually being involved in mundane activities. Ascetics of various types are still a very visible part of the Indian landscape, and in particular in the various *tīrthas*. The importance of asceticism is indicated by the number of different terms used to denote ascetic practices. The generic term for such practices is *sannyāsa*, and those who have adopted a life of abstinence and austerity are referred to as *sannyāsins*. While this typology is not absolute, and there is a degree of overlap between the categories, I suggest that there are three main types of holy men and women: *sādhus*, *swāmis*, and *gurus*.

Sādhus and *Swāmis*

The term *sādhu* is usually used to refer to those ascetics who adopt a peripatetic lifestyle and/or adopt very rigorous forms of asceticism. *Swāmi* is generally used as a title of respect, most frequently to refer to ascetics who have adopted a more monastic lifestyle. All *sādhus* and *swāmis* must undertake a ritual of initiation, which frequently entails the performance of the initiate's funeral and the adoption of a new name. This rite signifies that the initiate is no longer a part of the social world, and therefore no longer concerned with the three mundane goals: pleasure (*kāma*),[8] wealth (*artha*) and social duty (*dharma*), but are intent on liberation (*mokṣa*). Most adopt a specific mode of dress, or in some instances no dress at all. Many choose to wear saffron robes, which signify a life of renunciation. In general, although there are exceptions, *sādhus* tend to wear their hair in long matted locks, whereas *swāmis* frequently shave their heads. Both are indicative of an ascetic lifestyle, and in particular of celibacy.

There is no way really to assess how many ascetics there are in India. Dolf Hartsuiker (1993, p. 7) suggests there are four to five million. Although this is a very small percentage of the population, the influence of these ascetics reaches far beyond their actual numbers. Louis Dumont (1970, p. 275) rather overstates his case when he suggests that the renouncer is 'the agent of development in Indian religion and speculation, the creator of values', nonetheless there is no doubt that both the continuity and transformation of many aspects of the Hindu traditions can be attributed to particular individuals who have renounced the world.

Gurus

Because of their ascetic practices, *swāmis* and *sādhus* are believed to have special access to the sacred. Consequently, they play a very significant role in the religious life of many Hindus. While the various types of priests such as *pūjāris* and *paṇḍas* are ritual specialists, the renouncers are the source of religious knowledge. Some renouncers come to be regarded as *gurus*. It is important to note that not all renouncers are regarded as *gurus*, and conversely not all *gurus* are necessarily renouncers. Etymologically, the term *guru* is regarded as being composed of two parts: *gu* meaning darkness and *ru* signifying removal. Consequently, the *guru* is one who removes darkness or ignorance. That is, *gurus* are regarded as having the capacity of helping others achieve liberation.

It is impossible to underestimate the role of *gurus* in both the maintenance and transformation of the Hindu tradition. Many began lineages known as *paramparās*, which constitute an unbroken chain of succession. In the contemporary world, some *gurus* like Mata Amritanandamayi (see Warrier, 2005), Sri Mataji Nirmala Devi (see Coney, 1999) and Satya Sai Baba (see Babb, 1991) have become transnational figures who draw devotees from beyond the Indian community. Swami Sivananda is the most well known of the *gurus* who settled in Rishikesh.

Sivananda is regarded by his devotees as a *Sat Guru* – or true *guru*. The implication of this is that Sivananda is believed to be a fully realized being, who has understood his true divine nature. Sivananda is often referred to by devotees as Guru Dev, literally the *guru* who is god. Individuals such as Sivananda are believed to be liberated souls (*jīvan-mukta*). These realized individuals do not die as such, as they have escaped the wheel of life, death and rebirth, and when they leave their physical body they enter a state known as *mahā samādhi*. The term *samādhi* refers to the highest meditational state, when it is thought that the mind becomes totally absorbed in *Brahman*. The term *mahā* means 'great' and when added as a prefix to the term *samādhi* refers to the state attributed to liberated souls after they have left their physical body. The implication of this for the devotee is that Sivananda remains a very real presence. In his speech after taking over as the President of the Divine Life Society, Swami Chidananda suggested: 'Though he (Sivananda) has left one akara (form) and become nirakara (without form), he has now come to dwell in his more pervasive akara, namely this Ashram' (cited in *The Divine Life*, XXV (9), August 1963).

The Samādhi shrine at Sivananda Ashram. The full-sized image of Swami Sivananda is positioned above the place where Sivananda is buried. Large pictures that illustrate the life story of Sivananda painted by a devotee line the walls.

Individuals, such as Sivananda, who are believed not to have died but to have entered a state of *mahā samādhi*, are either buried or the body is submerged in the Gangā and not cremated as is the normal Hindu custom. Sivananda was buried in meditational pose and in a chamber that was then filled with salt, camphor and sandalwood. There is now a large hall with a shrine directly above the spot where Sivananda is buried, with a life-sized statue of Sivananda seated in meditation. This Samādhi Hall is the spiritual centre of the ashram.

Āśrams and *Sādhana*

The *āśram* founded by Sivananda, initially to provide accommodation for a growing number of devotees, is now the centre of a large multi-national and modern organization. The *āśram* is headquarters of the Divine Life Society (DLS), which was founded by Sivananda in 1936. It now has branches throughout India and the world, including most European countries, the USA, South Africa and Malaysia.[9]

The origins of ashrams can be traced back to the Vedic period, and in the contemporary period they have become important institutions for the maintenance, transmission and transformation of Hinduism. Ashrams in contemporary India are a very diverse phenomenon. Some, like Kailash *Āśram* in Rishikesh, are very traditional institutions. The latter was founded in 1880, and is primarily focused on learning Sanskrit, the study of the sacred texts (*śāstras*) and the philosophical schools (*darśanas*), particularly *Vedānta*. The head of Kailash *Āśram* is regarded as the most senior religious figure in the Rishikesh area. Other ashrams do little more than provide accommodation for pilgrims. However Sivananda Ashram, like many of the institutions that have sprung up around the spiritual preceptors of the late nineteenth and twentieth centuries, is a thoroughly modern institution. Sivananda's motto, 'Serve, Love, Meditate and Realize',[10] gives a good indication of the main focal points of most modern ashrams and many forms of contemporary Hinduism.

Serve

The concept of service (*seva*) as a spiritual practice (*sādhana*) has become a central defining core of many forms of contemporary Hinduism. In large part, Swami Vivekananda reformulated the notion of service, and made it a central aspect of modern ashrams and the lives of contemporary renunciants (*sannyāsins*). The underlying rationale for *sannyāsa* is to seek liberation from the wheel of life, death and rebirth (*saṃsāra*). Consequently, for the traditional *sannyāsin* the phenomenal world, including the suffering of others, is a mere distraction from the soteriological goal of liberation. Furthermore, if *Advaita Vedānta* provides the philosophical framework for renunciation, then not only is the world, including the physical body, a distraction, but it is also regarded as fundamentally unreal. There seems no place in this worldview for the *sannyāsin* to become involved in the world at all, not even to help alleviate the suffering of others.

While it would be an oversimplification to identify a single individual or organization as responsible for reinterpreting this paradigm, nonetheless Swami Vivekananda and the founding of the Ramakrishna Mission were deeply influential in fomenting the idea of selfless service as a spiritual practice (for a full discussion of this see Beckerlegge, 2006). The young Vivekananda in a period of wandering was shocked by the living conditions of many Indians that he encountered. In a letter written in 1894 to one of his fellow devotees of Ramakrishna, Vivekananda observed that Hinduism is a 'religion that fails to remove the misery of the poor'. Later on in the same letter Vivekananda suggests that he had a plan to use 'disinterested Sannyasins, bent on doing good to others ... disseminating education and seeking in various ways to better the condition of all down to the Chandāla' (Vivekananda, 1984, Vol. VI, pp. 254–5).

Vivekananda worked out a philosophical foundation for this practical idea that involved a radical reinterpretation of *Advaita Vedānta*. Swami Vivekananda termed this reworking 'Practical Vedanta', and presented it in a series of lectures given in London in 1896. His argument runs that 'Vedanta teaches Oneness', and that since every individual is part of that sacred unity, each individual has to be concerned for everyone's welfare, as ultimately there is no real distinction between the individual's existence and everyone else's. *Sannyāsa* is not therefore about retiring from the world and living in the remote Himalayas, but actively engaging in the world, and in particular helping to ameliorate the suffering of others. In 1897, the newly founded Ramakrishna Mission organized the first systematic programme of aid for victims of a famine (see Beckerlegge, 2006, pp. 27ff.).

The ideal of service (*seva*) pervades many forms of contemporary Hinduism. Like Swami Vivekananda, Swami Sivananda (2007, p. 67) suggests 'the basics of Hindu ethics is this: "There is one all-pervading Atman. It is the inner soul of all beings."' Consequently, 'Feed the hungry. Clothe the naked. Serve the sick. This is the Divine Life'

(Sivananda, cited in *The Divine Life*, August 2008, p. 21). Sivananda, a trained physician, operated a free dispensary for the *sādhus* in Rishikesh. In 1950 he opened the Sivananda Charitable Hospital, which remains an integral part of the ashram. The ashram also runs four leprosy colonies, and an educational trust to fund school and college fees. All of these services are provided free. Sivananda suggests that service to others is integral to the divine life. It not only creates harmony in this life, but also is important for the achievement of liberation. The *sannyāsins* living on the ashram are expected to fully engage with any number of mundane activities, from basic administrative tasks to working in the kitchen or hospital.

Love

The second term in the motto of the Divine Life Society is 'love', and this clearly refers to *bhakti* – or loving devotion to God. 'Bhakti has succeeded in becoming the religion of the Indian masses, undermining caste distinctions and providing forms of worship with a common language of ritual practice' (Geaves, 2008a, p. 89). Many Hindus' religious life is centred on images, and Hinduism still retains a vibrant visual culture. The area around Rishikesh is replete with brightly coloured statues of various gods and goddesses, many of them more than life sized. One of the most popular places for pilgrims to visit is Parmarth Niketan, a large ashram on the opposite side of Gangā to the Sivananda Ashram. In its well-tended gardens are a large number of painted images depicting scenes from various Hindu narratives. Many pilgrims wander quietly around these gardens, often slightly bowing their heads with hands joined together in respect before each image (*pranām*). They might well remind each other of the stories associated with the image and throw a coin at the base as an offering.

There is clear evidence of the importance of *bhakti* on Sivananda Ashram. The most important places for devotional practice are the *Samādhi* Shrine, The Visvanath Mandir, and the *bhajan* hall. The *Samādhi* Shrine is both the symbolic and physical centre of the Sivananda Ashram, as it is here that the body of Sivananda is interred, and Sivananda is regarded as having a real, albeit incorporeal, presence. Consequently, devotees come to the hall for *darśan* of Guru Dev. A number of ritual activities take place here, the most important of which is called *satsang* – which literally means 'good company'. There are three overlapping connotations to the term: it indicates the importance of being in the company of the *guru*; it suggests the importance of keeping company with fellow devotees; and it also is used as a general term to indicate a group of people gathered to listen to a religious discourse (Geaves, 2008b, p. 774).

In many ways the *satsang* in the Samādhi Hall at Sivananda Ashram includes all three aspects. The *satsang* begins at about 7.30 in the evening and finishes at about 9.30. It is the only activity which visitors staying on the ashram are expected to attend. The presence of Swami Sivananda is emphasized by large paintings of various aspects of Sivananda's life that adorn most of the wall space, and by the life-sized statue of Sivananda above the spot where he is buried. In the middle of the long wall, there is a small throne, with a garlanded picture of Sivananda with the *mantra Om Namo Bhagavate Śivanandaya* (Om Salutations to the God Sivananda) inscribed on the wall above.

Devotees gather for *satsang* not only to be in the presence of Sivananda, but also because many of the senior *swāmis* attend, and being in their august presence is also regarded as beneficial for the religious life. Being in the company of other devotees is also important. Many devotees feel a very real connection to other devotees, and often use the term *guru bhai*, literally 'guru brother'. The ritual of *satsang* at Sivananda Ashram involves congregational singing and chanting (*kīrtan*); often a chapter of the *Bhagavad Gītā* is chanted; a short extract from one of Swami Sivananda's many works is read; there will be a discourse in either Hindi or English given by one of the senior *swāmis* or a guest speaker; and the evening ends with *āratī* and the distribution of *prasād*.

Temples

Although it is an often cited aphorism that it is perfectly possible to be a good Hindu without ever going to a temple, the temple still plays a very important role in the lives of many contemporary Hindus. This remains the case across the wide spectrum of class, caste, and educational background. In Rishikesh, as well as the *ghāts*, temples are an important arena for ritual activity. As in all Indian towns, there are numerous temples in Rishikesh.

The Bharat Mandir claims to be the oldest temple in the region. The name refers to a form of Viṣṇu holding his most identifiable iconic objects: a conch, mace, discus and lotus. It is here that it is said that Viṣṇu appeared to the sage Raibhya. Furthermore, this *mandir* claims that the central image (*mūrti*) was installed by the great medieval philosopher Śankarācārya. This claim is important as it both substantiates its claim to being an ancient temple, and also links *bhakti* to *Vedānta* philosophy. Like most temples, the Bharat Mandir is actually a small complex. The main shrine is dedicated to Viṣṇu, and to the side there is an image of the child Kṛṣṇa (Bāla Kṛṣṇa) in a swing. There are small separate shrines, one dedicated to the elephant-headed Gaṇeśa, the other containing a small Śiva *linga*. This might seem surprising as Gaṇeśa and Śiva are both clearly located within the Śaivite tradition rather than Vaiṣṇava tradition. On one level this is a clear indication that these two broad traditions are not as distinct as some scholars suggest. On another, as these shrines are satellites to the main shrine containing the images of *Viṣṇu*, it could be regarded as a visible signifier of henotheism.

A *pūjārī* can be found in the temple. His position, like those of most ritual specialists, is hereditary: he follows in his father's footsteps, and is training his son to take over from him. He performs a simple *āratī* in the morning and evening, and the rest of the day is available for anyone that visits the temple. Throughout the day worshippers visit the temple. These visits mostly entail a simple bow of the head with hands held together in front of the chest before the image (*pranām*). The *pūjārī* spoons a small amount of sacred water into the right hand of the worshipper, who sips it. The *pūjārī* then marks the forehead of the worshipper with a spot of red powder made from turmeric (*kumkum*) and gives them a few sugar crystals as *prasād*. The worshipper generally gives the *pūjārī* a few rupees, makes a final *pranām* and leaves. They then may visit the other shrines, where a similar routine will be followed. The whole ritual process may take only a minute or two. It might seem very perfunctory to Western eyes; however, for the devotee, they have had *darśan* of the sacred and received the grace of the deity in the form of *prasād*.

Rishikesh is a town not only of temples, but also of shrines. There are wayside shrines throughout India. These might simply be stones placed under trees, a rock roughly hewn in the shape of a deity and painted bright orange (frequently Hanumān in North India), or a fully realized carving housed in a fairly permanent structure. There are three interconnected differences between shrines and temples. First, shrines are obviously far less grand and imposing than most temples. Second, in shrines the demarcation between sacred and profane space is not as clearly defined as for temples. Third, an intermediary ritual specialist is not normally present at shrines.

Swami Sivananda clearly believed that the temple was an important requisite for the divine life and consecrated the Visvanath Mandir on the ashram in 1943. Visvanath is an epithet of Śiva – and literally means 'Lord of the Universe'. According to the ashram's website:

> In India, there is a tradition and common practice to have a family deity or Kula-Devata. So, we find a temple in most of the

> Ashrams and the main Deity of the temple is like the presiding Deity of the Ashram. In this sense, Lord Visvanatha is the presiding and protecting Deity of Sivananda Ashram and the entire Sivananda family of devotees spread all over the world. (Sivananda Ashram, 2005).

The main *mūrti* is a Śiva *liṅga*, but there is also a prominent image of Kṛṣṇa, as well as an image of Śiva in his form as Lord of Yoga, and images of Gaṇeśa, Devi and Śankara. The Visvanath Mandir is where the more traditional religious activities of the ashram take place. The temple day begins at 4.00 a.m. when a *brahmacarya* rings the bell to awaken the deity. From around five, devotees start to drift in, most of whom are women. After a ritual bow (*pranām*) or a full prostration before the main shrine, they begin the chanting of the six-syllable Śiva *mantra Om Namah Śivaya* (Om, homage to Śiva) to the accompaniment of the harmonium.

Performing *pūjā* at a wayside shrine dedicated to Śiva. A Śiva *liṅga* can be seen in front; on the shelf behind is an anthropomorphic representation of Śiva flanked by two smaller images of Gaṇeśa.

Mantras

Repetition of *mantras* is known as *japa* and is widely practised. Harvey Alper (1991, p. 2) goes as far as to suggest that 'the history of religious life in India might plausibly be read as a history of mantras'. Although the precise definition of what constitutes a *mantra* is contested (see Alper, 1991) I will take a *mantra* to be a syllable, phrase or short verse that is believed to possess power, and the repetition of which can produce religious, spiritual or magical effects.

Many *mantras*, such as the six-syllable Śiva *mantra*, are short phrases that are normally associated with a particular deity. Perhaps the most well known of these is the *mantra* that is chanted by the International Society for Krishna Consciousness (ISKCON)

> Hare Krishna, Hare Krishna, Krishna Krishna Hare Hare;
> Hare Rama Hare Rama, Rama Rama Hare Hare.

These are different names for God. In ISKCON understanding, just as the *mūrti* is not simply a visual representation of God but is God, the *mantra* is not simply an aural representation, but is also God. 'Simply put, Kṛṣṇa *is* his name, and anyone who utters that name at once directly associates with Kṛṣṇa' (Deadwyler III, 1996, p. 81). In the *bhajan* hall on Sivananda Ashram, repetition of this *mantra* has been continued, night and day, unbroken since December 1943.

The repetition of *mantras* (*japa*) takes three different forms. The first is silent or mental repetition, and is often used as a form of meditational practice. A rosary of beads (*mālā*) is often used in the silent repetition of a *mantra*. The second form of *japa* is the recitation of *mantras* aloud. While the silent repetition of *mantras* tends to be an individual and meditational practice, the vocalization of a *mantra* tends to be a collective practice which is incorporated into ritual performance. Almost all forms of Hindu ritual practice include the chanting of *mantras* at some point in the ritual performance. The third form of *mantra* repetition is the writing out of *mantras* as a meditational practice, and this is known as *likhita japa*. While this is not as common as the other two forms of *japa*, it is still fairly widely practised. In Sivananda Ashram there is a small room housing thousands of notebooks sent by devotees, filled with the *mantra* of the individual's chosen deity (*iṣṭa devatā*). Sivananda (1994, p. 86) suggests, 'The very presence of these Mantra-notebooks will create favourable vibrations requisite for your Sadhana.'

Rituals: Abhiṣeka, Āratī *and* Yajña

At six o'clock in the morning the *abhiṣeka* is performed in the Visvanath Mandir. *Abhiṣeka*, the ritual anointing of an image of the deity (*mūrti*) can be quite a simple affair, or like most forms of Hindu ritual can be elaborated into a highly complex ritual. It is performed in one way or another in virtually all Hindu temples. At Sivananda Ashram, devotees are able to sponsor the performance of the *abhiṣeka*. This means that they are permitted to sit within the main sanctum and around the Śiva *liṅga* with the *pūjārī* who conducts the ritual. This is highly unusual, as in most temples the central sanctum is the preserve of the priests, and worshippers are not normally allowed to cross into this most sacred space.

The *pūjārī* greets those who have sponsored the *abhiṣeka* and seats them around the *liṅga*. The ritual lasts about an hour, in which various offerings are poured over the *liṅga* by those in attendance while the *pūjārī* chants various *mantras*. The most important offerings are the five nectars (*pañcāmrita*); these are curds, ghee, milk, honey and unrefined sugar (this last nectar is often dissolved and mixed with a fruit pulp). There are three explanations for this offering. The first is that these five substances are believed to have cooling properties.[11] The second is that they directly relate to the five elements (earth, water, fire, air and ether). Finally, the number five is particularly sacred to Śiva. In some forms of Śaivism, Śiva is said to perform five activities: veiling (the true nature of reality), granting grace, creation of the cosmos, maintenance, and destruction.

The *liṅga* is carefully washed after the anointing with the five nectars, and a silver coiled serpent is placed over it. The serpent is associated with Śiva, and is also regarded as having cooling properties. The serpent represents death and signifies Śiva's mastery over death. Furthermore, the serpent symbolizes the yogic power known as *kuṇḍalinī*, which normally resides as a dormant force at the base energy centre (*cakra*) of the human body. The hooded serpent that shades the *liṅga* like an umbrella represents the awakening of this yogic power, and its rising to the highest *cakra*, signifying liberation. The *pūjārī* then decorates the *liṅga* with garlands of flowers, anoints it with three horizontal lines of sacred ash (*vibhūti*) and a sacred mark (*tilak*) made from a red powder (*kumkum*) and sandalwood paste. The participants are each provided with a tray of flowers and bilva leaves (also known as bael). Bilva leaves normally have three leaflets and therefore vaguely resemble the end of a trident, and are consequently sacred to Śiva. These are scattered around the *liṅga*, as the *pūjārī* chants further *mantras*. This signals the end of the *abhiṣeka* and the participants are instructed to leave the sanctum, where they wait in the main hall of the temple with other devotees who have been gathering. The *pūjārī* finally finishes the adornment of the *liṅga* with offerings of fruit.

The *pūjārī* at Sivananda Ashram performing *āratī* before an image of Kṛṣṇa at the end of *abhiṣeka*. The Śiva *liṅga* can be just seen, swathed in garlands of flowers and decorated with coconuts. In front of the Śiva *liṅga* is Nandi, the bull who is regarded as Śiva's vehicle. To the right are images of Rāma and Sītā.

It is now time for the *āratī*, which is announced by a cacophony of bells, gongs, drums and the blowing of a conch. The *pūjārī* rings a bell in his left hand and waves various lamps in front of all the images in the main shrine. The *āratī* culminates with the lighting of a lamp that has 108 wicks, which after it has been presented to the images is taken to the awaiting devotees, who proffer their hands to the flames and then bring them up to touch their foreheads. As the devotees file out of the temple, they get a mark of sacred ash on their foreheads, a sip of sacred water and a small sweet (*prasād*).[12] The *āratī* at Sivananda Ashram is a very organized and ordered ritual. Men and women are kept in separate lines on either side of the main shrine, and although the devotees are eager, there is none of the pushing and shoving that can occur in the performance of some *āratīs*. Because Sivananda was originally from the state of Tamil Nadu, the rituals of *abhiṣeka* and *āratī* are very much in a South Indian style. Consequently, many of the *darśan* tour buses from South India touring some of the sacred sites of northern India make a stop for the *āratī* at Sivananda Ashram.

There is a small room in one corner of the Visvanath Mandir, which contains a small square pit, surrounded by a low wall, for making a ritual fire. This room is known as the Yajña Hall (*Yajña Shala*). The term *yajña* means sacrifice, and often is used to refer specifically to the Vedic fire ritual. Although *pūjā* remains the core ritual of devotional forms of Hinduism, *yajña*[13] still plays an important role in contemporary ritual life. However, the place and understanding of *yajña* in contemporary forms of Hinduism is very different to that of the Vedic period. For example, in the Vedic period the *yajña shala* would not have been a permanent structure and would have been specially consecrated for a single ritual performance. At Sivananda Ashram, the *yajña* is performed every Monday morning, and any other morning when there is a sponsor. The ritual itself is quite lengthy, lasting for over two hours. The main part of the ritual involves 108 repetitions of a *mantra*. At each repetition, the sponsors and priests pour some ghee using long-handled spoons into the ritual fire. The couple who sponsored the *yajña* that I witnessed informed me that the ritual was dedicated to Lord Śiva, and they performed it for the sake of good health and a long life.

Performing a *yajña*, the ancient fire ritual that has its roots in the Vedic period.

Bhakti, or the loving devotion to a personal deity, therefore remains an important aspect of many forms of contemporary Hinduism. It is also true that many of the ritual practices associated with *bhakti* remain a significant part of the religious life for most Hindus and cut across many demographic divides. Ritual performance is an important expression of *bhakti*. This might simply mean going for *darśan* in a temple and receiving a few sugar crystals as *prasād*, or can involve long and complex rites.

Meditate

The third aspect of Sivananda's Yoga of Synthesis is meditation. Sivananda means something quite specific by this term. The most commonly used Sanskrit term for meditation is *dhyāna*, and this is one of the stages in the systemization of yoga expounded by Patañjali.[14] This systematized form of yoga is sometimes referred to as Kingly Yoga (Raja Yoga), and also eight-limbed yoga (*aṣṭānga yoga*) as it involves eight different spiritual practices.

1. *Yama* – abstentions
2. *Niyama* – observances
3. *Āsana* – posture
4. *Prāṇāyāma* – control of the breath
5. *Pratyāhāra* – withdrawal of the senses from sense objects
6. *Dhāraṇā* – concentration
7. *Dhyāna* – meditative absorption
8. *Samādhi* – union (enstasis)

Abstentions and observances pertain to social relationships, and constitute an ethical code. The most well known of these is non-violence (*ahimsa*), which Gandhi famously made a central tenet of his philosophy. *Āsana*, the physical postures, are what most people in the West think of as yoga. Yogic thought suggests that controlling the physical body (*āsana*) and the breath (*prāṇāyāma*) helps to control the mind. Withdrawal of the senses (*pratyāhāra*) is the transition point between external and internal practices. The analogy that is sometimes used to describe this stage is that of a tortoise drawing its limbs into its shell. Concentration (*dhāraṇā*) refers to concentrating the mind on a single point. This is followed by a state of meditative absorption (*dhyāna*). The difference between concentration and meditative absorption is very subtle. An analogy that is often used is the comparison between pouring a steady stream of water as opposed to oil. The final goal of yoga is known as *samādhi*, in which all distinctions between the meditator, the act of mediation and the object of meditation collapse. *Samādhi* enables the meditator to grasp the true nature of reality that underlies all phenomenal existence, undistracted by what Patañjali terms the fluctuations of consciousness. Swami Vivekananda used the term superconsciousness to try to convey the meaning of the term *samādhi*.

Elizabeth De Michelis (2004) has identified distinctive forms of modern yoga, which she argues are quite different from classical forms. It is important to note at this point that classical forms of yoga can still be found in India, and, as with many aspects of Hinduism, the new does not necessarily replace the old; rather, modernity and tradition exist side by side, interacting in highly complex ways. Yoga and meditation are traditionally associated with *sannyāsins*, and not householders. However, modern forms of yoga do not advocate ascetic practices beyond sometimes suggesting a vegetarian diet and avoidance of intoxicants.

Yoga is very popular in that it is perceived as an authentic aspect of Hindu culture. It is authentic, because its roots can, in theory, be traced back to an ancient past. Many modern yogis point to the enigmatic Indus Valley Seal of the so-called 'proto Śiva' as evidence of the ancient origins of yoga. It is further represented as being scientific, and also superior to Western forms of medicine. The practice of yoga is now firmly identified with the ability to prevent and cure diseases, and to alleviate the stress of modern living. One of the foremost proponents of what might be called therapeutic Hinduism is the highly popular Swami Ramdev, who not only holds regular yoga camps, but also has a regular slot on cable television. 'His popularity demonstrates the power of yoga to satisfy a national and transnational nostalgia for tradition' (Chakraborty, 2007, p. 1174).

While Sivananda Ashram provides facilities for both yoga and meditation, the majority of visitors do not avail themselves of these facilities, and the yoga classes are predominately attended by Western seekers. Nonetheless, yoga and meditation play an important symbolic role in the minds of many Hindus. It could be argued that they have become increasingly significant in the contemporary period. There are three main interconnected reasons for the growing salience of yoga and meditation. The first reason is what Agehananda Bharati (1970) has called the pizza effect. By this he means a process of re-enculturation whereby a cultural phenomenon is exported and transformed, is then re-imported to the original cultural milieu in its transformed state and re-evaluated accordingly. The second reason is that yoga and meditation have been reframed in terms of being both rational and scientific, and consequently are commensurate with a modern ethos. Third, these practices have been divorced from ascetic practices and rearticulated with discourses on physical health and psychological well-being.

Realize

Sivananda's final term, 'realize', encapsulates three interrelated concepts that play an important role in many forms of contemporary Hinduism. These are absolute monism (*Advaita Vedānta*), knowledge (*jñāna*) and liberation (*mokṣa*). These three concepts play an important symbolic, rather than actual role in contemporary forms of Hinduism. *Advaita Vedānta*, the absolute monistic school of philosophy as espoused by Śankara (8th–9th century CE), has been reinterpreted in the apologetic discourses of modern forms of Hinduism, and represented as the acme of all religious thought. This discourse begins with the premise that *Advaita Vedānta* recognizes that there is only one fundamental reality that underlies the diversity of the phenomenal world (*Brahman*). The corollary is that this absolute reality can be expressed and accessed in an infinite number of ways. All expressions of this absolute cannot fully encapsulate its reality *in toto*, consequently all religious expressions have an equal, but partial validity. However, because *Vedānta* recognizes the relative and partial nature of all modes of religious expression, this places it in a privileged position.

This assertion facilitates the gathering of all modes of religious practices under the umbrella term of Hinduism, and underpins the often cited phrase that Hinduism is characterized by 'unity-in-diversity'. *Vedānta* is represented as a sort of meta-religion. Consequently, Hinduism in the modern world is frequently represented as being tolerant. *Vedānta* does not evaluate different modes of religiousness in terms of right and wrong, but suggests that each person's religiousness is expressed in terms of what is appropriate to their own religious development. Ultimately, each person has the capacity to realize the truth, and this is referred to as knowledge (*jñāna*).

Clearly the *summum bonum* of *Vedānta* is the knowledge (*jñāna*) that is encapsulated in the great Upaniṣadic sayings (*mahāvākya*), such as 'I am the Absolute' (*aham brahmāsi*). This is sometimes expressed in various metaphors such as the drop realizing its oneness with the ocean. *Jñāna* means something other than knowing a fact; it is the knowledge that leads to liberation (*mokṣa*) from the eternal cycle of life, death and rebirth (*saṃsāra*). It is a knowledge based upon experience, and the discourses of many modern *swāmis* tend to emphasize experience.

While most Hindus acknowledge the Vedas as the source of Hinduism, and recognize them as a source of knowledge, their role in contemporary Hinduism is minimal. There are a few places, like the Kailash Ashram in Rishikesh, where exegesis of Sanskrit texts (*śāstras*) is still the main focus of religious practice (*sādhana*). However, the Vedas tend to be a symbolic, rather than an actual, source of authority, and this enables almost anything to be regarded as authoritative in religious matters.

Four sources of religious authority have come to be prominent in contemporary Hinduism: religious experience itself, various *gurus*, the *Bhagavad Gītā* and the *Rāmāyaṇa*. The religious experience of sages might be regarded as a paradigmatic model. The Vedic *ṛṣis* in many ways provide a template, as it is their experiences that revealed the truth embodied in the Vedas. Many contemporary *gurus* are regarded as authoritative as they speak from their own religious experience. This has given them a special status, and consequently knowledge is derived from the articulation of the *guru*'s experience and not necessarily from any textual source. Some *gurus* spend a great deal of time discoursing on various topics such as *Vedānta*. However, for many devotees, having a sacred sight (*darśan*) of the *guru* is more significant than any didactic discourse. The importance of being in the presence of the *guru* is especially significant in movements like the Sathya Sai Baba and Mata Amritananandamayi movements. It is of course the love of the *guru* for his or her devotee and vice versa that is the main emphasis in these particular modern movements.

It is clear that the *Bhagavad Gītā* had a special status in premodern times, but it has also come to play a particularly significant role in contemporary Hinduism. John Brockington (1997, p. 28) observes, 'To most Vaiṣṇavas, and indeed to most modern Hindus, the *Bhagavad Gītā* is their main religious text and the real source of many of their beliefs.' There are a number of interconnected reasons for this increasing salience. The *Bhagavad Gītā* was one of the very first Sanskrit texts to be translated into English. It had a deep impact on a wide variety of Westerners, including the Romantics, the Transcendentalists and academics. In other words, it was the first Hindu text to not only be made accessible in the West, but also be evaluated positively amongst certain sectors of the Western intelligentsia (see Sharpe, 1985). The *Bhagavad Gītā* has been allocated a special place by many prominent Hindus themselves. For example, Mahatma Gandhi often extolled its uniqueness and significance, not only for Hindus in general, but in his own life. The *Bhagavad Gītā* is a very short text, particularly in comparison to the Vedic corpus. Consequently, many commentators have suggested that this short composition encapsulates Hindu beliefs. However, it also has a universality, and as Will Johnson (1994, p. viii) indicates, it has 'an apparently limitless capacity to inspire new and necessarily valid meanings'.

While many Hindus might know more of the content of the *Bhagavad Gītā* than the Vedas, it still plays a largely symbolic role in the majority of Hindus' lives. However, almost all Hindus know at least the basic story of the *Rāmāyaṇa*. It is a very compelling narrative that tells how Rāma rescues his wife Sītā from the ten-headed demon Rāvaṇa. This narrative is recited, told in comics, and acted out in street performances. It has also been filmed and made into a television series. The central theme of the *Rāmāyaṇa* is *dharma*, which will be the theme of the next chapter.

Chapter 3

Hindu Dharma *in the Contemporary World: Caste, Gender and Political Hinduism*

There is no word in any of the Indian languages that is equivalent to the term religion. It is fairly common to hear Hindus suggest that there is no such thing as Hinduism, and that the term in itself is a misnomer. In fact many Hindus find the very term Hinduism rather insulting. The reason for this is that it is claimed, with some justification, that it is a foreign term imposed during the colonial period. It is suggested that the correct term for the religious culture of Hindus is *Sanātana Dharma*. *Sanātana* can be translated as 'Eternal'; however, there is no single word in the English language that is equivalent to the term *dharma*.

Dharma has the connotation of order as opposed to *adharma*, which implies chaos. When combined with *Sanātana*, the term *dharma* is best understood in terms of 'truth'. Therefore the closest translation of *Sanātana Dharma* is the 'Eternal Truth'. This gives us a clue as to why many Hindus suggest that Hinduism is not a religion. The argument goes that all other religions can be traced to a founder or foundational event. However, the truth that is articulated in the Vedic corpus is eternal, and was revealed to the ancient Vedic seers (*ṛṣis*). It is therefore not a composition of a founder, but the truth that transcends both time and space.

In particular, *dharma* is concerned with the maintenance of the social order. This social order is linked both to individual behaviour and to the maintenance of the cosmos. In other words, the individual, the social and the cosmological are inseparable. The correct behaviour of the individual is perceived as bringing balance and order to both society and the cosmos.

Dharma is often regarded as applying to specific groups and is referred to as *varṇāśramadharma*. This rather ponderous word is actually three words joined together: *varṇa* – which is often translated as caste; *āśrama* – which means stage of life; and *dharma* – which in this context can be translated as duty. Therefore *varnāśramadharma* roughly translates as 'one's duty as determined by one's caste and stage of life'. I will not be discussing the *āśrama*[1] system, as it is largely an ideal and is rarely adhered to. However the concept of caste continues to play a significant, albeit contested, role in contemporary Hinduism.

Caste

Caste is perhaps the most widely misunderstood aspect of Hinduism. There are two interconnected reasons for the misunderstanding. First, the term caste is not an Indian term but is derived from the Portuguese term *casta*, which roughly translates as race or tribe. However, the Portuguese '*casta*' does not correspond with the social structures of Hindu society. Second, the term caste has come to stand for two distinct systems of social structure: *varṇa* and *jāti*. *Varṇa* refers to the division of society into four groups, whereas *jāti* refers to thousands of groups that were originally determined by occupation.

Varṇa and *Jāti*

Varṇa refers to a system that divides society into four hierarchically arranged groups: the priests (*brāhmins*); warriors and rulers (*kṣatriyas*); artisans, farmers and traders (*vaiśyas*); and those who serve the other groups (*śūdras*). Louis Dumont, in his seminal work on caste, argues that the underlying principle of this hierarchy is the opposition between purity and pollution. Furthermore Dumont (1980, p. 74) argues that this opposition 'is a religious, even a ritualistic affair'.

The origin of *varṇa* can be traced back to a hymn found in the *Ṛg Veda* called the Hymn of the Cosmic Man (*Puruṣa Sūkta*). This hymn suggests that creation is due to the sacrifice and dismemberment of the cosmic man. 'His mouth became the Brahmin; his arms were made into the Warrior, his thighs the People, and from his feet the Servants were born' (O'Flaherty, 1981, p. 31).

This hymn, although it does not use the term *varṇa*, suggests that society is an organic whole, homologous to the structure of both the cosmos and the body. However, there is no unequivocal evidence that the Vedic society was actually organized according to this structure.

A clearly defined social structure in terms of four distinct *varṇas* is only outlined in the later *dharma* texts, and in particular *The Laws of Manu*, which clearly delineates the duties (*dharma*) of each *varṇa*. *The Laws of Manu* (1:88–91) indicates that the duty of the priests (*brāhmins*) is to learn the Vedas and perform the sacrifice, the duty of the warriors (*kṣatriyas*) is to protect society, the duty of the people (*vaiśyas*) is to farm and engage in trade, and the duty of the servants (*śūdras*) is only to serve. The three highest *varṇas* are sometimes collectively referred to as twice born (*dvija*). This refers to the fact that at about the age of eleven all males of the three highest *varṇas* undergo an initiation in which they receive a sacred thread. This is a triple loop of thread, which is worn over the left shoulder and under the right arm. This initiation is generally perceived in terms of a spiritual birth. Beneath the four *varṇas* is a fifth stratum of society, not formally classified as a *varṇa*, which is sometimes referred to by the generic term 'Untouchable'. Members of this stratum, because of their occupations, are regarded as ritually impure. The structure of the *varṇa* system can be diagrammatically represented as in Table 2.

Table 2: *The structure of the* varṇa *system*

	Varṇa	**Duty**	
Twice born (*Dvija*)	*Brāhmin*	Learn the Vedas and perform the sacrifice	Purity
	Kṣatriya	Protect the people	
	Vaiśya	Tend cattle and trade	
	Śūdra	Serve the twice born	
	Untouchables		Pollution

The *jāti* system is a taxonomy of all life forms including animal, human and celestial beings. Members of the same *jāti* are believed to share the same bodily substance, which distinguishes them from members of all other *jātis*. While the *varṇa* system divides society into four basic strata, there are literally thousands of *jātis*. In fact, the number of *jātis* is not fixed. *Jāti* was originally determined by locality and occupation. However, nowadays, many members no longer perform their traditional occupation, and might well have moved away from their original locality. *Jātis* are endogamous groups, and the practice of marrying only within one's own *jāti* is still prevalent. *Jāti* is both ascriptive and immutable. However, this does not mean to say that there is no social mobility within the system.

In this highly complex system, each *jāti* might be also subdivided into sub-castes. In the colonial period the British tried to map the *jāti* system onto the *varṇa* system, despite the fact that there is no direct correlation between the two systems. Although the *jāti* system is also hierarchical, it is often highly problematic to categorize specific *jāti* in terms of a particular *varṇa*.

Caste is an incredibly sensitive issue, mainly because many outsiders, without fully understanding the nuances of either *varṇa* or *jāti*, have been extremely critical of the caste system. A new apologetic on caste is emerging amongst Hindus. This involves a discourse about both *jāti* and *varṇa*. It is widely acknowledged that *jāti* is not confined to the Hindu community, but extends to other religious communities. This has led many Hindus to argue that *jāti* is not a religious, but a socio-cultural phenomenon. In a survey conducted by the Hindu Forum of Britain, one respondent suggested: 'Varna is within the construct of Hinduism. Jaati [*sic*] on the other hand is just a social and cultural phenomenon. It has nothing to do with the core principles of Hinduism' (Kallidai, 2008, p. 7).

Hindus sometimes suggest that it is only natural that one would want to interact most closely with those who are perceived to share an equivalent cultural background. This argument is often used to indicate why marriage within the same *jāti* is normally preferred. This view of *jāti* denies the conceptualization of *jāti* as a group of people who are considered as sharing the same 'bodily substance'. In other words, there is a shift from thinking about *jāti* in physical terms to a cultural conception of caste, whereby *jāti* is conceived of in terms of lifestyle. There is therefore a move away from thinking about marriage within a specified group as physiologically predetermined, to the idea that selection of a marriage partner within a specified group is a matter of cultural preference. In this way the concept of *jāti* is preserved, but reinterpreted so that it is more compatible with the ethos of the contemporary world.

On the other hand, it is recognized that *varṇa* is a Hindu concept, but this is also reinterpreted by many Hindus in the contemporary context. This interpretation suggests that the Vedic seers recognized that society is an organic whole, and that societies require different people to fulfil different functions. These functions are determined by attitude and aptitude, rather than by heredity. However, it is suggested that, over time, this model of society was appropriated by the *brāhmins*, who reframed it in terms of heredity, in order to maintain positions of power. Consequently a true understanding of caste would look to the Vedic origins, and not to the later corruption of this social system. This allows for caste to be seen as an ancient and authentic Indian phenomenon, and at the same time as entirely compatible with the ethos of meritocracy that structures modern Western societies. Nonetheless, caste still contributes to the social and economic disenfranchisement of large numbers of Indians.

Dalits, Ādivāsīs and Other Backward Classes

There are three categories of groups that are recognized by the Constitution of India as being socially and economically deprived. In the official idiom these are known as Scheduled Castes (SC),[2] Scheduled Tribes (ST)[3] and Other Backward Classes (OBC).[4] It must be stressed that all of these categories are diverse and each is composed of a wide range of different *jātis*. All have a certain degree of legal protection under the Constitution, not only in terms of outlawing discrimination, but also in terms of having reserved seats in the legislative assemblies at state and national levels. There are also certain proportions of places in education and other institutions that are reserved for those classified as SC, ST or OBC. In other words, the Government of India has adopted a policy of positive discrimination. This itself has contributed to the politicization of these groups. It has also led to some backlash, which has sometimes been violent. Some anti-reservation demonstrations by higher-caste Hindus have relied simply on a rhetoric of the inherent inferiority of Untouchables. However, most critiques of reservation have adopted a discourse that refers to more contemporary themes such as 'fairness' and 'merit'.

Untouchability

There are some aspects of life, particularly those associated with birth, death, menstruation and bodily excretions in general, that are considered as especially defiling. Consequently, those people engaged in activities such as laundry, leather work and so on are considered as especially polluting. They are regarded as untouchable, as their touch is thought of as being ritually polluting. Although caste discrimination has been outlawed by the Constitution of Indian, there is no doubt that still today many Untouchables are economically deprived, and suffer from social stigmatization.

Before looking at untouchability in more detail, it is necessary to say something about nomenclature. The term 'Untouchable' has of course derogatory connotations. The names of particular untouchable *jātis*, such as *chamar* who are traditionally leather workers, are also sometimes used as disparaging terms. Mahatma Gandhi, although he did not critique the *varṇa* system itself, was acutely aware of the social injustices created by the concept of untouchability. In an attempt to circumvent the social stigmatization implicit in it, he coined the term *Harijan*, literally 'children of god', to denote untouchable groups. However, many untouchable groups find this term very patronizing. The Indian Government uses the term Scheduled Castes as a legal designation for untouchable groups. However, in recent years, many Untouchables have adopted the term *dalit*, literally 'oppressed ones', as a self-designation, and although this has not been universally adopted by all Untouchables, I will primarily use this term interchangeably with the more formal terminology of Scheduled Castes.

There are numerous different *jātis* classified as *dalit*. In other words, the *dalits* cannot be considered as a homogeneous group. The 2001 Census of India indicates that there are 166,635,700 people, about 16 per cent of the population, who are classified as Scheduled Castes.

Resisting Oppression

The *dalits* and other deprived groups have also adopted four broad strategies of resistance to their condition of exploitation. I have termed these: rejection, opposition, rearticulation and politicization. These are not necessarily alternative strategies, but are a range of possibilities upon which different individuals and groups draw in various combinations and degrees.

Rejection

Rejection refers to a strategy whereby oppressed individuals and groups argue that Hinduism is inherently hierarchical and exploitative, and the only possibility of improving one's social status and economic condition is to reject Hinduism. This frequently involves adopting another religious tradition that is perceived to be intrinsically egalitarian. There has been, and continues to be, a practice of individuals and groups converting to Islam, Buddhism or Christianity in an attempt to opt out of the caste system. However, this strategy has not necessarily been effective in alleviating the social plight or economic status of low-status *jātis*. Furthermore, this strategy has not only been controversial, but has also in some instances caused a violent backlash in certain parts of India.

For example, in 2008 in Orissa, violence broke out between Hindus and the Christian community.

Resistance by *dalits* to the overarching exploitation of the caste system cannot be understood without a brief mention of Dr Bhimrao Ambedkar, who has become an icon to all *dalits* who totally reject the hierarchical structures of the caste systems. Ambedkar was an extraordinary individual. Although he was a Mahar, which is classified as an untouchable *jāti*, he gained a PhD from Columbia University in 1917 and passed his bar exams in London in 1923. He was a member of Jawaharlal Nehru's first independent government, and was largely responsible for drawing up India's Constitution. In a speech in 1935, Ambedkar suggested that because 'we have the misfortune of calling ourselves Hindu, we are treated thus. If we were members of another Faith, none would dare treat us so' (cited in Zelliot, 2001, p. 206). Shortly before his death in 1956, Ambedkar converted to Buddhism, and this has inspired roughly three million *dalits*, mostly Mahars, to convert to Buddhism in turn.

In 1972 in the state of Mahrashtra, the Dalit Panthers was formed. As its name suggests, it was modelled on the Black Panther movement in the USA. It was a revolutionary movement that drew on Marxist ideas and acknowledged Ambedkar as an important symbolic leader in the struggle against oppression. The Dalit Panther Manifesto suggested that: 'To eradicate untouchability, all the land will have to be redistributed. Age-old customs and scriptures will have to be destroyed and new ideas inculcated' (cited in Joshi, 1986, p. 141).

The Dalit Panther movement did not last long; this was partly because of the fragmentation of the *dalit* community, and partly because their agenda to completely overturn the socio-religious structures was perhaps too radical, even for those at the bottom of the heap. However, the Dalit Panthers did stimulate the flourishing of a *dalit* literary tradition known as *dalit sahitya*, literally 'the literature of the oppressed'.

Opposition

Opposition is a strategy that attempts to resist exploitation primarily through various forms of artistic expression which critique the hierarchical structures of caste. The use of poetry and literature as a way of expressing opposition to the hegemonic narratives of caste-based Hinduism has a long pedigree, and is intrinsic to certain forms of *bhakti*. *Bhakti* in general has been seen as a way of expanding the soteriological franchise of Hinduism. According to the Brahminical texts, such as *The Laws of Manu*, the best lower castes can hope for is a better rebirth. However, many forms of *bhakti* suggest that true devotion to the sacred can lead to liberation for all, regardless of caste status.

David Lorenzen (1995, p. 20) observes that devotion to the sacred with attributes (*saguṇa bhakti*) has 'served to justify *varṇāśramadharma* and the status and privileges of Brahmins and other upper caste groups'. On the other hand, the ideology and theology of those who extol devotion to the sacred without attributes (*nirguṇa bhakti*) have tended to explicitly oppose the hierarchical structure of *varṇa* and the privileged status of the *brāhmins*. The founding figures of the various strands of *nirguṇa bhakti* mostly date from around the fourteenth to fifteenth century CE, and are often referred to as *Sants*.[5] *Sants* such as Kabir (1398–1448) and Ravidās (15th–16th century CE) suggest that devotion is the only path to salvation; the Vedas, ritual and yogic practices are all ineffectual; and the *brāhmins* are dishonest hypocrites. For example, Kabir challenges the concept of untouchability:

> Pandit, look in your heart for knowledge.
> Tell me where untouchability
> came from, since you believe in it ...
> We eat by touching, we wash
> By touching, from a touch
> the world was born.
> So who's untouched? asks Kabir.
> Only he who has no taint of Maya.
>
> (Cited in Hess and Singh, 1986, p. 55)

The compositions of *Sants*, such as Kabir and Ravidās, are an important resource for *dalits* and OBCs to express opposition to their exploited condition.

Rearticulation

Rearticulation involves the construction of various narratives that provide an account for the exploited condition of marginalized groups. These narratives can take two slightly different forms. The first narrative form challenges a *jāti*'s position in the hierarchical structure. For example, the Yadavs, who are formally classified as *śūdra*, claim to be *kṣatriya*, and to have been wrongfully denied their true status. The Yadavs suggest that they are in fact descended from Kṛṣṇa, making them as pure as, if not purer than, *brāhmins*. They support this claim by referring to the stories that Kṛṣṇa was a cowherd, which is the traditional occupation of Yadavs (Luce, 2006, p. 124).

A claim to a higher-caste status within the hierarchical *varṇa* structure is often accompanied by a change in name and a change in lifestyle. The renowned Indian sociologist M. N. Srinivas has called this strategy Sanskritization, which he defines as 'the process by which a "low" Hindu caste, or tribal or other group, changes its customs, ritual, ideology and way of life in the direction of a high, and frequently, "twice born" caste' (1972, p. 6). This could include lifestyle changes such as adopting a vegetarian diet and no longer drinking alcohol. The strategy of Sanskritization is often adopted when a *jāti* classified as relatively low in the hierarchical structure of *varṇa* finds itself in a fairly successful economic or social position. Srinivas (1972, pp. 96–7) observes that 'Sanskritization was able to resolve the inconsistency between the newly acquired wealth and low ritual rank.' Furthermore, this form of narrative and accompanying lifestyle change, unlike either rejection or opposition, aspires only to a positional change, and does not challenge the structure itself.

The second narrative form provides an account of the origin of the relative position of the various *jātis*. Robert Deliége (2001, pp. 73–5) provides several versions of the same basic narrative that Paraiyars, a South Indian Scheduled Caste, relate as an explanation of their untouchable status. The basic version of the myth goes as follows:

> In the beginning, there were two brothers who were poor. They went together to pray to God. God asked them to remove the carcass of a dead cow. The elder brother answered: *Een thambi papaan* (My younger brother will do it), but God understood: *Een thambi paappaan* (My younger brother is a Brahmin), and that very day the younger brother became a Brahmin (*paapaan*), and the elder brother became a Paraiyar. (Cited in Deliége, 2001, p. 73)

The doctrine of *karma* is often mobilized by higher castes to provide an explanation for the relative status of various groups and individuals. In other words, Untouchables somehow deserve their exploited status because of something they have done in a previous life. The Paraiyar narrative clearly rejects this notion, and suggests that their exploited status is purely due to a mistake that occurred in the dim and distant past.

Politicization

Politicization of the SCs, STs and OBCs began with what Srinivas (1972) has called 'horizontal solidarity'. Two factors have contributed to horizontal solidarity. First, the educational, economic and political opportunities that were created by British rule and later by the secular nature of post-Independence India. Second, horizontal mobility has been facilitated by the vastly expanded possibilities of communication created by modern transport and media. The political structures of colonial India were ostensibly caste free, and this continued after independence. However, this paradoxically created a context where it was apparent that an effective strategy for making the most of the new political, economic and educational opportunities was to politically mobilize caste identities. This political mobilization was facilitated by modern transport and media, which enabled regional caste groups to communicate effectively with similar caste groups in other parts of India. The political context of colonial India, coupled with the growing ability to communicate across greater distances, led to the formation of caste associations. Lloyd and Susan Rudolph (1984) have characterized these as paracommunities that 'enable members of castes to pursue social mobility, political power and economic advantage' (p. 29). Caste associations are structured as modern institutions with managerial positions and elected board members.

Possibly one of the most successful of these caste associations has been the All India Yadav Mahasbha (AIYM), which was formed in Allahabad in 1923. The Yadavs were in origin relatively low-status pastoral groups. To contest this status, they adopted a range of interconnected strategies that enabled them to become a powerful political force in the states of Bihar and Uttar Pradesh, and to a certain extent in national politics as well. The AIYM is both a product of and an agent for horizontal mobility. The AIYM is active in 17 of the Indian states, and has subsumed a number of different sub-castes to form a numerically strong constituency, comprising possibly around 10 per cent of the total population. In 1998, the AIYM called for 15 per cent of seats to be reserved for Yadavs in the state assemblies of Rajasthan, Delhi and Madhya Pradesh (Michelutti, 2004, pp. 50–1).

The Yadavs claim to be descended from a common ancestor and therefore to share a common blood, thus in Hindu terms constituting a *jāti*. The primordial ancestor of the Yadavs is said to be Kṛṣṇa. This not only substantiates their claim to *kṣatriya* status, but also enables a discourse that suggests that Yadavs are natural fighters. Furthermore, the narrative of Kṛṣṇa, and in particular his defeat of the tyrant Kamsa, is represented in terms of democracy and social justice (see Michelutti, 2004). The Yadavs have been particularly successful in utilizing familiar discourses in the formation of a paracommunity, which is active not only at state and national level, but also globally. There are now Yadav associations in both the United Kingdom and the USA.

Perhaps the most significant consequence of the formation of *jātis* into paracommunities has been that they have become vote banks in the political process. India is the largest democracy in the world, and in the elections held in April 2009, over seven hundred million people were entitled to vote. Though it is important to note that, for most Indians, *jāti* is not the only consideration when it comes to voting, some politicians and political parties have been able to mobilize caste identities to support their campaigns. This has been both a strength and a weakness for the poor and exploited. It is clearly a strength in that in ensures low-status *jātis* have a chance of being represented in political institutions at local, state and national levels. For example, the charismatic, but highly controversial, Lalu Yadav[6] and his wife Rabri Devi have been the major political power in the state of Bihar because they have been able to mobilize support from an alliance between the Yadavs and the Muslim community. The mobilization of *jātis* in the political process has also been a weakness, because the poor and the dispossessed are split into numerous *jātis*. Deliége (2001, p. 5) argues that 'this fragmentation is one more curse for Untouchables, making it impossible for them to play on their numerical strength to win a significant role in Indian politics'.

The Bahujan Samaj Party (BSP), founded by Kanshi Ram in 1980 and now led by Mayawati, does aim to represent all Scheduled Castes, Scheduled Tribes and Other Backward Castes, as well as religious minorities. Under the leadership of Mayawati, who is affectionately referred to by her followers as Bahenji (Sister), the BSP has raised its profile. Mayawati was the first *dalit* to become chief minister for any of the Indian states, when she became the chief minister in Uttar Pradesh, India's most populous and one of its poorest states, in 1995. However, it is clear that like many other parties that represent only one particular constituency, the BSP has had to broaden its appeal. Consequently in the 2009 elections, Mayawati toned down her anti-high-caste rhetoric, inviting all 'to ride the elephant' – which is the symbol for the BSP.

What these strategies make clear is that *dalits* are not simply passive victims of oppression, but actively resist their social and religious position in a variety of ways. The same can be said for the position of women in Hinduism.

Gender: Women and Marriage

For women, as for the four *varṇas*, normative tradition prescribes a set of rituals, protocols and duties; this is referred to as *strīdharma*. In particular, *strīdharma* indicates women's obligations in marriage. In the *dharma* texts women are not represented as autonomous individuals, but are always dependent upon and subservient to men. *The Laws of Manu* suggests that 'in childhood a woman should be under her father's control, in youth under her husband's, and when her husband is dead, under her son's' (*Laws of Manu* 5:148, Doniger and Smith translation, 1991, p. 115). The term used for the ideal wife is *pativartā* – which literally means 'she who makes a vow to her Lord'. In other words, a wife vows to serve her husband as her lord and master. Furthermore *The Laws of Manu* (9:17) suggests that the nature of women is inherently lustful, crooked and malicious. The only way to overcome this nature is for women to be devoted wives and produce sons. Although *The Laws of Manu* is not widely read, or even known about, this text continues to have a profound impact upon the ways in which women understand themselves, and in men's perceptions of gender (Knott, 1996, p. 19).

Sītā as Role Model

While *The Laws of Manu* provides the normative framework for gender roles, most Hindus are much more familiar with texts such as the *Rāmāyaṇa*, and these narratives often indicate ideal role models for women. In particular, Sītā is regarded as the epitome of the ideal woman and wife. In the most well-known versions of the *Rāmāyaṇa*, Sītā is represented as being totally devoted to Rāma, and her whole life is portrayed as revolving around him. This is perhaps best illustrated in the point in the narrative when Rāma is informed that he must be exiled into the forest for 14 years. Rāma accepts his fate with equanimity, as it his *dharma* as a dutiful son to obey his father. However, Rāma suggests that Sītā stays in the city of Ayodhya, as she would find life in the forest difficult, uncomfortable and dangerous. She responds to Rāma:

> A wife alone follows the destiny of her consort, O Bull among Men; therefore, from now on, my duty is clear, I shall dwell in the forest! For a woman, it is not her father, her son, nor her mother, friends nor her own self, but the husband, who in this world and the next is ever the sole means of salvation. (*Rāmāyaṇa of Valmiki* 2:27, cited by Kinsley, 1987, p. 71)

It is apparent that Sītā recognizes that her *dharma* is to remain at her husband's side, no matter what the circumstances. Sītā also indicates that her salvation lies through her ability to directly serve her husband. Mary McGee (1991) indicates that many of the women she interviewed suggested that if they fulfilled their marital duties successfully, this, rather than any other religious practice, would lead to salvation. 'For a woman, liberation is not separate from her request for a good husband, a healthy child, or a happy marriage. Marital felicity and liberation go hand in hand' (McGee, 1991, p. 87).

When Sītā is kidnapped by the demon Rāvaṇa, Vālmikī suggests that she loses her radiant beauty, as she is separated from Rāma. Nonetheless she keeps Rāma in her thoughts throughout her ordeal, and resists Rāvaṇa's advances. When Sītā is eventually rescued from Rāvaṇa, rather than being pleased at being reunited with his consort, Rāma appears disgruntled. Sītā has been, albeit as a prisoner, staying in the house of another man, and this has repercussions for his honour, and therefore he cannot welcome her back into his house. The distraught Sītā, apparently scorned by Rāma, who as her husband and lord is her very *raison d'être*, instructs Rāma's brother to build her funeral pyre. Because of her purity and fidelity, Sītā is unscathed by the flames, and having proved her faithfulness and honour, is accepted back by Rāma.

However, during his glorious reign, Rāma hears some citizens gossiping about Sītā's sojourn with Rāvaṇa, and despite her being pregnant, he banishes her from Ayodhya. This narrative seems to reinforce the notion that the duty (*dharma*) of the ideal wife should be faithful obedience to her husband. It also seems to suggest that Sītā has no independent existence apart from Rāma. However, as we shall see later, there are different and resistant readings of this narrative.

Widows and *Sāti*

If narratives such as the *Rāmāyaṇa* and texts such as *The Laws of Manu* suggest that women have no independent existence apart from men, and it is the *dharma* of a woman to ensure the health and well-being of her husband, the death of a husband before his wife can be perceived as a failure. This is often represented in terms of bad *karma* and/or failure to properly follow the *dharma* of the good wife (*pativratā*). The low social status of widows is often exacerbated by their economic plight. While it is possible for women to inherit land, this often only happens if there are no male heirs. Consequently, the predicament of women who survive their husband's death is potentially extremely problematic. Susan Wadley (1995, p. 92), in her study of widows, cites one of her informants as saying '[the husband] is the main pillar of life. When he dies, then there is nothing for women.'

The Laws of Manu indicates that women must remain faithful even after the death of their husband. However, as Wadley (1995) observes, actual practice does not necessarily follow normative prescriptions, and whether or not a widow marries again is more often contingent upon the customs of the specific *jāti*. Nonetheless, widows will often break the signifiers of married status, such as glass bangles and toe rings, and will sometimes cut their hair and wear white. While women can attain a degree of authority in the domestic sphere, this often becomes attenuated over time, with daughter-in-laws gradually assuming authority. Frequently widows will also have the lowest status in an extended household.

The most extreme response of a woman surviving her husband's death is to ritually immolate herself on the funeral pyre of her deceased spouse (*sati*[7]). There is a considerable body of literature on *sati*,[8] in fact the amount of literature seems to be way out of proportion to its actual occurrence. *Sati* was officially outlawed in 1829. However, the last well-documented case of *sati* was in 1987 when an 18-year-old girl called Roop Kanwar from a village in the state of Rajasthan burned to death on the funeral pyre of her deceased husband. There is still a great deal of controversy about this tragic event. Questions are still raised about whether she was a 'voluntary' *sati* or whether there was force or coercion involved in her death.

Immediately after Roop Kanwar's death, the state government passed legislation prohibiting the glorification of *sati*, which included building a shrine or temple or organizing any ceremony that celebrated the death of a *sati*. Eleven people were accused under this legislation in connection with glorifying the Roop Kanwar *sati* but, much to the chagrin of various women's organizations, all the accused were acquitted in their trial in 2004. Although it is almost impossible to assess the actual number of *satis*,[9] it remains a very marginal phenomenon. However, the symbolic importance of *sati* remains significant in certain parts of India, where a *sati* may be venerated by some, not only as the embodiment of the perfect wife, but also as a goddess (*satimata*). *Sati* has also become a symbolic motif for mobilizing various groups of feminists and intelligentsia who oppose not only *sati*, but also other aspects of Hinduism that are perceived as being incompatible with the concepts of social rights and human justice. *Sati* has become a significant point of contestation between tradition and modernity (see Courtright, 1994).

Alternative Readings and Resisting Patriarchal Norms

It would be wrong to perceive Hindu women as simply passive victims of male dominance, and within the broad Hindu traditions there is scope for resistance. For example, it is possible to find alternative readings of the relationship between Sītā and Rāma. While on the surface Sītā may seem to be too subservient and passive to act as a relevant role model for contemporary Hindu women, her passivity is equivocal. When Rāma is banished to the forest, he suggests that she stays behind in the comfort of the palace at Ayodhya, but she insists that she follow Rāma. Sītā also clearly resists Rāvaṇa's advances, and she is represented as being very strong willed.

Sītā as a Symbol of Resistance

A study by Madhu Kishwar (2001) suggests a rather different evaluation of Rāma and Sītā. One of Kishwar's interviewees is somewhat equivocal. She indicates that Sītā does represent the ideal wife, but she thinks that Sītā could have stood up more to Rāma. She is highly critical of Rāma, especially his demand to test Sītā's virtue after she had been rescued from the clutches of Rāvaṇa. Kishwar's interviewee is especially scathing about Rāma banishing the pregnant Sītā because of gossip.

> It is because he had these unworthy doubts in his mind that the second time round he got swayed by the comment of a mere dhobi (washer man). The condition in which he abandoned her, and the way that he did it can by no means be considered dharma. (Kishwar, 2001, p. 287)

The *Rāmāyaṇa* is used by this young contemporary woman, not so much as a model to either aspire or adhere to, but as a resource for not only reflecting on gender relations and the nature of marriage, but also considering the nature of *dharma*. She considers that while Sītā was true to her *dharma*, Rāma was not. The concept of *dharma* has been appropriated by this young woman to critique Rāma's behaviour as a husband. She later goes on to state that 'an ideal wife cannot by herself make an ideal household. It takes both to make one' (in Kishwar, 2001, p. 288).

Most versions of the *Rāmāyaṇa* continue the narrative by recounting how Rāma eventually summons Sītā back from her exile from the forest for a final ordeal to publicly exonerate her. However, at this point Sītā becomes totally exasperated by Rāma's fickleness and asks to be taken back into the bosom of mother earth. A throne emerges and Sītā is swallowed by the ground. Although Sītā's prayer to be swallowed by the earth could be interpreted as Sītā giving up, and possibly even committing suicide, another of Kishwar's interviewees suggests that this last act was one of resistance to Rāma's unreasonable demands. She suggests that it is a statement equivalent to saying 'no more of this shit' (Kishwar, 2001, p. 289).

The Status of Women and Goddess Worship

Like the *dalits*, women are often represented as being an exploited group. Hindu culture is frequently perceived as being irredeemably patriarchal and androcentric. On the other hand, goddess worship has a significant place in Hinduism. Some outsiders with a little knowledge of Hinduism point out that the subordination of women and the importance of the goddess seem to be totally incongruous. There are a number of responses to this observation. While I would not deny that there is considerable need for the improvement of women's condition, both in the normative discourses and in the lived reality of women's lives, there is substantial diversity in women's experience. Caste, region, class and a whole variety of other demographic factors impact on the experiences of Hindu women. Even the *Laws of Manu* is not as unequivocally patriarchal as it might first appear. As indicated above, *Manu* suggests that women are always subservient to men and are inherently perverse in nature. Yet *Manu* (3:55–8) suggests that women should be revered, otherwise all religious rites are fruitless, and that the family only thrives if women are not miserable. This, of course, does not necessarily contradict the overall patriarchal and androcentric worldview of the *Laws of Manu*.

Goddess worship does not necessarily entail that women themselves are revered or have an equitable position in society. Nonetheless 'the ubiquitous presence of female deity has coloured the notion of Hindu womanhood in subtle ways' (Sherma, 2000, p. 25). There is, of course, a variety of different goddesses that can provide very different models of womanhood and gender relations.

The concept of *śakti*, the animating principle of creation, is also perceived in feminine terms. Many Hindus, both men and women, suggest that women, simply by being female, embody *śakti*. This can be a basis for the empowerment of women. June McDaniel (2007, p. 173) indicates that she has seen 'shakta religious widow matriarchs, who are called holy women by members of the extended family, who dominate both their households and the Brahmin priests called in to perform rituals'. However, this is rare and the dual concepts of the divine and the animating principle of creation in feminine terms do not necessarily ameliorate the subordinate position of women in Hindu society.

Nonetheless, the concepts of the goddess and *śakti* can function as a resource for women to resist the exploitation, oppression and subordination of patriarchal discursive practices. Kathleen Erndl (2000) indicates that Indian women are increasingly drawing on the symbolism of *śakti* and the goddess to construct a specifically Indian form of feminism that is not reliant upon Western feminist discourses. Not only can the conceptions of *śakti* and the goddess provide a resource for the empowerment of women but they can also, although not necessarily, instil men with respect for women. For example, the dual concepts of *śakti* and the goddess also facilitate the acceptance of holy women and female *gurus*. This recognition can be found in two broad traditions: certain forms of *tantra*[10] and *bhakti*.

The tantric texts are generally classified as *Vaiṣṇava*, *Śaiva* or *Śakta*. The *Vaiṣṇava* and *Śaiva* texts take the form of the goddess asking questions of Viṣṇu and Śiva respectively. This 'narrative structure reflects the importance and centrality of the guru in Tantrism' (Flood, 1996, p. 159). However in the *Śakta Tantras*, it is Śiva who questions the goddess. This not only provides a textual affirmation that women can achieve enlightenment independently of men, but also constitutes a model of woman as *guru* (Sherma, 2000, p. 42).

Bhakti and Escaping the Constraints of the Domestic Sphere

There is a long tradition of women *gurus*, not only within the *tantric* traditions, but also within certain forms of *bhakti*. The compositions of women *bhaktas*, like the poetry of untouchable and lower-caste *bhaktas* discussed above, provide a resource for women to express opposition to exploitation. It is no coincidence that *Manushi*, a journal and publishing company concerned with issues of social justice and in particular women's issues, has published a collection of the poetry of women *bhaktas*. Vasudha Narayanan (2007, p. 185) observes that there is 'a growing awareness of women poets'. These poets indicate that women can approach the sacred directly, and that liberation can be achieved independently of men in general, and husbands in particular. This awareness of women *bhaktas* has led to the formation of a growing number of women's groups that meet to learn and sing the devotional compositions of these *bhaktas*. This has also led to public performances, which Narayanan (2007, p. 187) suggests are a new mode of ritual which is becoming increasingly popular, and thus 'highlighting women's piety and public role in religious expression'.

Consequently, women's religious activities are not simply confined to the domestic sphere.

The normative traditions of Hinduism suggest that women must marry, and that an unmarried woman is a social anathema. Often, marriage circumscribes women's independence. It is often also perceived that Hindu women are confined to the domestic sphere. The most obvious manifestation of this is the institution of *pardā* (often anglicized as purdah), which literally means curtain or veil: the practice whereby women are kept screened from the gaze of men. Many richer houses in rural India are built around a courtyard, and it is not uncommon for pre-menopausal women to virtually never venture unaccompanied beyond the walls of the domestic compound. On the rare occasion when they do enter a public domain, women may well cover their faces with the ends of their saris. Of course women from poorer backgrounds cannot afford to be confined to the domestic sphere, as they often have to contribute to the family's income.[11]

Bhakti, and in particular devotion to various forms of the goddess, can facilitate a degree of freedom for women from the constraints of *pardā*. Joyce Flueckiger (2007) in her study of two women in South India describes how their devotion to the goddess has freed them from the normal restrictions of marriage. Flueckiger (2007, p. 40) relates how the giving by the groom of a gold pendant, known as a *tali*, in the wedding ritual not only binds the new bride to the groom, but also delimits her activity to the domestic sphere. The two women in Flueckiger's case study also exchange *talis* with the goddess. This enables them to extend their sphere of activity. In the words of one of the women, 'the goddess keeps taking me from hill to hill, valley to valley, village to village' (cited by Flueckiger, 2007, p. 48). In other words, devotion to the goddess is an accepted and recognized strategy which enables women in this part of rural India to have a degree of independence and autonomy from the normal constraints that are imposed upon them.

The appropriation of *bhakti* as a strategy to challenge patriarchal norms is not confined to impoverished rural contexts as described by Flueckiger. Mary Hancock's (1995) study of urban *brāhmin* women also details a similar strategy, albeit not always successful, of circumventing male authority. Hancock's study shows how *bhakti* enabled these relatively privileged women to challenge some aspects of the gender hierarchy. In particular, Hancock's study focuses on a middle-class *brāhmin* woman, called Sunithi, who became possessed by the goddess, and in her possessed state gave advice to a gathering of friends, relatives and neighbours.

Possession in the rural context is often a quite frenzied phenomenon, but in the genteel suburbs of Chennai it is a much more restrained affair. This appropriation of what are predominantly rural practices becomes transformed in the contemporary middle-class urban context. Possession by the goddess is perceived as an effective means for some women to establish some form of authority, but it must operate within the decorous protocols of the urban middle-class household. Sunithi's possession by the goddess therefore draws on a range of different idioms: goddess possession, urban, middle class, Brahminical, domestic and personal, to create a syncretic ritual performance, which not only enhances her authority in the domestic setting, but is also recognizable and meaningful to her followers. Hancock observes that in many ways Sunithi's enhanced status derived not only from her ability to be the (genteel) conduit for the goddess, but also from her status as a respectably married woman.

The normative discourses on *dharma*, drawing on the conceptualization of society as a sacred and organic whole, suggest that society is contingent upon everyone performing their sacred duties. The four *varṇas* equate to different parts of the body, and it is a social, moral and religious obligation for *brāhmins* to perform rituals: *kṣatriyas* to protect society, *vaiśyas* to generate wealth, and *śūdras* to serve. Similarly, it is incumbent on women to marry, serve their husbands and produce sons. However, these social structures are neither as rigid nor immutable as the *dharmic* precepts suggest. There is a degree of agency, and various individuals and groups have reinterpreted the concept of *dharma* and/or adopted various strategies of resistance to the dominant paradigm. Before leaving our discussion of *dharma*, it is necessary to look at the way in which the concept has been politicized and linked to the idea of the nation-state.

Political Hinduism

The term *dharma* has a religious, a social and a moral connotation; however, the term also has a political connotation. A considerable portion of *The Laws of Manu* outlines the *dharma* of the ruler. Consequently, there has never been the same degree of functional differentiation between politics and religion in the Indian context as there is in the Western world. Mohandas (Mahatma) Gandhi (1982, p. 453), in the conclusion of his autobiography, famously suggested 'that those who say that religion has nothing to do with politics do not know what religion means'. This blurring of boundaries between religion and politics can still be identified today, despite the fact that India has a secular constitution and a modern political system of governance.

In particular, this blurring of boundaries between the political and the religious manifests itself in a collection of loosely affiliated organizations collectively referred to as the Sangh Parivar. The term derives from the umbrella organization called the Rashtriya Swayamsevak Sangh (RSS), which roughly translates as 'The National Volunteer Association', and the term Parivar which means 'Family'. The Sangh Parivar includes trade unions, a student group, a women's organization, a group that ostensibly supports tribal people, and a specifically religious organization. 'These offshoots have allowed it [the RSS] to intervene in nearly every public domain' (Bacchetta, 2005, p. 111). Perhaps the most significant of the Sangh Parivar groups is the Bharat Janata Party (BJP), which was the leading political party in the coalition government between 1998 and 2004, and still constitutes one of the leading parties.

What unifies all of these groups, other than various and shifting degrees of affiliation to the RSS, is their commitment to an ideology known as Hindutva, which roughly means 'Hinduness'. The core of this ideology was most clearly articulated by V. D. Savarkar (1883–1966), who attempted to define who is a Hindu. Savarkar suggested: 'A Hindu means a person who regards this land of Bharat Varsha[12] from the Indus to the seas as his Fatherland as well as his Holyland, that is the cradle land of his religion' (cited in Keer, 1966, p. 143).

Savarkar expands on this idea in a pamphlet entitled *Hindutva*. In this pamphlet, Savarkar suggests that the Hindu community is defined by a common nation (*raṣtra*), a common ancestry (*jāti*) and a common culture (*sanskṛti*). What is interesting in this definition and understanding of the parameters of Hinduism is who it includes and who it excludes. For example, Sikhs would be included, whereas Muslims – whose most sacred place is in Saudi Arabia – would be excluded, not only from Hinduism as a religious tradition, but also from Bharat Varsha as a political entity (*raṣtra*). Here, Savarkar imagines the nation in Hindu and ethnic terms. It is also significant that Savarkar extends the concept of *jāti* to include all Hindus, and that it is not confined to a particular endogamous group. The significance of this lies in the fact that an important theme in the Hindutva rhetoric is that the Hindu community is divided, and that there is a need for Hindus to unite in the face of stronger unified forces, such as Islam and secularism.

India as the Goddess Bhārat Mātā

The idea of the Hindu nation is emphasized by the conceptualization of the nation in terms not only of a holy land, but also of a goddess – Bhārat Mātā (Mother India). There are now a number of temples dedicated to Bhārat Mātā, the most important being in the two sacred cities of Hardwar and Banares. The Bhārat Mātā Mandir in Banaras has a vast relief map of India installed as a *mūrti*. However, the Bhārat Mātā Mandir in Hardwar represents Bhārat Mātā in anthropomorphic form as a goddess holding a milk urn in one hand and a sheath of grains in another, representing the fecundity of the nation. She is further represented as mother to 'Bold and gallant sons and daughters ... who sacrificed their lives for the patriotic cause of protecting the Sanatan Dharma and the glory of the Mother land' (Bharat Mata Mandir, n.d.). The Bhārat Mātā Mandir in Hardwar was a project instituted by the Vishva Hindu Parishad (VHP), one of the most vocal organizations in the Sangh Parivar. The VHP's stated objective is 'to organise – consolidate the Hindu society and to serve – protect the Hindu Dharma [*sic*]' (VHP, n.d.).

Bhārat Mātā is also prominent on the RSS website, where she is portrayed holding a red flag, with a lion and an outline of India behind her. This iconographically equates India with the goddess, and thus reinforces the notion of India as inherently a Hindu nation (*raṣtra*). The lion equates Bhārat Mātā specifically with the Goddess Durgā, a fearsome goddess, who in popular narratives and iconography is represented as defeating the demon Mahiṣa. However, Bhārat Mātā is depicted as a benign goddess: her right hand is raised in the gesture indicating blessing, and she holds none of the weapons normally associated with the iconography of Durgā. The implication is that while Bhārat Mātā bestows her blessings, she also needs protecting.

The RSS

The RSS was founded in 1925 by Keshav Baliram Hedgewar, primarily as a response to communal violence that erupted between Hindus and Muslims in Nagpur. Hedgewar perceived the Hindu community to be divided and weak, in contrast to the Muslim community, which he considered to be strong and organized. However, Hedgewar did not see the problem as a political, but as a psychological one. Consequently, the solution was not to form a political party, but to organize at a grass-roots level in order to imbue the Hindu community with a sense of unity and strength from the bottom up. The idea was to cultivate a sense of self-discipline. This was not the self-discipline of the individual yogi directed to personal salvation, but the development of team discipline directed towards the salvation of the nation.

The fundamental unit of the RSS is the *shakha*, which is a local group (see Andersen and Damle, 2005, pp. 35–6). The *shakha* remains the very basis of the RSS organization. The RSS 2009 report suggests that there are 43,905 *shakhas*. It presents itself as the largest voluntary organization in the world, with a membership of over one and a half million (Chitkara, 2004, p. 168). Members of the *shakhas* are called *swayamsevaks*, which roughly translates as volunteers (literally self-servants). The notion of *swayam*, or self, is radically different to the concept of self indicated by the term *ātman*. *Swayam* connotes the embodied self in the world, rather than the transcendent Self conveyed by the term *ātman*. The embodied self is not, however, selfish, but must serve a higher purpose, namely the nation.

Membership numbers of *shakhas* are kept low, normally between fifty and a hundred members. The idea is to cultivate a spirit of camaraderie. The intent is that strong identification with a local group will foster loyalty to the wider RSS organization and the ideology of Hindutva. This camaraderie is fostered through the wearing of a distinctive uniform of khaki shorts, white shirts and black caps, by physical and ritual activity, and by ideological talks. The *shakhas* meet on a daily basis and *swayamsevaks* play various types of team games. The rituals are very militaristic in style and involve saluting a flag, and chanting *Bhārat Mātā Ki Jai* (Victory to Mother India). The uniform, the physical games and the military-style rituals make the *shakhas* very appealing to boys. There is some evidence to suggest that many only stay involved in the RSS for a relatively short period of time. However, those who do stay in the RSS for longer display considerable loyalty and dedication to the organization.

The *shakhas* also involve ideological talks given by senior members. The ideology is clearly derived from Savarkar's notion of Hindutva. RSS ideology also suggests that Hindu culture is superior to all other cultures. However, Hindutva rhetoric also reflects a siege mentality. In particular, the advocates of Hindutva suggest that the Hindu nation, personified as the Mother (*Bhārat Mātā*), has to be defended against the forces of secularism and the proselytizing of Christian and Muslim missionaries. It is after all the duty (*dharma*) of all good sons to protect their mother. This has led to the formation of a militant and muscular form of 'matriotism', which Lise McKean (1992, p. 252) characterizes as, 'the devotion of a loyal citizenry' to the nation 'figured as a loving Mother'.

The Iconography of Rāma and the Dispute over the Babri Masjid

This militant and muscular matriotism is perhaps embodied most fully in the figure of Rāma and the conflict over the alleged site of Rāma's birthplace. The narrative of the *Rāmāyaṇa* indicates that Rāma was born in a town called Ayodhya, which was where he ultimately reigned as a righteous king. There is also a town in the state of Uttar Pradesh called Ayodhya. The evidence is equivocal as to whether Rāma was a historical figure, and whether or not this town is the actual place described in the mythic narrative. The significant fact is that many Hindus believe it is the historical site of Rāma's birth and reign, and Ayodhya has become an important pilgrimage place.

In the centre of Ayodhya there once stood a mosque known as the Babri Masjid. The VHP suggests that there is clear archaeological evidence indicating that a Hindu temple was destroyed in the sixteenth century to make way for the building of this mosque. Specifically, they argue that this temple marked the actual spot of Rāma's birth[13] (VHP, 1990), and demand that the temple should be rebuilt. This dispute has a long and complex history (see Jacobs, 2008). The dispute culminated in December 1992 when a large group of Hindu nationalists broke through the police cordon and literally demolished the mosque with pick axes, shovels and their bare hands. The army eventually regained control, and the site has been cordoned off. The destruction of the Babri Masjid led to the worst communal violence in India since the Partition in 1947.

The government delegated the judiciary both to investigate the cause of the events that led up to the destruction of the Babri Masjid, and to suggest possible solutions. In March 2002, the Supreme Court ruled that no religious activity 'symbolic or active' could be permitted on the disputed site (Noorani, 2003, Vol. II, p. 297). Despite hopes of building a temple, the dispute is still unresolved. In 2009 the BJP once again raised the issue in their manifesto for the national elections. However, this was clearly not a pertinent issue for many people, and the BJP-led coalition did surprisingly poorly in the election.

Rāma is represented by the Sangh Parivar as a universal symbol of the Hindu community. However, theirs is a very specific understanding of Rāma. In the iconography of Hindutva, Rāma has become a hyper-masculine symbol intended to rally the besieged Hindu nation, which is iconographically represented as the benign goddess who bestows her blessings on her dutiful sons. If the iconographic representation of Durgā has become transformed into a benign goddess devoid of weapons, the Hindu nationalist representation of Rāma has moved in the opposite direction. In Hindutva iconography, Rāma is transformed 'from a tranquil, tender and serene god to an angry punishing one, armed with several weapons' (Kapur, 1993, p. 75). This is not a wholly fabricated representation of Rāma, but it does emphasize one particular aspect of Rāma's character that is commensurate with the ideology of Hindutva. Hindu nationalists have utilized the narrative of the *Rāmāyaṇa* as a symbolic resource to validate their understanding of *dharma* as the need to robustly defend the Hindu nation (*raṣtra*) and culture (*sanskṛti*), even if this entails demolishing mosques and attacking Christians.

Dharma is a complex, contested and multifaceted concept. However any understanding of Hinduism today must be based on knowing something of what is meant by this term. It is possible to argue that many of the central issues detailed in texts such as the *Rāmāyaṇa* and the *Mahābhārata* are concerned with *dharma*. It is also possible to suggest that many of the contemporary issues faced by Hindus today can also be understood in terms of debates that relate to *dharma*. Here, *dharma* is understood as the way in which the individual should act in the world in order to maintain balance and harmony in society, and by extension the cosmos. These issues largely pertain to questions of identity, such as caste, gender and nation. Clearly, there is a tradition, derived from the *dharma* literature, which is very prescriptive about the place of different groups within society. However, the nature of these prescriptions has not gone unchallenged. *Dharma*, while it is in many ways a fixed and even sacred point of reference, is also contested and contextual. One of the most significant contexts for understanding Hindu *dharma* in the twenty-first century is what many people now identify as globalization.

Chapter 4

Hindusim in a Global Mass-mediated Context

This chapter is concerned with how Hinduism is mediated, and in particular explores the impact that the move from traditional modes of communication to the growing use of new media has had on the ways in which Hinduism is understood and practised. This chapter will also cover the emergence of what Maya Warrier (2005) calls transnational devotional movements. These are movements that are clearly facilitated by new modes of communication, and that see the spread Hinduism not only beyond the subcontinent but also beyond the Indian constituency.

Communicating Hinduism

It is often said that the central aspect of religion is the belief in some form of transcendent reality and that this transcendent reality is considered to be ineffable, yet without some way of communicating religious ideas, religion could only be an individual and private phenomenon. While not denying that religion has a personal experiential aspect, it is also a thoroughly mediated phenomenon. There would be no such thing as Hinduism or the Hindu community without communication through both time and space.

Oral Communication

The Vedas were primarily oral compositions, and were probably communicated orally for about a thousand years before they were actually written down. The Vedic corpus is often referred to as *śruti*, literally meaning 'that which is heard'. This indicates that it is the enunciation and hearing of these compositions which is regarded as being primary. Julius Lipner (1994, p. 25) suggests that, 'no doubt in India scripture has been written down for incidental purposes. But as such it loses its vitality; the sacred word springs to life and exerts power when it is spoken and heard.' Even today, the Vedas are still primarily taught orally in the few remaining Sanskrit schools. Chanting *mantras* and singing *bhajans* remain central practices for most contemporary Hindus.

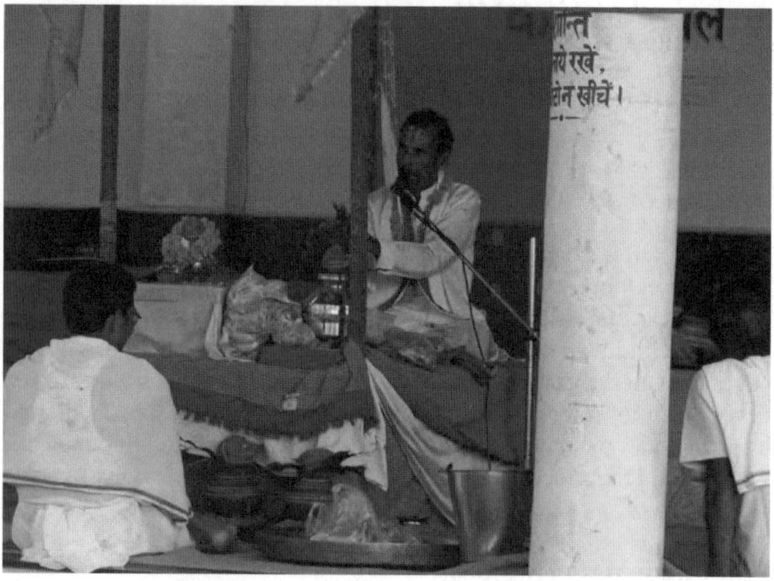

A *Rāmkathā* on the *ghāts* at Rishikesh.

Recitation of texts (*kathā*) is also still important. Recitation of the *Rāmācaritmānas* (literally The Lake of the Deeds of Rāma), which is the retelling of the *Rāmāyaṇa* in Hindi attributed to Tulsīdās (1532–1623), is particularly popular. The recitation normally takes place over a period of eight or nine days, and is referred to as *Rāmkathā*. The tale of Rāma is of course a good story, but listening to a recitation is also intended to develop an attitude of devotion. The reciter will often interject explanations and anecdotes that relate events in the narratives to contemporary issues. Philip Lutgendorf (1995, p. 227) observes that 'the source text serves merely as an anchor for an improvised verbal meditation that may include almost endless digressions and elaborations'.

Through these digressions and elaborations the mythological narrative is made fresh on each retelling, and retains relevance for the contemporary audience. These retellings ensure that the *Rāmkathā* not only elicits an attitude of devotion, but is also a means of both maintaining and transforming religious knowledge. *Rāmkathās* can also be highly entertaining. The continuous retelling of a familiar narrative in part explains the continuing popularity of the *Rāmāyaṇa*. A number of people have become famous for their ability to recite the whole of the *Rāmācaritmānas*, for example Morari Bapu, a Gujurati Hindu, who travels throughout India and the world.[1]

The story of Rāma is not only recited, but is also acted out in events known as *Rāmlīlā* (literally the Play of Rāma). These performances are immensely popular in northern India; the most spectacular of them takes place on 31 consecutive evenings at Ramnagar (literally Rāma's town) on the opposite bank of the Gangā from the sacred city of Banaras.

There are two significant points to be made about *Rāmkathā* and *Rāmlīlā*. The first point is that they are still very popular today. This popularity derives from the dual aspect that both these modes of retelling are familiar and new at the same time. Familiar, because the basic story is well known, and new because the narrative of the Rāma story and the forms of *kathā* and *līlā* are flexible enough to be constantly reshaped according to particular contexts.[2] The second point is that the conventions of these more traditional forms of communication have informed the style in which mythological narratives are produced for new media forms, such as cinema and television.

Performance: Ritual or Concert?

The singing of devotional songs (*bhajans*) is an important aspect of Hindu religious practice. *Bhajans* are sung in temples, in *satsangs* on ashrams, and in domestic spaces. However, the singing of *bhajans* is also performed in public. Certain singers, such as Vinod Agarwal, have developed reputations as great musicians, and sing for audiences. It is rather a misnomer to call these events concerts. While there is a performative element to the singing of *bhajans* by renowned singers, it is more than a concert, as the audience are by no means merely passive listeners.

Musicians like Agarwal perform in halls and outside venues, not necessarily associated with temples or other types of sacred space.[3] Agarwal and his accompanying singers sit on a stage. The audience are seated on the floor, many sway and very quietly clap their hands together, some hold their hands in the air, and have their eyes half closed.[4] The normal convention is that the lead singer will be followed by a refrain by the rest of the participants. The refrain at this type of event is mostly sung by the accompanying musicians on stage, while the audience often very quietly joins in or silently mouths the words. This is in stark contrast to performances in temples and during festivals like the celebration of Kṛṣṇa's birthday (*Janmāṣtamī*) where the evocation and refrain can often become rather frenzied. During celebrations associated with Kṛṣṇa, dancing can become quite wild. Although the performance by Agarwal, and its reception, is more staid than traditional ritual performance, it would be wrong to think that this is simply an aesthetic experience like a Western concert. For many in the audience, this is a deeply religious event.

It could be said that the ostensibly secular space of the hall becomes sanctified through the singing of the *bhajans*. However, the ethos of both the space and the character of the middle-class Hindu audience creates a dynamic that is different from both the concert hall and the ritual space of the temple.

In a study of Bharatam Natyam dance, a form of dance traditionally associated with devotional performance in the temple, which is now perceived as an art form to be watched, Vasudha Narayanan (2007, p. 178) observes that 'ironically, the secular stage became transformed into a shrine replete with icons of the dancing Shiva or Krishna, lighted lamps, incense and flowers'. Narayanan also describes a popular television show in South India in which young girls take part in a dance competition. The studio is decorated with a floor-to-ceiling image of Shiva as Lord of the Dance (*Naṭarāja*). Narayanan (2007, p. 195) concludes by suggesting that 'the public stage and the television platform have become the new hybrid spaces – extensions of the temple space and domestic altars in secular forums'. Music and dance have become both entertainment and ritual performance in these new hybrid spaces.

Orality and traditional modes of expressing religiousness remain a vibrant part of Hinduism today. However, the changing context, especially the emergence of a growing educated and urban middle class in India, has transformed some aspects of these traditional modalities, and opened up new spaces for religious expression. This sector of Hindu society has also contributed to the increasing salience of print.

Hinduism in Print

In our investigation of print technology, it will be necessary to divide the discussion between printing of the word and printing images. In the contemporary context, print is utilized widely. Contemporary published material within the Hindu tradition falls into a number of different types; these include: the writings of contemporary *gurus*, the transcription of discourses given by modern *gurus*, recollections of devotees, hagiographical accounts of the lives of *gurus*, and sacred texts.

Modern Gurus *and the Printed Word*

In particular, print has come to be used by modern *gurus*. The Divine Life Society in Rishikesh, specifically states that the one of their primary aims is:

> *To Disseminate Spiritual Knowledge*
> (a) By publication of books, pamphlets and magazines dealing with ancient, oriental and occidental philosophy, religion and medicine in the modern scientific manner, and their distribution on such terms as may appear expedient to the Board of Trustees. (DLSHQ, 2005)

Swami Sivananda himself started the Yoga Vedanta Forest Press at the ashram, and three hundred titles are attributed to Sivananda. An anecdotal tale indicates that when the ashram was experiencing some financial problems, Sivananda suggested closing the kitchen, rather than halting the publication of books (Ananthanarayan, 1987, p. 115). The Yoga Vedanta Forest Press continues to publish works by Sivananda and his direct disciples, and there is a large book store by the banks of the Gangā that sells these publications at a very low cost. Numerous pamphlets are distributed free, indeed it is impossible to visit the ashram without being given a handful of pamphlets. There is also a monthly magazine *The Divine Life*, which is published in both English and Hindi. Books can also be ordered online, and *The Divine Life*, together with many of the titles by Sivananda, can be downloaded for free. Although most modern *gurus* are not as prolific as Sivananda, they usually publish some form of teaching. This is often in the form of discourses that have been recorded and then transcribed by devotees. The proliferation of this type of literature is instrumental in the formation of what Sarah Strauss (2005) identifies as transnational communities of practice.

Hagiographical accounts of the lives of many *gurus*, written by devotees, tend to follow a fairly similar pattern. Namely, at an early age these individuals display a natural affinity for religious practices, a certain precociousness, and often the ability to perform miracles. At some point in their lives, these individuals become disillusioned with the mundane life, renounce the world and become a *pavirājaka*, literally 'one who wanders'. This period involves visiting many of the most significant pilgrimage places (*tīrthas*), particularly those in the remote Himalaya, studying the sacred texts (*śāstras*) and undertaking extreme forms of asceticism (*tapas*). Sometime during this period, the aspirant will be initiated either by another *guru* who recognizes the true nature of the aspirant, or directly by God. Gradually, according to these accounts, people are drawn to these individuals, who accord the teacher a very special status. Once a following has gathered, these individuals spend the rest of their lives involved in disseminating their teachings. In order to spread their teachings and to cope with a growing number of devotees, these teachers found institutional organizations.

There are, of course, variations to this basic hagiographical account of the life trajectory of *gurus*, but the biographies of *gurus* draw on the majority of elements listed above. Devotees might also write about their own personal encounters with their *guru*. These personal accounts invariably indicate how the *guru* has transformed the devotee's life. Both hagiographies and the personal accounts of devotees act to legitimize the special status accorded to the *guru*.

Hinduism Today: Global Dharma

There are of course numerous books, pamphlets and magazines published by Hindus about Hinduism. Possibly the most high profile of these is *Hinduism Today*, which is published by The Himalayan Academy, a small monastic community based in Hawaii. This quarterly, and highly professional-looking magazine, was begun in 1979. It has a print run of 25,000 and an estimated readership in the region of 125,000, with a further 5,000 accessing the free online edition. The Editor suggested that he likes to think of these 'as a "leadership" more than a readership, as our readers tend to be the movers and shakers in their various communities'.[5] There are subscribers in 65 countries and readers who access the online edition in another 20 countries.

In an article about the history of *Hinduism Today* Levani Melwani (n.d.) proclaims:

> The age-old Hindu philosophy passed from mouth to mouth in tiny villages across India is now going high-tech, thanks to Hinduism Today, the preeminent global journal of Hindu Dharma. This Hawaii-based publication is shedding its broadsheet image after 18 years and transforming into a sleek, easy-to-carry, full-color magazine.

This suggests that in the new global context new modes of mediating Hindu ideas have to be found. Furthermore, this statement suggests a continuity between the global dissemination of 'Hindu Dharma' using modern print technology and the oral tradition. The founder of *Hinduism Today* suggested that 'it was apparent there was nothing to satisfy contemporary Hindus, to articulate in modern language India's ancient wisdom' (cited in Melwani, n.d.). One of the explicit mission statements of *Hinduism Today* is 'to foster Hindu solidarity as a unity in diversity among all sects and lineages'. Not only does *Hinduism Today* suggest that there is a need to promote a sense of collective identity amongst the multiplicity of sects and lineages, but it also advocates a unified global Hindu community.

Each edition of the magazine begins with a section entitled 'Global Dharma', which reports on various activities and issues relevant to the Hindu community in various parts of the world. For example, in the second quarter edition of 2009, 'Global Dharma' contains reports not only on Diwali celebrations in London, a dispute about priests at a very important Hindu temple in Nepal, and how a *swāmi* in India claimed to have reconverted fifty thousand Christian tribals back to Hinduism, but also on how Barack Obama carried a small image of Hanumān as a good luck charm on the campaign trail. This edition, which is fairly typical, contains features on The American Hindu Foundation, an advocacy group working for Hindu Rights in the USA, and the worship of a temple ox in a small village in India. The contents clearly indicate that the patterns of worship found in village India and the functioning of a modern and sophisticated organization based in the USA are both inherent dimensions of a global Hindu community.

The Gita Press: Printing Sacred Texts

Finally, it is important to briefly mention sacred texts. Like all religious traditions, the sacred texts of Hinduism can now be obtained in print. Texts can be obtained in Sanskrit, and many have been translated into most of the vernacular languages and English. Printing and translation clearly enables many more people to access sacred texts. In 1923 the Gita Press was founded in order to publish relatively cheap copies of the Bhagavad Gītā. It is still an important publishing company, which now produces a wide range of different texts, primarily the *Purāṇas* and Epics, which are translated into Hindi and other vernacular languages. The publications of the Gita Press are relatively inexpensive. Its stated aim is to disseminate the texts to the widest possible readership.

> The institution's main objective is to promote and spread the principles of Sanatana Dharma, the Hindu religion among the general public by publishing Gita, Ramayana, Upanishads, Puranas, discourses of eminent Saints and other character-building books & magazines and marketing them at highly subsidised prices. (Gita Press, n.d.)

Printing and translation not only facilitates access to texts, but also enables individuals to study these texts and draw their own conclusion as to the texts' meaning.

The Gita Press also publishes a monthly magazine, *Kalyan*, which has been in continuous publication since 1927. It claims a circulation of 250,000 (Gita Press, n.d.). It publishes commentaries on various texts, and articles on a wide range of topics such as aspects of yoga, *bhakti*, gender, particular deities, cow protection and so on. These translations, commentaries and discussions bypass the traditions (*sampradāya*) of communicating teachings orally. The publications of the Gita Press represent a 'new, yet conservative, concept of Hinduism which is easily acceptable and accessible to the general public' (Horstmann, 1995, pp. 296–7).

Visual Images

While the printing of the word has now become a significant aspect of Hinduism today, the printing of the visual image has had an even greater impact. Hinduism has a vibrant visual culture. Arriving in India, one cannot but be struck by the rich abundance of images of the various deities and saints of Hinduism. These images are not just confined to temples and shrines, but can be found in almost every Hindu home, shop, café, and office as well as on the dashboards of cars, trucks and buses. Images can be found in a great variety of materials including: brass, wood, clay, papier-mâché and plastic. However, perhaps even more striking are the brightly coloured posters of the deities that are readily available in bazaars across India, and calendars with images of gods and goddesses that are often distributed free by various companies. I will use the term god poster to refer to the mass-produced two-dimensional reproductions of saints, *gurus*, gods and goddesses.

The Hindu artist does not perceive himself as a creative individual as such, but as part of a lineage, firmly located within a particular tradition. Stephen Inglis (1995) notes that many of the artists who produced god posters in the early to mid-twentieth century did not sign their own names, but that of their teacher or studio. This clearly parallels the concept of a *guru* lineage (*paramparā*). Perhaps more importantly, the mechanical reproduction is not regarded as somehow less authentic than the original. God posters are not ritually installed in people's homes and places of work in the same way that images (*mūrtis*) are in temples. Nonetheless, the sacred nature of what they portray also transforms the nature of the god poster itself. For many Hindus, god posters are regarded in some way as being the sacred, and not simply as a representation of the sacred. God posters are therefore not merely aesthetic, although they may be considered decorative, but are also integral to the religious life of many contemporary Hindus.

The possibility of producing vast numbers[6] of god posters coupled with their relative cheapness and transportability, has contributed to their ubiquity. H. Daniel Smith (1995, p. 37) argues that the ubiquity of god posters has been responsible for what he calls 'a new and pervasive "omnipraxy"'. Many Hindus will begin their day by offering some lighted incense sticks before the various chosen god posters on their walls. This, Smith (1995, p. 37) suggests, constitutes 'a democratic devotionalism, a populist piety, of extraordinary proportions'. As we have already noted, mechanical reproductions transcend the limitations of time and space. This means that the devotee can have sacred sight (*darśan*) in his/her domestic space or place of work, rather than having to go to the specific temple associated with that deity. Most temples now sell small framed photographs of the installed image (*mūrti*). Many pilgrims will buy one of these framed images, which not only act as a souvenir but will also be placed in their shrines at home and incorporated into domestic worship.

The mass production of god posters has also contributed to an increasing mobility of particular deities. Many Hindu deities have begun their life, so to speak, as the focus of relatively local devotional movements. The ability to produce many thousands of images cheaply has contributed to the spread of these images beyond the immediate locale. Where once, images of deities such as Venkateswara would probably have been only recognized in a relatively localized area, now posters of Venkateswara have proliferated throughout South India, and they are also spreading up into North India.

This mobility has led to an increasingly available pantheon of deities, from which Hindus can choose their particular focus of worship. This has facilitated more individualized and tailored modes of devotionalism, whereby Hindus can 'pick and mix' a personalized pantheon of deities which resonate with their life and personality. It is very common to see a miscellany of posters of various gods, goddesses and saints that traditionally have no connection on the walls of people's homes and places of work. Some of these non-traditional combinations themselves have become so popular that they themselves are now reproduced as posters. For example, it is relatively easy to find posters and postcards depicting the elephant-headed deity Gaṇeśa alongside the Goddess Lakṣmi.

Audio-Visual Recording

Hinduism is both a rich oral and visual culture. Consequently, it is hardly surprising that Hindus were quick to take advantage of new recording technologies. Initially, cassette tapes of *bhajans* and *mantras* were very popular, but this media form has now almost been entirely superseded by compact discs (CDs). With the convergence of digital technology and the increasing number of Indians who have access to a computers and DVD players, video compact discs (VCDs) and DVDs, which combine the visual and oral, are also becoming relatively easy to obtain, and are bound to become ever more available.

These VCDs and DVDs often show video footage of concerts by famous singers such as Vinod Agarwal. The ability to record concerts of *bhajans* and easily distribute these recordings has contributed to the fame of singers like Vinod Agarwal. Shots of a concert are interspersed with images from popular poster art and images of *mūrtis* of the relevant deity. For example, a film of a concert by Vinod Agarwal featuring *bhajans* dedicated to Kṛṣṇa is accompanied by shots of god posters of various well-known episodes of the Kṛṣṇa story, such as Kṛṣṇa playing his flute, and Kṛṣṇa's sport (*līlā*) with the milkmaids (*gopīs*). The VCD also has scenic shots of various locations around India, often showing Hindus at prayer.

The recording of *bhajans* and *mantras* by highly accomplished musicians, such as Vinod Agarwal, enables these events to reach a much wider audience. In addition, just as the mass production of god posters undermined the distinction between decoration and religious icon, the recording of sacred sounds has the potential to conflate the aesthetic appreciation of music with ritual activity. Listening to a beautiful rendition of *bhajans* on a CD player is not only a leisure pastime, but also a religious occasion. This conflation is reinforced if the oral and the visual are combined through the use of the new media technologies such as VCD and DVD. The fusion of the sacred and the profane is of course facilitated by the fact that these distinctions have never been clear-cut in the Hindu context.

The distinction between the sacred and profane is perhaps more obvious when considering the recordings of religious discourses given by various *gurus* and teachers. In the Sivananda bookstore, and online, it is now possible to buy a range of recorded talks by some of the leading *swāmis* of the ashram. These talks are on a range of topics, such as discourses on various texts, the meaning of the various Hindu festivals, or various aspects of yoga and *Vedānta*. There are a very few recordings of Swami Sivananda, mainly because the technology was not readily available when he was alive. However there are a considerable number of audio recordings by Swami Chidananda and Swami Krishnananda, who were both direct disciples of Sivananda and who both attracted a number of devotees themselves. There are also a number of video recordings of the later discourses given by both of these revered *swāmis*. Considerable effort has been made to make these audio and video recordings readily available to devotees. Video technology is now relatively cheap and easy to use, and many contemporary *gurus* have almost their every word recorded and filmed.

These audio-visual recordings of religious discourses have a number of important consequences. The first, of course, is that the direct words of a particular teacher are preserved verbatim, as they are spoken. The second consequence is that it is no longer necessary for the listener to be physically present in the same place as the speaker. In other words, recording enables the teachings of particular *gurus* to transcend the limitations of both time and space. A vast audio-visual archive is now directly available to devotees of many recent and contemporary *gurus*. However, this is not simply a matter of just hearing the teachings of a particular *guru* in order to develop a greater knowledge and understanding. Audio-visual recordings of discourses enable devotees to have *darśan* of their *guru* from the comforts of their own homes. Viewing audio-visual recordings of religious discourses is not only an individual activity, but can also be a group activity. Followers of a particular *guru* may gather together to watch a recording of a discourse of their teacher in what can be said to be a new form of *satsang*. Audio-visual recordings have become an important resource for devotees who live far from the ashram of their *guru*, and particularly for the diaspora communities.

Hinduism and Film

Hinduism, as we have seen, has both a very rich visual culture and an exuberant mythology, each of which has provided a rich resource in the development of cinema in India. This has produced a genre, unique to India, known as the mythological film. Mythologicals can be defined as films that depict the stories of gods, goddesses and heroes, whose narratives can mostly be found in the *Purāṇas* and the Epics (Dwyer, 2006,

p. 15). The visual look of mythologicals is very much influenced by the aesthetic of god posters and draws on the conventions of folk theatre, and in particular *Rāmlīlā*. Rachel Dwyer (2006) also identifies a second genre of religious films, which she terms devotionals. These largely derive their narratives from the *bhakti* traditions, and typically depict the hagiographic accounts of the lives of *Sants*, such as Tukaram.

The heyday of Hindu mythological and devotional films was from the 1940s to the 1970s. One of the last significant mythological films to be made was *Jai Santoṣī Mā*. It was the surprise hit of 1975. The narrative was not derived from the Sanskrit traditions of the *Purāṇas* and Epics, but was a free adaptation of a narrative of a local goddess. The film is important, in that it was largely instrumental in spreading the popularity of Santoṣī Mā throughout India. John Hawley (1996, p. 4) suggests, 'as her film bought her to life, Santoṣī Mā became one of the most widely worshipped goddesses in India'. Santoṣī Mā is now fully incorporated as an accepted form of the goddess.[7]

In the film, a young woman called Satyavati, a devotee of Santoṣī Mā, is badly mistreated by her in-laws. Birju, her husband, leaves the family home to seek his fame and fortune. The three Sanskritic goddesses, jealous of the devotion offered to Santoṣī Mā by Satyavati, make Birju forget all about his wife. Satyavati takes a vow (*vrat*) not to eat anything on 16 consecutive Fridays. She offers the goddess unrefined sugar and chickpeas, both of which are inexpensive and readily available foods. Pleased with her devotion, Santoṣī Mā intercedes by restoring Birju's memory. He returns home, having amassed a fortune, and demands that his family treat Satyavati with respect. This *vrat* has now become a very popular practice for Hindu women throughout India, as it is believed that Santoṣī Mā will intercede directly and fulfil the wish of the devotee. Sometimes the fast is replaced by a simple avoidance of eating sour foods on each of the consecutive Fridays. Since the film there have been a number of new temples dedicated to Santoṣī Mā, and her image has become increasingly popular as a god(dess) poster.

Although mythological and devotional films are no longer such popular genres in the cinema, it is possible to discern religious themes in what are more ostensibly secular narratives. Stories from the Epics and the *Purāṇas* often inform the narratives of modern films (see Lothspeich, 2009). Moreover, the majority of Indian films do, at some point in the narrative, represent religious practices. There are often scenes depicting characters performing *pūjā*. *Bhajans* and *mantras* can also form the basis of popular songs performed in most Indian films. Religious practice and beliefs are therefore significant and visible features of Indian cinema.

Television Epics

Hardly any mythologicals and devotional films are made now, however their longevity has been preserved by being freely available on video-cassettes, and more recently on DVDs. They have also had a direct influence on a number of television shows. In particular, the conventions of mythological cinema have had a major influence on the televising of the *Rāmāyaṇa*, which was broadcast in 78 episodes in 1987–8. The series, produced and directed by Ramanand Sagar, has become a myth itself, India reportedly having come to a standstill at the times the show was broadcast. Some people have dubbed Ramanand Sagar as the Tulsīdās of the media age. Just as Tulsīdās retold the original Sanskrit epic in a vernacular language to make the narrative more accessible, Sagar has retold the *Rāmāyaṇa* in an idiom that is apposite for the contemporary context.

The conventions used for the televising of the *Rāmāyaṇa* clearly derived from the aesthetics of god posters, as well as more traditional formats such as *Rāmkathā* and *Rāmlīlā*. Purnima Mannekar (1999, p. 168) suggests that these very deliberate televisual techniques 'reveals that the "preferred" viewing of the serial, the structure of feeling it aimed to produce, was that of devotion, or *bhakti*'. As such, it was remarkably successful, in that many Hindus did consider the viewing of the series as much a ritual act as a leisure activity. In some instances, the television set itself was treated as an icon, with people taking a ritual bath before the show, draping television sets with garlands of flowers and lighting incense. The show was watched with a reverent hush, as the audience had *darśan* of Rāma and all the other familiar figures of the narrative.

The televising of the *Rāmāyaṇa* was predictably followed by the serializing of the *Māhābharata*, directed by B. R. Chopra, and broadcast on state television between September 1988 and July 1990. It gained an audience of over two hundred million. However, it did not evoke the same sort religious response as the *Rāmāyaṇa*.

Ramanand Sagar, following on from his success with the *Rāmāyaṇa*, made two serials: one on Sri Krishna and the other on Jai Ganga Maiya. In 2008 Sagar's company broadcast their most ambitious project since the *Rāmāyaṇa*, which was a serial based on the life story of the very popular teacher Sai Baba of Shirdi[8] (1842–1918) whose images can be found throughout northern India. The self-proclaimed intent of the show is 'to spread Baba's social and spiritual messages with a judicious blend of entertainment' (Sagar Arts, n.d.).

As with the mythological films, the longevity of these mythological serials has been extended through video-cassettes and DVDs. It is not unusual in rural India to find groups of people gathered around a television screen in a small roadside café watching Sagar's *Rāmāyaṇa* or some other mythological. This electronically mediated form, while drawing on the conventions of recitation (*kathā*) and street performance (*līlā*), is clearly very different to the more traditional modes of telling. In particular, such recordings give no room for the improvisations that constantly make the retellings of popular tales fresh and relevant. Consequently, it is not surprising that in 2008 Sagar remade the *Rāmāyaṇa*, which was broadcast on NDTV every weekday evening at 9.30. The media context is of course quite different to that of the late 1980s. Satellite television has arrived in India, and this means that Indian viewers have a choice of stations, whereas there was only the one government station, Doordarshan, when the original series was screened. More Indians have now had a much greater exposure to all media forms, making the original series seem naïve and very dated. Nonetheless, the investment in the remaking of the *Rāmāyaṇa* does indicate the belief by the production company of the enduring appeal of the narrative. Although some viewers suggest that it is not as good as the original, others indicate that they find it inspiring. For example one viewer suggests:

> I watch this serial everyday and always try to understand the valuable teachings given by saints during those days. I am finding a tremendous change in my attitude and character after watching this New Ramayan. I hereby request other persons to watch this new Ramayan and understand the essence of this serial. (Subrat, 2008)

In other words, this series not only contributes to keeping the narrative alive as part of a rich mythological tradition, but also has the potential to provide a resource for Hindus to reflect on their beliefs and practices.

Satellite technology has also made it possible for a number of the larger temples to televise and broadcast *āratī* and other rituals. Tata TV, for example, has a station called Virtual Darshan which broadcasts live from the Sai Baba Temple in Shirdi, the ISKCON temple in Mathura and the Sri Vishvanath Mandir in Banaras. There are also a number of religious channels, such as Sanskar TV and Aastha, which broadcast discourses by famous teachers such as Sri Sri Ravi Shankar and Swami Ramdev, as well as *kīrtans*, *kathās* and *āratīs* from various ashrams, temples and places of pilgrimage. Sanskar TV claims that it 'is dedicated to the Indian Philosophy, Religion and Spiritual solidarity, Culture and dissemination of the vast and timeless knowledge of our great "Sanatana Dharma" to the people of the world'. Aastha indicates that it 'brings you meditation, yoga, devotional music and spiritual programs that will uplift your spirit and stimulate your mind'.

Hinduism in Cyberspace

Hinduism, like all religious traditions, has a considerable online presence. Although I agree with Dawson and Coward (2004, p. 7) that 'it is increasingly difficult to separate the mere provision of information from the practice of religion in cyberspace', I will maintain this distinction as a starting point to try and make some sense of the proliferation of Hindu websites. Information can be broken down into general information about Hinduism and information about specific temples, groups or organizations. Again this distinction is not absolute, since many groups represent themselves as speaking for all Hindus. Consequently, it is important that students are extremely cautious when coming across sites that claim to represent 'all Hindus'. The most common type of practice in cyberspace is the performance of online *pūjās*. Listening to a discourse by a *guru* online could be considered to be both a source of information about religion and a ritual performance at the same time.

Information Online

Type the term 'Hinduism' into a search engine like Google, and one of the foremost sites in the list generated will be *The Hindu Universe*.[9] There is no indication of who is responsible for this website. It has a fairly commercial look to it, with various types of merchandise, such as Hindu Universe T-shirts and mugs, advertised. There are prominent links to Vedic astrologers, numerologists and dating services. The Hindu Universe Resource Centre has links to the arts (which they call Darshan Gallery), and links to pages on gods, sages, *pūjā*, philosophy and so on. *The Hindu Universe* itself has sections of information specifically targeted at women and children.

Most generic sites from within the Hindu community promote a modern *Sanātana* view of Hinduism. This modern Sanātanist perspective is unaffiliated to any particular *guru* lineage (*paramparā*) or sect (*sampradāya*), and might be characterized as an ecumenical form of Hinduism. The modern Sanātanist perspective suggests:

1. Hinduism is more than a religion in the Western sense; it is 'a way of life'.
2. Hinduism is a misnomer and the correct name for the religious tradition is *Sanātana Dharma*.
3. The roots of *Sanātana Dharma* can be traced to the Vedas.
4. If properly understood, *Sanātana Dharma* is rational and in accord with the scientific paradigm.
5. The various gods and goddesses of the Hindu pantheon represent different functions or powers of one supreme Absolute Reality.
6. Caste (*varṇa*) in ancient India was based on the understanding that society is an organic whole, and that different people had to perform different tasks according to their individual attitude and aptitude. However, over time, this system became corrupted.

While modern Sanātanism is an important form Hinduism today, it is not representative of all Hindus. There are, as we have seen, many diverse forms of Hinduism, many of which challenge this particular version of Hinduism.

As well as generic information about Hinduism, many different groups also have an online presence with detailed information about their beliefs and practices. Caste associations, specific sects (*sampradāya*), individual temples, particular *guru* lineages (*paramparā*) and so on all have an online presence. Some of these sites are very sophisticated. For example, on the Divine Life Society's website there are not only details about visiting the ashram in Rishikesh, but links that allow you to download books, watch short video clips of Swami Sivananda, and listen to recordings of Swami Sivananda chanting and discourses given by some of the senior *swāmis* of the ashram. There is a spiritual calendar on the site which not only gives details about the important festivals, but also gives links to Sivananda's writings about them.

Seeing and Hearing the Guru in Cyberspace

Accessing audio recordings of discourses of *gurus* online has an informational dimension. The listener is informed about the teachings and beliefs of a particular *guru*. However, the Internet also has the facility to recombine the oral and the visual. The concept of *darśan*, combined with beliefs about the nature of the *guru*, makes viewing a discourse on the Internet something more than simply learning about the *guru's* teaching. In an opening sequence of a short video presentation about the nature of the *guru* on the Divine Life Society website, an image of the earth in space is accompanied by the narrator indicating that 'the guru is God himself manifesting in personal form'.[10] This suggests that the nature of the true *guru* transcends time and space. However, the human form of the *guru* might also be considered as a concentrated manifestation of sacredness, and to have *darśan* of the embodied *guru* is especially auspicious. Later in the video, the narration suggests that contact with the *guru* 'reforms and refines those who approach them with a sincere heart'.

While in theory the *guru* is present everywhere, even after having shed their physical body, it is clear that images of the *guru* are also regarded as concentrations of sacredness. Like god posters, images of the *guru* are incorporated into the ritual life of the devotees. This concentrated presence is even more apparent in video clips of the *guru*, which are perpetually available online. The incorporation of the visual and the oral in video recordings of the *guru* combines the concept of *darśan* with that of *satsang*, as the devotee not only sees the *guru*, but also hears the *guru*'s enlightened discourse. The ability to access the *guru* from anywhere at any time, via a computer terminal, reinforces the notion of the omnipresence of the true *guru*. The devotee not only sees and hears the *guru*, but is reminded that they are also in the sight of the *guru*, who resides everywhere, even in cyberspace.

Virtual Pūjās *and Online* Pūjā *Services*

Not only *gurus*, but also deities exist in cyberspace. *The Hindu Universe* web pages have a link to what they call 'E-darshan'; this provides a facility for performing virtual *pūjās*. Opening the link presents the viewer with a list of deities, including Lord Shiva, Lord Ganesha, Lord Krishna, Goddess Saraswati and so on. This is commensurate with the concept of a chosen deity (*iṣṭa devatā*). Lord Ganesha is the first option, as he is regarded as 'The Remover of Obstacles', and is typically propitiated before all other deities. Clicking on the link reveals an image of Ganesha looking straight at the viewer. This is of course the perfect position for *darśan*. Sitting at the computer, the devotee not only sees the virtual image (*mūrti*), but is also directly in the sight of the virtual deity. There is an animated halo behind Ganesha, who is seated on a lotus, between two pillars that are joined by a decorated arch. There are animated oil lamps flickering on either side of the virtual shrine. A *mantra* to Ganesha can be heard being chanted in the background. There are clip art images of flowers, a coconut, some bananas and an *āratī* lamp. Click on the image of the flowers, and animated flowers fall at the feet of Ganesha. The virtual coconut will virtually break at the base of the *mūrti*, and the virtual bananas can be dragged and placed in front of Ganesha. The oil lamp will, at the click of the mouse, be waved in front of the image. This obviously replicates in cyberspace the practice of performing a *pūjā* in temple or at a domestic shrine located in the physical world.

A virtual *mūrti* located in a cyber-shrine has obviously not been brought to life in the same way as a *mūrti*, which has been ritually installed in a temple. However, accessing the virtual *mūrti* can be considered as homologous to the use of god posters in domestic and work spaces. Cyberspace can be thought of as a new dimension to the 'pervasive omnipraxy' that Daniel Smith (1995) has suggested pertains to the ubiquity of printed images of Hindu deities. The web designer of a virtual Hindu temple suggested: 'I do believe that virtual *darshan* is possible ... I see the Virtual Temple as an in-home-shrine, and just as one can do *darshan* from their in-home shrine, the same can be done with a Virtual Temple' (cited in Jacobs, 2007).

There is an obvious difference between virtual *mūrtis* and god posters, namely that online images are not nearly as visible or prolific as god posters. While there are a growing number of sites where it is possible to have cyber-*darśan*, these are still relatively few. Furthermore, although many Indians have increasing access to computers, the majority of Indians do not. We know how god posters are integrated into patterns of worship, but as yet there are no studies that investigate how these sites are actually used. The web designer of the Virtual Temple clearly envisages the possibility of cyber-*pūjās* when he suggests, 'Hindus use any form of worship available ... Why not, then, use the Internet as another venue of worship?' (cited in Jacobs, 2007). However, there is no evidence, as yet, that Hindus are actually integrating this possibility into their daily patterns of worship.

Perhaps an even more interesting use of the Internet is the emergence of online personalized *pūjā* services.[11] It is now possible to pay for someone else to perform a *pūjā* on your behalf at a chosen temple. For example, one *pūjā* service suggests:

> In spite of earnest desire, it is not possible for everybody to come all the time physically to the holy places ... The matter of distance, shortage of time or the over engagement with a very busy schedule becomes a big factor for this inability. However, now through our online puja shop and services you can easily offer puja directly from

> your home and get "Prasad", "Pushpa", Sindoor etc. directly at your home. You can offer your puja at Holy Temples in India through us. Distance or time will not be a matter [*sic*]. (Kaalighat, n.d.)

Logging on to one of these sites, the devotee is given a selection of temples; these are normally the most renowned temples, such as the Venkateshwara Mandir at Tirupati. Having selected the temple of choice, the devotee is given a brief description of the temple and main deity. The devotee is then required to send personal details including name, kinship group (*gotra*), astrological sign, date of birth, purpose of performing the *pūjā* and the accompanying fee. The site then indicates that it will send one of its ritual specialists to the selected pilgrimage place to perform the *pūjā* on their behalf. The service will then send the devotee what they would normally have received in the temple had they attended themselves. This could include, as the quote above indicates: *prasād* (normally some sugar crystals), some flowers (*puṣpa*) and the red powder (*sindoor*) used to make an auspicious mark (*tīlak*) on the forehead at the end of performing *pūjā*. The service will also send a picture of the image of the chosen deity.

On the surface, this appears to be an example of what might be called the commodification of religion. The cynical interpretation of online *pūjā* services would suggest that relatively wealthy urban middle-class Hindus, living both in India and in other parts of the world, have adopted the prevailing consumer culture of the globalized marketplace, and that purchasing this service is not fundamentally different from buying any other type of product or service. However, one must be very wary of such a simplistic evaluation. It is a part of the Hindu tradition that devotees give some contribution for religious services. This might be giving a few small coins to the *pūjārī* in a small temple, or quite sizeable donations to temples and ashrams.

In her study of Rajasthani pilgrims, a number of Anne Grodzin Gold's interviewees indicated that the benefits of the pilgrimage derived as much from the donation of money as from being in a pilgrimage place. Furthermore, they suggested that giving money at places of pilgrimage is more efficacious than simply giving to worthy causes at home (Gold, 1988, pp. 289–90). An online payment to a third party facilitates a direct pecuniary link between devotee and place of pilgrimage. Consequently, it is possible to suggest that these online *pūjā* services represent a resourceful appropriation of a new media technology in support of the more traditional practice of pilgrimage. Pilgrimage places can be considered as nodes in the sacred geography of India. However, information technology and the spread of the Hindu community beyond the sacred borders of India have entailed that pilgrimage places are not only sacred nodes, but also centres of a global communication nexus.

Hinduism on YouTube

The Hindu community is clearly very adept at using new media technologies and fora. The magazine *Hinduism Today* has made considerable use of new media technologies. The editor indicated:

> Facebook, Twitter, YouTube, we have moved into these communication worlds for a number of reasons, foremost among them the Hindu youth around the world. If they want information about their faith, they don't go to a library, the bookstore, grandmother or other traditional sources. They go online. Most of what they learn is there, online. We want them to find their faith there, in its most authentic expression, articulated intelligently, presented in a way they will find engaging. (Paramacharya Palaniswami, personal correspondence, May 2009)

The editorial of each quarterly issue of *Hinduism Today* is available as a videoed discourse on YouTube. *Hinduism Today* is published by a small monastic community, based in Hawaii, that is part of the Śaiva Siddhānta tradition. This raises the issue of whether this small monastic community, belonging to a very specific tradition (*sampradāya*), will have a disproportionate influence to its size on the ways in which Hinduism is understood, due to its significant online presence and its highly sophisticated use of media technologies.

YouTube is an appropriate forum for other aspects of Hinduism too. Numerous short video clips of a wide selection of *bhajans* and *mantras* have been uploaded to YouTube; for example, over 760 video postings of the *Gāyatrī Mantra*.[12] Some of these videos have had tens of thousands of viewings over a year, and have elicited a range of different responses. Most simply say, 'thank you for the posting'. Others suggest that some Hindus begin their day by accessing videos of *mantras* or *bhajans*. Many suggest that the video clips bring peace and relaxation. This leads to a necessary warning about some of the clips and comments, namely that many postings are uploaded not by Hindus, but by those who might loosely be identified with the 'New Age'[13] – a fact that suggests various Hindu beliefs and practices have been influential in the development of 'New Age' philosophies.

As with other forms of computer-mediated Hinduism, it is difficult to assess how the videos clips uploaded to YouTube are actually integrated into the religious life of Hindus. At a recent gathering of the Hindu Student Forum at the University of Wolverhampton, a YouTube video of a popular *bhajan*, *Jaya Jagadiśa Hare*, was used by the Hindu students as a reminder of the words in the *āratī* performed at the end of the meeting. The words were transliterated and translated into English. This clearly helped those students who were unfamiliar with Hindi.

Transnational Gurus

Some of the most sophisticated use of new media technologies can be identified with groups referred to by Maya Warrier (2005) as modern transnational *guru* organizations. As the term implies, these are organizations that have transcended the boundaries of the Indian subcontinent. This is partly due to the fact that Indians themselves have migrated in fairly substantial numbers to other parts of the world. It is also due to the fact that there are a growing number of non-Indians who are drawn to various facets of Hinduism, especially yoga and meditation. These organizations are focused on a charismatic individual, who is regarded by their followers as both spiritually enlightened and at the same time possessing the ability to progress the devotee along the path to spiritual awakening. These groups are organizations in that they have modern institutional structures, and what could be called a corporate identity.

Transnational *guru* organizations are modern in that individuals choose to join because they perceive that these organizations fulfil a particular need. Warrier (2005, p. 18) also points out that 'devotion to a guru is one of the means by which individuals come to terms with modernity'. Furthermore although the *guru* figure is often attributed with miraculous powers, the teachings of the *guru* are said to be perfectly commensurate with science and rationality.

There are a number of different organizations that fall within the category of modern transnational *guru* organizations. Perhaps the best known are:

1. The International Sai Organization, which is the organization that has grown up around the controversial *guru* Sathya Sai Baba. Lawrence Babb (1991, p. 160) suggests that Sathya Sai

Baba is 'among the most important of modern India's religious personalities'.

2. The Mata Amritanandamayi Mayi Mission, that centres on Mata Amritanandamayi, simply Mata (Mother) to her devotees, who is renowned for physically embracing her devotees as a signifier of her divine love (see Warrier, 2005).
3. Sahaja Yoga, which was founded by Sri Mataji Nirmala Devi in 1970. Her devotees believe that she has the capacity to awaken the spiritual power in people. Sahaja literally means 'spontaneous'. The implication is that self-realization no longer requires severe yogic and ascetic practices, but through the teachings of Mataji Nirmala Devi 'this experience has become effortless and available to everyone, for the first time in the history of human spirituality' (Sahaja Yoga, n.d.) (see Coney, 1999).

Sri Sri Ravi Shankar and the Art of Living Foundation

The Art of Living Foundation is a fairly typical transnational *guru* organization. It was founded in 1981 by Sri Sri Ravi Shankar.[14] Clearly the most obvious thing about this organization is that the name itself has no obvious Hindu terminology. This suggests that Sri Sri Ravi Shankar wishes to have an appeal beyond the Hindu community. A quick look around his official website reveals that the most prominently used word is 'spirituality'. Many contemporary Hindus suggest that Hinduism is not a religion as such; consequently for some Hindus, spirituality seems a more appropriate term. Many Westerners also find the word 'religion' an anathema; 'spirituality' is more acceptable. For many individuals disillusioned with the institutions of traditional religions, both from within the Hindu community and outsiders, spirituality has become regarded as a 'panacea for the angst of modern living' (Carrette and King, 2005, p. 1).

Many of Sri Sri Ravi Shankar's ideas are clearly derived from various aspects of the Hindu tradition, though direct references to specific Hindu concepts are few. Sri Sri Ravi Shankar does utilize some Sanskrit terminology, but this is kept to a minimum. Furthermore, he often explains Sanskrit terminology in Western terms. For example, he explains 'samadhi is being completely immersed in the mystery of life and in this creation' (Office of His Holiness Sri Sri Ravi Shankar, 2009). While one can perceive *samādhi* in these terms, a more traditional yoga understanding would be quite different. In traditional yoga, *samādhi* is understood in terms of complete absorption in the object of meditation, where the concepts of subjectivity and objectivity no longer pertain. The minimal use of Sanskrit paradoxically distances the teachings of Sri Sri Ravi Shankar from Hinduism, and at the same time legitimizes his ideas by rooting them in the perceived ancient Sanskritic tradition.

The biography of Sri Sri Ravi Shankar is also fairly typical of *guru* hagiographies. He is said to have been precocious, often found in deep meditation, as a youngster. At the age of four, according to his biography, he recited the *Bhagavad Gītā* without apparently having ever read it. Between the ages of six and seventeen he studied the Vedas (Office of His Holiness Sri Sri Ravi Shankar, 2009). He told friends at school 'that people all over the world are waiting for me'.

Sri Sri Ravi Shankar's followers clearly accord him the status of a *guru*, but what this actually means is ambiguous. Narratives about Sri Sri do legitimize his special status as a *guru* in a number of specific ways. First, he is recognized as special by other acclaimed teachers. There are also numerous accounts of miracles performed by Sri Sri, most pertaining either to foreseeing some future event or to healing. Sri Sri is further represented as being intensely human, yet also inscrutable. He is said to have a prodigious memory and extraordinary stamina.

However, perhaps the most significant dimension of narratives legitimizing a modern *guru*'s status is their ability to transform individuals' lives. This transformation is often couched in secular terms such as overcoming an initial scepticism, inducing a sense of well-being, a reduction of stress, and a deep inner connection with both the *guru* and other devotees. Sri Sri is sometimes referred to as Gurudev by his followers, indicating that at least some of them regard him as the manifestation of the divine in human form.

Sri Sri himself reinforces his position as a teacher by wearing his hair and beard long. However, unlike the wandering ascetic (*sādhu*), his hair is groomed and not kept in matted locks. Sri Sri always dresses in immaculate white dhoti and cotton shawl, rather than the more traditional saffron that is worn by most *gurus* and renunciates. White is associated with celibacy, rather than actually renouncing the world. This particular look cultivated by Sri Sri is very similar to that of Mahesh Yogi, the founder of Transcendental Meditation, with whom Sri Sri was associated for a while prior to setting up on his own. White clothing and long well-cared-for hair therefore signifies not a withdrawal from the world, but being in the world yet not of it.

While the actual Hindu side of Sri Sri's teaching has been downplayed to some extent, therefore giving it an appeal beyond the Hindu community, his teachings are based on ideas derived from the Hindu tradition. The very concept of a *guru* is of course distinctly Hindu. However, Sri Sri and other transnational *gurus* are clearly very different from the original conceptualization of the spiritual preceptor found in the Vedic corpus, though they still play a significant pedagogical role in the transmission and transformation of religious ideas. They are also in many ways the most visible face of Hinduism to those outside the Hindu community.

Sri Sri Ravi Shankar's teaching is based around a breathing practice called *Sudarshan Kriya*, which is claimed to be both an effective antidote to stress, and scientific. In other words, *Sudarshan Kriya* is represented as being both modern and a panacea for the anxieties caused by modern lifestyles. The Sanskrit term links it to ancient yogic practices. Courses in Sri Sri Ravi Shankar's teachings are held at various centres around the world. They are run by members of the Art of Living Foundation who have taken advanced and teacher training courses, indicating that the organization is something quite different from the more traditional transmission of teachings in a *guru* lineage (*paramparā*). Direct vision (*darśan*) of the *guru*, while desirable, is not essential for devotees. Furthermore, there is almost no mention, in any of the literature, of liberation or other soteriological goal. The prime *raison d'être* for the Art of Living Foundation is expressed in terms of realizing one's full human potential, finding inner peace and joy, physical and mental well-being, eliminating stress, and so on.

Like many modern Hindu organizations, service (*seva*) is a core aspect of the Art of Living Foundation. Sri Sri suggests, 'our first, and foremost commitment is to do seva in the world. When you make service your sole purpose in life, it eliminates fear, brings focus in your mind, purposefulness in action, and long-term joy' (Art of Living, 2007–8). The Foundation has established a number of initiatives, such as disaster relief, prisoner reform and educational programmes.

Transnational *gurus*, such as Sri Sri Ravi Shankar, are both indexes and agents of what might be termed the reinvention of tradition. In other words, the tradition of the *guru* can be traced back to the Vedic period. However, traditions only survive if they adapt to changing contexts. The transnational *guru* is therefore both traditional, in the sense that the idea of a spiritual preceptor can be traced back to the Vedic period, and new in that the significance and role of the transnational *guru* is very different from the way that the *guru* was perceived in ancient times. However, because of their perceived status as religious experts, transnational *gurus* are not only indexes of the way that traditions have adapted to the new global context, but also agents of change. For example, whilst the ashram (*āśram*) also has an ancient antecedent, the ashrams of modern transnational *gurus* are thoroughly modern institutions that exist at the centre of global networks of devotees.

As should be clear from the discussion in this chapter, the Hindu community is not confined to the Indian subcontinent. If we accept that the wider cultural, social, economic and political context has an impact on the ways in which religion is practised and understood, then a change in context will bring about some changes in religious beliefs and practices. The next chapter will explore how the context of contemporary Britain has impacted on the beliefs and practices of Hindus.

Chapter 5

Hinduism in Diaspora

Hindus have now spread across the globe. While statistics are notoriously unreliable, the Adherents.com website indicates approximately 72 million Hindus outside India,[1] spread across almost every continent. When considering Hinduism outside India, we have to take into account the complex relationship between three communities: the sending community, the community of people who actually relocate, and the host community. The first thing to emphasize is that none of these three communities is homogeneous. The fact that Hinduism outside India must be understood in terms of this complex relationship suggests that it is necessary to look at the specific context of migration. This context is both spatial and temporal.

In spatial terms, the experience of the Hindu community will be different in, for example, Trinidad (see Vertovec, 2000 and Baumann, 2004), the United States (see Eck, 2000), and the United Kingdom (see Burghart, 1987 and Ballard, 1994). In temporal terms, it is necessary to investigate how the Hindu communities outside India have developed over time. In particular, generational issues must be taken into account. Do Hindus who have been born outside India have a different understanding of Hinduism from their parents or grandparents who originally migrated? Furthermore, it is necessary to assess how some of the variables that cut across the Hindu community have impacted on the diasporic experience. As well as the usual demographic variables, such as gender, there are numerous other variables to consider when investigating Hinduism in diaspora, such as region and caste.

Terminology

Before looking more specifically at what happens to Hinduism and the Hindu community when it relocates from its original cultural context, it is necessary to briefly discuss terminology. The term diaspora was originally used to refer to the Jewish exile in Babylon in the seventh century BCE. However, it has come to be the preferred term used by most academics to indicate any religious, cultural or ethnic group that has moved from an original homeland yet still retains some sense of identification with that homeland. Clifford (cited by Ramji, 2006, p. 647) suggests that diasporas 'mediate, in living here and remembering/desiring another place'. This can sometimes lead to individuals in diaspora becoming what Dhooleka Raj (2003, p. 27) calls 'double outsiders'. In other words, there is a sense in which individuals in diaspora do not fully belong to either sending or receiving cultures, yet at the same time they are in continuous dialogue with both.

Some scholars are critical of the wider use of the term diaspora, because in origin it referred to the traumatic and forceful dispersal of the Jewish people and cannot be applied to more benign forms of dispersal from an original homeland. Other scholars, such as Robin Cohen (1997), argue that religious communities cannot be considered as diasporas *per se*, as diasporic identity has to have an ethnic dimension, and the Hindu community cuts across a variety of different ethnicities. However, India has a sacred geography and therefore a very special place in the minds of all Hindus, even if they may not hold any desire to return to or even visit India. Consequently, I will continue to use the term diaspora to indicate Hindu communities living outside of South Asia. However, the question has to be addressed of whether for second, third and subsequent generations of Hindus born outside India the relation with a perceived homeland/sacred land becomes so attenuated that the term diaspora community is no longer apposite. Linked to this is the question of whether we can now identify distinctive forms of diasporic Hindu identity: British Hindus, American Hindus and so on.

In order to address the issues that pertain to Hinduism outside of India, this chapter will primarily focus on Hindus and Hinduism in Britain, and more specifically the Hindu community in the area of Wolverhampton. According to the United Kingdom 2001 census, there were 559,000 people who reported themselves as being Hindu, which is about 1 per cent of the population. The 2007 *Religions in the UK Directory* lists almost 400 separate Hindu organizations and temples.

These range from temples serving the local Hindu community, to caste organizations and various UK-wide bodies such as the Hindu Council UK.[2] In Wolverhampton, 9,198 people recorded themselves as being Hindu, which is about 3.89 per cent of the population (Office for National Statistics, 2003).

A Brief History of the Hindu Community in Britain

Hindus, like other South Asian groups, have ventured to the West for many centuries, and it is a mistake to think that there has only been a South Asian presence in the United Kingdom since the Second World War. In the seventeenth century, a number of adventurous travellers from the subcontinent found their way to Europe. However, these were very few and it was not until the colonial period that any significant numbers of South Asians, from all the different religious communities, arrived in Britain. The East India Company and later the British Government employed South Asian sailors as deckhands. These sailors of Indian origin were known as *lascars*. Many had to wait in British ports for ships returning to the subcontinent, some jumped ship and some set up boarding houses for other *lascars*. Michael Fisher (2006) suggests that there were about 10,000 *lascars* living in Britain by 1813.

In the late nineteenth and early twentieth century, many Indians, realizing that a Western education was necessary to gain any position in the institutions of the Raj, came to Britain. Also in this period, a number of Indian *gurus* visited the West, primarily to teach Westerners about aspects of Hinduism. The most influential and well known were Swami Vivekananda, who travelled to the USA in 1893 and later visited Britain, and Paramahansa Yogananda, who lectured in the USA in the 1920s.[3]

Substantial mass migration to Britain from the subcontinent did not really begin until after the Second World War. In this immediate postwar period, it was predominately only men that came to Britain, primarily to avail themselves of job opportunities. The pattern of migration of Hindus can be termed 'chain migration'. With the prospect of work in postwar Britain, a number of South Asians began to arrive; once arrived, they informed relatives and friends back on the subcontinent of employment and accommodation opportunities. The result of this pattern of immigration was that there were highly concentrated areas of settlement in which the population was derived from a particular locality and/or specific caste group. The main concentration of Hindus settled in places like the West Midlands, Leicester and London, where there were plentiful job opportunities. Today, these are still the main centres of the Hindu community.

The majority believed that their sojourn in Britain would be temporary, and that once they had earned sufficient money, they would return to India, where their main focus lay. They tended to live in communal and sometimes very crowded conditions, sending as much money as they could back home and living as frugally as possible. There were no established places of worship at the time, and certainly no purpose-built temples (*mandirs*). Sojourners tended to either abandon religious practice or practise religion on an individual rather than collective basis.

In 1962 and again in 1968, the British Government tightened up legislation on immigration. In anticipation of the implementation of the new laws, immigrants from South Asia sent for their wives and families. By the mid-1960s, the gender ratio was just about even. This completely changed the whole ethos of the diaspora communities. In particular, with the arrival of wives and families, it gave a sense of permanence and undermined the 'myth of return'. With the notion of returning to India becoming more remote, religion became increasingly significant. Although most privileged positions in the various Hindu traditions are almost invariably occupied by men, women tend to have a more active lay-role in the perpetuation of religious life. By the mid-1960s, many Hindu devotional groups had become established, generally meeting in private houses. A number of trust funds were begun and Hindus began to pool their resources in order to obtain premises that could become dedicated places of worship and community centres. The first Hindu temple was consecrated in Leicester in 1969. This was followed shortly after by temples in London, Coventry, Leeds and Bradford.

In the 1960s, East African countries that had formerly been part of the British Empire gained independence. During the colonial period, the British had shipped large numbers of South Asians to East Africa to work as indentured labour and, by the 1960s, these communities had become well established. However, the newly formed independent governments of countries such as Kenya and Uganda instigated a policy of Africanization, which rendered the South Asian situation less stable. This culminated in 1972 when Idi Amin ordered all South Asians out of Uganda. Many of the South Asians who left East Africa migrated to Britain, and are generally referred to as twice migrants. Most were of Gujarati origin and Rachel Dwyer (1994, p. 182) suggests that about half of the approximately half a million Gujaratis in Britain 'have strong East African connections'.

The Challenges of a New Context

There are several interlinked issues that face all religious groups when they relocate to a different cultural context. From being an integral, and possibly majority, religious community in the original context, diaspora communities often find themselves in a context dominated by the values of a different worldview. Consequently, what was considered normal and unproblematic in one cultural context may well be perceived as strange and unfamiliar in the new context. Diasporic contexts give rise to a situation where 'religion is less "caught", but increasingly taught' (Baumann, 2004, p. 80). Although it is relatively easy to maintain religious beliefs in a different context, there might be difficulties in maintaining certain practices in the new context. For example, in India it is common practice for Hindus to cremate the recently deceased on open funeral pyres, and then scatter ashes in the Ganges or another river, which at the present time is not possible in Britain. Therefore, certain practices have to be modified or abandoned altogether.[4] Not only practices but also beliefs can become transformed in the new context. A religious diaspora community's need to explain its beliefs to the receiving community, in terms that the host community can understand, can actually transform the nature of those beliefs.

Strategies

George Chryssides (1994, p. 59) suggests that there is a range of strategies that individuals from diaspora traditions adopt in the new cultural context. He labels these apostasy, accommodation and renewed vigour. Apostasy refers to abandoning all the beliefs and practices of the original tradition and adopting the values and mores of the host community. At the other end of the scale, renewed vigour refers to becoming more committed to beliefs and practices of the original home culture. A strategy of renewed vigour is adopted in a context that is perceived as alien and possibly hostile, where there are pressures to assert a more clearly defined sense of collective identity. For example, individuals who might never or rarely have attended temple in India become regular attendees in the new context. Raj (2003, p. 76), in her ethnographic study of Hindu Punjabis in Britain, cites one of her interviewees, who suggests, 'compared to India, we are more Hindus. We are more Hindus because we feel that we have to stick to something.' Between these poles, accommodation is a strategy of retaining some aspects of the home culture but transforming or abandoning other aspects, while adopting some, but not all, aspects of the culture of the receiving community. This strategy is contingent upon identifying which aspects of a religious culture are essential and which are peripheral. There are, of course, no clear criteria for determining where this line lies, and consequently different people will draw the line in different places. Furthermore, this line can shift over time as the community becomes more established. An example of this can be seen in the way that the festival of Holi is celebrated in Britain.

Celebrating Holi in the UK

In March 2009 about two hundred people, of all ages, gathered at the Sri Venkateswara (Balaji) Mandir just outside of Wolverhampton. They had gathered to celebrate the festival of Holi, a spring festival mostly associated with Kṛṣṇa. The festival itself is linked to a number of different narratives. In particular, it is associated with Prahlād, son of the demon (*asura*) king Hiraṇyakaśipu. Prahlād, despite his father's prohibition, was a devotee of Viṣṇu. Hiraṇyakaśipu, in his fury at the continued devotion of his son, ordered him to be killed. However, Prahlād miraculously survived all attempts on his life. At one point in the narrative, Hiraṇyakaśipu instructs his sister Holikā, who has a special power making her invulnerable to fire, to sit on a pyre, holding Prahlād in her lap. Because of his devotion to Viṣṇu, Prahlād survives and the demoness Holikā burns to death. Holi is said to celebrate this particular event, as well as Kṛṣṇa's sporting with the milkmaids (*gopīs*). Holi is primarily celebrated in North India. Although there are regional variations, the festival invariably involves throwing coloured powder, and lighting a bonfire into which coconuts are offered. The roasted coconuts are then offered around as *prasād*. The celebrations can include taking *bhang*, a drink made with marijuana, and can get very wild, even aggressive, in India. The origins of this festival remain obscure, but it is clearly a spring festival associated with fertility.

In 1977, Robert Jackson wrote an article describing how Holi was celebrated at the Shree Krishna temple in Coventry (UK). He notes (p. 206) that 'there was none of the traditional paint throwing and certainly no ribaldry linked traditionally with inter-caste or inter-sex rivalry'. Jackson suggests five possible explanations of the changes to the way that Holi was celebrated in Coventry. First, the rumbustious elements have in some instances become toned down in India, although in many regions there is no real evidence of this. Second, the wilder aspects of the celebration would be misunderstood by the host community, and therefore could cause friction. Third, Holi in India is normally celebrated over several days, and in Britain this is no longer possible. In the British context, some sort of celebration lasting a few hours will be arranged at temples on the nearest weekend to the actual date of Holi. Fourth, as people need warmer, and therefore more expensive clothing in Britain, celebrants are less inclined to risk ruining their clothes. Finally, Hindus in Britain tend to come from a narrower band of castes. In particular, the majority of Hindus come from the higher castes.

Victor Turner suggests that rituals include a liminal stage in which the usual hierarchical structures of society can be simplified, eliminated or reversed. This liminal phase can be characterized as 'anti-structure', which Turner suggests (1995, p. 177) reaffirms the order of social structures and the relative places of individuals within that structure. The wild colour throwing during Holi can be thought of as an exemplar of this liminality that ultimately affirms social structure and an individual's status within that structure. However, in the British context the social structures are more often articulated in terms of class, rather than caste, and this diminishes the need for rites that temporarily eliminate hierarchical distinctions.

However in 2009, members of the Venkateswara temple, in Wolverhampton, were invited to participate in 'colour splashing'. This was organized by the Balaji Youth Group. There were several differences in the way in which this festival was celebrated here. The colour throwing was timetabled to a designated hour and restricted to the grounds of the temple, whereas in India the colour throwing is a free-for-all on the streets that continues for the whole day. While all those involved participated with great enthusiasm, virtually all participants ending up covered from head to toe in multi-coloured powder, it was a less rumbustious event than can be the case with the celebrations that take place on the streets of Northern India.

Furthermore Holi, as I have indicated, is primarily a North Indian festival but Shree Venkateswara is a deity that is mostly found in South India. The fact that 'colour splashing' is a part of the way in which Holi is celebrated at the Venkateswara temple indicates that diaspora Hindus feel more confident about what ritual practices can be performed in the context of the UK. In other words, the line of accommodation has shifted over the last few decades. However, this does not indicate that the religious beliefs and practices will necessarily, or even probably, coincide with the way in which Hinduism is understood and practised in India.

Diversity in Diaspora

Just as Hinduism is a very diverse religious tradition in India, it is not homogeneous either in the UK. While there is a tendency for Hindus to represent themselves as a unified community in the British context, variables including region of origin, caste and sectarian affiliation can be identified. However, the distinction between these variables is also influenced by time and place of settlement. In terms of time, all forms of variables that cut across the South Asian diasporas were less significant in the early days of migration after the Second World War. Faced with both ignorance and sometimes open hostility from the wider British community, internal differences that divided the South Asian communities were relatively unimportant. However, with the passage of time, and as these communities have become more established and secure, such differences have become more significant. The impact of regional, caste and sectarian affiliations are contingent upon the relative size of the Hindu community. In places, such as the West Midlands, where there is a relatively large Hindu community, networks of identification can fragment along these lines. However, where the community is relatively small there is a need to pool resources, and it is possible to identify a more ecumenical form of Hinduism.

Region

By far the majority of Hindus in Britain originate from the state of Gujurat in the West of India. According to Paul Weller (2007, p. 170) between 55 and 70 per cent of Hindus in Britain originate from Gujarat. This community, as indicated above, is itself divided between those who came directly from India in the late 1950s and early 1960s, and the twice migrants who came from East Africa in the early 1970s. Dwyer (1994, p. 182) warns 'not to overestimate the differences between once and twice migrants'. Though the patterns of settlement were quite different – 'once migrants' tended to arrive as single men, whereas most twice migrants arrived in family units – shared caste and sectarian affiliations have increasingly attenuated these differences. The next largest group of Hindus to have settled in Britain are from the Punjab, which Weller (2007, p. 170) indicates as being between 15 and 20 per cent of the total number. This leaves a maximum of 30 per cent of Hindus originating from all the other states of India and Sri Lanka.

Place of origin does make a difference, and Punjabi and Gujarati forms of Hinduism tend to have a quite different ethos. In Gujarat, the overwhelming majority tends towards Vaiṣṇava forms of Hinduism.

Many Gujaratis identify with one of two sects (*sampradāya*): Puṣṭi Mārga or the Swaminarayan *sampradāya*. Puṣṭi Mārga (Path of Grace) was founded by Vallabhācārya (1479–1531). It has become one of the most significant sectarian groups in Western India. It combines a focus on devotion to Kṛṣṇa with a reinterpretation of *Vedānta*, which Vallabha termed 'pure non dualism' (*śuddhādvaita*). Vallabha argued against Śankarācārya's concept that the world is unreal (*māyā*). Vallabha argued that as everything is in fact an emanation of Kṛṣṇa, who is regarded as synonymous with *Brahman*, then the material world must fundamentally be real.

The Swaminarayan *sampradāya* was founded in the nineteenth century by Swamirarayan. Its central focus is on the lineage of *gurus* begun by Swaminaryan. The *guru* is regarded as the complete manifestation of the Supreme Being (*Puruṣottam*). Consequently, the current *guru* Pramukh Swami is regarded as both the manifestation of *Puruṣottam* and Swaminarayan. Temples play a very important role in the Swaminarayan movement, and the main images (*mūrti*) are always those of Swaminarayan and his successors. Overall, Gujaratis have been very successful in Britain. Followers of Swaminarayan are expected to tithe between 10 and 20 per cent of their earnings to the movement. Consequently, it has been able to build a magnificent temple in north London, which was opened by Pramukh Swami in 1995.[5]

This was the first temple in Britain built according to the prescriptions of the texts known as the *Śilpa Śāstras*. Italian marble and Bulgarian limestone were shipped to India, where they were hand carved by craftsmen and then shipped to Britain for assembly. The temple itself is very imposing and one cannot but be impressed by this beautiful, ornately carved, gleaming white marble edifice in an otherwise unprepossessing neighbourhood. Deservedly, the temple has gained a very high public profile, and has become a centre for school visits. However, this one, albeit very important, *sampradāya* has come to represent for many outsiders the 'authentic' version of the richly diverse traditions subsumed under the umbrella term Hinduism. The movement itself has, of course, no objection to being represented as the universal face of Hinduism. Indeed, it contributes to this perception with an interesting exhibition in the temple ambitiously titled 'Understanding Hinduism'. This exhibition, with its tableaux depicting various scenes from both Hindu mythology and the life of Swaminarayan, is of course highly selective, and while it gives an insight into the worldview of the followers of Swaminarayan, it cannot be said to represent the beliefs and practices of all Hindus.

The ethos of the Punjabi traditions is quite different to that of the Gujarati community. As Roger Ballard (1996) notes: one of the most significant features that all Punjabis share is a common language, which 'provides the foundation of their common world view'. Another aspect of Punjabi traditions is that the boundaries between Sikhism, Islam and Hinduism were never as clearly defined as many scholars have suggested (see Ballard, 1996 and Oberoi, 1997). Although certain prototypical groups can be identified as belonging to one clearly defined religious community, even in diaspora, other groups are not so easily classified.

Not far from the centre of Wolverhampton is a temple known as Ek Niwas, literally 'One Place'. Stepping through the doors of this relatively unassuming building one is transported into another world. Against the backdrop of a fibreglass landscape, intended to represent the Himalayas, are not only a number of images (*mūrtis*) of Hindu deities, but also various stuffed animals. The immediate impression is that Ek Niwas is clearly a Hindu place of worship. This is reinforced by the fact that the central shrine is dedicated to Baba Balaknath, who is identified with Skanda (also sometimes known as Kartikeyya), who is regarded as the son of Śiva and brother to Gaṇeśa, which clearly links Ek Niwas to the wider Śaivite traditions. However, a closer look around reveals images that are more associated with Sikhs. For example, there are images of Guru Nanak and Guru Gobind Singh.[6] There is also a *Guru Granth Sahib*, the holy text for Sikhs, installed in a small upstairs room. The charismatic founder of Ek Niwas states that he is a Jat Sikh.[7]

Caste

Caste is an extremely sensitive and contested topic amongst Hindus in Britain. A report made for the Dalit Solidarity Network indicated 'that there was a lot of reluctance to discuss caste as it relates to communities living in the UK as it is seen as an issue only for Dalits in India' (Borbas, 2006, p. 8). Three types of response can be identified when raising issues of caste amongst British Hindus: caste is completely irrelevant, caste is misunderstood, and caste still continues to create injustices. Many Hindus will say that caste identity has become totally meaningless in the British context. In a recent broadcast on caste for the BBC Asian Network (*Asian Network Report*, 2 March 2009) the presenter Satnam Sangera suggested that '[i]n Britain it [caste] means no more to me than the brand of socks that I wear'.

Caste, as well as being a hierarchical ordering of society, also designates whom one can (or cannot) marry. Some British Hindu parents will indicate that they are not concerned about the caste status of prospective partners for their children, pointing out that there are increasing numbers of young Hindus who even marry outside the Hindu community. The important thing is that there is a good match between the two individuals. This clearly draws upon a Western conceptualization of marriage as a partnership between two individuals, rather than an Indian view that suggests marriage is the joining of two families. However, *jāti* does seem to be important in finding a life partner for many Hindus living in Britain. Hindus posting on matrimonial and dating websites for Hindus will often provide their caste identity.[8]

There is no doubt that caste has been a factor in oppression and social injustice in India, which raises the question of how far this has been imported into the UK. Annapurna Waughray (2009, p. 182) observes that 'for some groups and individuals within the UK caste exerts a divisive force, albeit one which is not readily acknowledged and which is largely invisible to the majority of the population'. CasteWatch UK suggest that caste and the concomitant injustices of this social system have been imported into Britain. Consequently, Waughray (2009, p. 184) argues that there is a need for 'explicit protection against caste discrimination' to be inscribed in British law.

It is very difficult to obtain any accurate figures for the number of *dalits* in Britain. A report for the Dalit Solidarity Network UK (DSN UK) suggests at least 50,000 *dalits* live in the UK (Borbas, 2006, p. 4), although some suggest numbers as high as 200,000 (see Puri, 2003). The problem of quantifying the *dalit* population is hardly surprising since the term *dalit*, though used as a signifier of collective identity in India, is 'not a common term of self-reference in the United Kingdom' (Dhanda, 2009, p. 49).

Collective identities tend to coalesce around different signifiers. For example, Valmiki is an important signifier of identity for some British South Asians.[9] Most Valmikis in the UK are originally from the Punjab, and many are twice migrants who came to Britain via East Africa. Like most migrants from the subcontinent, Valmikis followed a pattern of chain migration and there are now Valmiki centres in the West Midlands, Coventry, Oxford, Bedford and Southall.

Like many Punjabi groups, it is not clear whether Valmikis are Hindu, Sikh, or neither, as they draw upon symbols and rites of both religions in order to construct their own tradition as a discourse of resistance. Even within the Valmiki community in Britain there are differences. Eleanor Nesbitt (1994, pp. 130–2) observes that the Coventry temple and rites seem more in the style of a Sikh place of worship (*gurdwara*) while the Southall temple appears to be much more Hindu in its style and ritual idiom. It is best to think of Punjabis as *bricoleurs*[10] who construct their various traditions from the wide and diverse pool of symbolic resources available in the Punjabi cultural milieu.

It is also equivocal whether the Valmikis can be classified as a caste (*jāti*[11]) or a tradition (*sampradāya*). In terms of being classified as a *sampradāya*, the Valmikis trace their tradition to the sage Vālmīki, who is regarded as the composer of the *Rāmāyaṇa*. However, some Valmikis believe that the most known versions of this epic tale are a Brahminic distortion of what Vālmīki actually composed. In the Valmiki tradition, Rāvaṇa is represented as a ruler of the indigenous Dravidian people. Rāma is depicted as being of mixed Dravidian and Āryan stock, but nonetheless represents the aggressive expansion of the Ārya into Central and South India (see Birmingham Valmiki Sabha, n.d.).

In terms of *jāti*, Valmikis are occupationally associated with street cleaning and refuse removal. Although many Valmikis in India, and almost certainly none in the UK, actually earn a livelihood as street cleaners, they are formally classified as being untouchable. Nesbitt (1994, p. 127) suggests that diaspora groups such as the Valmikis suffer a 'double exclusion'. In other words, they are marginalized in the discursive practices of both the dominant white majority and the higher-caste South Asians. Consequently, Valmikis are caught in a double bind. On the one hand, this double exclusion necessitates the formation of strong supportive community networks, yet on the other hand this strong sense of community can potentially emphasize their distinctive caste status, and marginalize them even further.

CasteWatch UK suggests that a 'disturbing number of the Indian Diaspora are actively perpetuating caste system in the United Kingdom' (*sic*). CasteWatch UK suggests that casteism in the UK can be identified in five areas:

1. Inter-caste marriages are frowned upon, if not forbidden.
2. Religious places of worship are divided along caste lines.
3. Children are bullied in schools through name calling, which sometimes leads to violence.
4. Caste masquerades as entertainment in Punjabi bhangra music.
5. Caste is manifest on the factory floor, and can lead to discrimination and violence.

Caste lines are, of course, maintained through the practice of endogamy, and to some extent it is immaterial whether or not the rationale for endogamy is cultural or physiological. The survey carried out by DSN UK of 'key members of the Dalit community' suggested that '85% of respondents felt that Indians[12] in Britain actively practise and participate in the caste system'. The research indicated that over 80 per cent of respondents perceived that temples in Britain were organized along caste lines, and the same proportion believed that British Indians tended to marry within caste. Over half the respondents suggested that they had experienced some form of caste discrimination (Borbas, 2006). A survey conducted by the Hindu Forum of Britain (HFB) suggested that over 92.6 per cent of respondents believed that there was no caste discrimination in the British context, and the remaining 7.4 per cent did not believe it to be a major issue (Kallidai, 2008, p. 14). A Lohana[13] respondent suggested that 'instances of caste discrimination are almost non-existent in the UK'.

There is some indication in the HFB report that there is still a preference, because of similar cultural perspectives, for marriage partners to be from the same caste. However, a clear distinction is made between forced and arranged marriages, with the HFB strongly condemning any form of coercion in respect to marriage. The report also suggests that the preference for a marriage partner from the same caste is becoming less significant. It could be argued that with second- and third-generation Hindus, a sense of being British and Hindu becomes a more significant shared cultural perspective than the cultural distinctions of caste.

The question arises as to why there is such a discrepancy between the two reports. It could be argued that, methodologically, both are flawed. The main criticism that can be levelled against them is that they are very limited in scope. It is clear that the DSN UK report only asked the opinions of those individuals and groups who can be classified as *dalit*. This is of course not unreasonable, as it is important to understand the perceptions of those who are believed to be discriminated against.

The Hindu Forum of Britain (HFB) represents itself as 'the largest representative body for British Hindus', and therefore aims to speak for all Hindus, regardless of caste. Its report suggests that it did include a wide range of caste and community groups in its research. It criticizes the DSN UK report, and similar reports on casteism, as being merely anecdotal. HFB more seriously accuses the DSN of obtaining funds from Christian groups, claiming that the caste discrimination lobby in the UK is predominately made up of Christians with an evangelical agenda. However, it is not at all clear from the HFB report how many individuals and groups that might be classified as *dalit* were included in the research.

It is hardly surprising that there are different accounts of the significance of caste in the UK, given the complex networks of interactions between the community of origin, the diaspora communities and the receiving community. Caste does seem to play a role in the British Hindu community. Overall, although there is some acceptance of inter-caste marriage, endogamy tends to be preferred, and there is some anecdotal evidence of caste discrimination. Meena Dhanda (2009, p. 57) interviewed a number of young '*dalits*' in Wolverhampton who, although they did not relate to the term *dalit*, 'reported experience of caste bullying at school, sometimes via exclusion, but mostly through name calling'.

There are British caste organizations: for example the Council of Valmiki Sabhas UK, already mentioned, and the Lohana Community UK (LCUK). Lohanas claim descent from Rāma's son Luv and therefore *kṣatriya* status. The majority of Lohanas in the UK originate from Gujarat, and almost all arrived via East Africa (Michaelson, 1987, p. 34). The LCUK has branches around the country, mostly in the Midlands and London. Besides organizing social and sporting events, it has a matrimonial service with its own website, and in March 2009 the LCUK organized a 'Matchmaker Event' in London. There is also a Shree Prajapati Association UK. The Prajapatis are traditionally potters by trade, although very few earn their livelihood in this way. The Shree Prajapati Association was founded in 1975 and has 13 local branches, which organize a wide range of social and cultural events. There are also a number of *brāhmin* groups. Some temples are also caste based, although every temple I have visited always indicates that it is open to all.

The question is: to what extent do these groups perpetuate caste divides, and create isolated socio-religious groups? This is a very difficult question to address. On the one hand, I think it is fair to say that many British Hindus, for cultural reasons, still prefer to marry within the same *jāti* and that various caste organizations do perpetuate caste identity. On the other hand, the British context does provide Hindus with other arenas of association, meaning that caste boundaries are far more malleable and permeable than the normative discourses around caste suggest.

Furthermore, though the wider British public in the twenty-first century may be able to recognize the distinction between Hindus, Sikhs and Muslims, albeit in a rather simplistic way, they really have no knowledge of the cultural distinctions between Brāhmins, Prajapatis and Lohanas, and this tends to create a cultural context that attenuates the significance of these distinctions. This leads to a situation where the distinctions between religious traditions, which at least in the Punjabi context have not always been clear-cut, become more reified, but where caste becomes little more than a social network whose members have little of real substance in common. This raises the question of whether it is possible to identify a distinct form of British Hinduism. However, before looking at this it is necessary to briefly consider the third significant variable that cuts across the British Hindu community, namely sectarian divide.

Sampradāya

The term *sampradāya* probably best translates as tradition and refers to religious teaching that is handed down through the generations; it can be thought of in terms of sectarian differences. I have used the term sect, not in the strict sociological sense of an exclusive religious group that demands a total commitment and whose members aspire to achieve personal perfection, but in the sense of a loosely connected group that claims a common origin, and has shared mythic narratives, doctrines, rituals and symbols, and some form of institutional structure. Most Hindus have some allegiance to a particular sect (*sampradāya*).

Both the Puṣṭi Mārga and the Swaminaryan movement, mentioned above, are important sectarian movements for the Gujurati community. In many ways the Swaminaryan movement, mainly because of the impressive temple in North London, is the most visible *sampradāya*. However, British Hindus identify with a wide range of sectarian movements, other important ones in Britain including the International Society for Krishna Consciousness (ISKCON) and the Sathya Sai Baba Movement. Both of these movements have attracted Western followers, and are sometimes classified as new religious movements. Kim Knott (1986) suggests that in Leeds in the 1980s the Shree Satya Sai Baba Mandal could be classified as a Hindu group, as its membership at the time was exclusively Gujarati. On the other hand, Knott suggests that ISKCON is a Hindu-related group; in other words it is basically a new religious formation that draws upon certain Hindu ideas in order to construct its worldview. I would argue that in the contemporary context, ISKCON is much more recognizably a Hindu group, as its roots lie in, and it still acknowledges and practices, a paradigmatically Vaiṣṇava form of devotionalism. However, the message of the International Sai Organization, as it is now known, has become so universalistic in its content and tone that its Hindu origins seem to have become almost lost. This, of course, raises the question of who is a Hindu.

The history of ISKCON in the West is well known.[14] It was founded by Swami Prabhupada, a follower of a Bengali form of Vaiṣṇavism who travelled to New York in 1965, at the height of the counter-cultural movement. He quickly achieved a following and/or the support of many of the leading voices of the counter culture. This culminated in a meeting with the Beatles, who had already begun to develop an interest in Indian culture. In 1969, the Beatles sponsored Prabhupadha's visit to Britain, and George Harrison became a devotee. Harrison recorded the song 'My Sweet Lord', which includes the Hare Krishna *Mantra*, which reached the number one spot on both sides of the Atlantic in 1970. This began the process of what John Zavos (2008) terms 'visibilization' of the Hindu community in general, and ISKCON in particular. Visibilization is termed by Zavos (2008, p. 328) as 'the process by which subterranean group identities become visible within a range of wider public spheres'.

In 1973, George Harrison donated a large manor house, with 17 acres of land in Hertfordshire, to ISKCON; this was renamed Bhaktivedanta Manor. While the majority of residents at Bhaktivedanta Manor were Western converts, it very quickly attracted substantial numbers of visitors from the Hindu community, especially during festival times.[15] ISKCON is a development of a form of Kṛṣṇa worship[16] that derives from Bengal. However, most of the Hindus who lived in the vicinity were twice-migrant Gujaratis. Nonetheless, devotion to Kṛṣṇa is also an important aspect of Puṣṭi Mārga, which is very popular with the Gujaratis. So, although Bengali in origin, the devotional practices at Bhaktivedanta Manor do have a resonance for Gujuratis. The large number of visitors led to an ongoing dispute over planning permission with the local council,[17] which to a certain extent involved the entire Hindu community (Nye, 2001).

This dispute was the first of several that acted as a focal point for British Hindus to gather together as a unified community in the face of perceived injustices. In May 2005, the UK-based Hindu Human Rights protested against the French company Minelli's use of images of Lord Rāma on shoes. Minelli agreed to withdraw the shoes, which left the group with a dilemma as to what actually to do with about five hundred pairs bearing such images. After discussion, they carefully picked off all the images of Rāma, which were then sent to India and disposed of in the Ganges, and the unadorned shoes were burned.

Later in 2005, there was a protest by British Hindus about the 68 pence stamp (the cost of postage to India), which was part of that year's set of special Christmas stamps. The image on the stamp was a detail from a seventeenth-century painting that depicts Joseph and Mary as having *tīlaks*, which suggests that they are Hindus, worshipping a clearly blond baby Jesus. The Hindu Forum of Britain suggested that the image was disrespectful and asked for it to be either amended or withdrawn. Although initially resistant, the Royal Mail did eventually withdraw the stamp. In his discussion of this and other protests, Zavos (2008, p. 335) concludes that 'these campaigns constitute a form of performance that operates to express and create the idea of the Hindu community'. Consequently, while it is possible to suggest that regional identity, caste organizations and endogamy are forces that maintain divides amongst Hindus in Britain, there are also countervailing forces that act to unify British Hindus.

Temples

One of the most visible signifiers of the Hindu community in Britain is the increasing number of purpose-built temples, of which the Swaminaryan Mandir in North London is the epitome. It is very difficult to assess the number of Hindu temples in Britain. The most recent *Religions in the UK Directory* records just over seven hundred local Hindu organizations (Weller, 2007), many of which are temples, or at least include some form of shrine. There are two main difficulties in trying to quantify the number of Hindu places of worship in Britain. The first is that many private houses are used for religious gatherings, especially for communal singing of *bhajans*. The second is that for some groups, particularly those of Punjabi origin, like Ek Niwas, it is difficult to unequivocally classify them as Hindu.

Temples can be classified in a number of different ways. I suggest three overlapping approaches, not as a way of placing specific temples into particular categories, but as a way of understanding the significance of the temple in the diaspora context. These three modes of analysis are: to look at which deity or deities are installed in the temple; to look at which particular community the temple is intended to serve; and to look at the architectural style.

Any understanding of a Hindu temple, whether in India or in diaspora, has to take into account the deity or deities to whom it is dedicated. This is not always as straightforward as it may seem. Most temples in India have a main shrine dedicated to a particular deity, and satellite shrines for those deities associated with the central deity. However, this is not always the case in Britain. On entering many temples in the UK, one might be greeted by a wide range of different deities. One would think that the devotional focus of the Shree Krishan Mandir in Wolverhampton would be unambiguous. Certainly the main *mūrtis* are of Kṛṣṇa and Rādhā. There are also images of Rāma and Sītā, which is not altogether surprising as both pairs of deities fall broadly within the Vaiṣṇava traditions. However, there is also a Śiva *liṅga* and a small image of Baba Balaknath, both of which fall within the Śaivite traditions. This diversity of images in single temples has led some commentators to suggest that one can identify an ecumenical form of Hinduism developing in diaspora communities. There is of course a fairly straightforward reason for this: temples are expensive to build and maintain, and in the British context there are fewer Hindus, and therefore it is necessary to ensure that temples will attract the widest possible range of devotees.

However, as particular communities grow and develop, this can also lead to the establishment of new temples. A fairly typical example of this is the development of the Shree Venkateswara (Balaji) Temple located between Birmingham and Wolverhampton. From about 1974 onwards, a small group of South Indians, all of whom were devotees of the important and very popular deity Venkateswara, whose main temple is in Tirupati in the southern state of Andhra Pradesh, met socially and for prayer meetings in the house of one of the group. The group decided that they wanted to be able to conduct their devotions in a more traditional way. In particular, they wanted to conduct the early morning devotion known as *Suprabhatam Seva*, which involves waking the deity to the sound of particular hymns.

In 1980, the Shree Geeta Bhavan, a temple in Birmingham, agreed to allow the group to install a *mūrti* of Venkateswara, and they met every Sunday to conduct their devotional rites. Consequently the group grew in numbers, and eventually decided that they needed to establish their own temple, where they would be freer to practise according to their own South Indian traditions. This led to the building of the Shree Venkateswara (Balaji) temple in the mid-1990s.

The second way of analysing temples in the diaspora context is to consider whether the temple is intended for a particular regional, caste or sectarian group. As indicated earlier, all the temples I have visited have always made it clear that they are open to all. At the celebration of Holi at the Venkateswara temple, there were not only Hindus from South India, but also Hindus from a Punjabi and Gujarati background joining in the celebrations. Nonetheless, language, culture and sectarian affiliation (*sampradāya*) do make a difference, and in places where there is a large enough community to support it, temples do tend to serve a particular group.

Joanne Waghorne (2004) identifies what she calls an increasing globalization of local temple traditions. In other words, there is a gradual move away from broad ecumenical places of worship to more distinctive temples that serve a particular constituency. These distinctive temples are now linked in a global network, often, as with the Venkateswara (Balaji) temple in Britain, having a particular temple in India at the epicentre of this network. With many South Indians having migrated to the United States, Waghorne (2004, p. 173) suggests that there is 'a virtual chain of Venkateswara temples that now stretches from coast to coast'. This virtual chain has subsequently expanded further to become global in extent.

Finally, it is necessary to look at the architectural style. There are three main architectural styles of temples in diaspora, which I have termed appropriation, vernacular and traditional. Appropriation refers to taking over an already existing building, such as a community centre or disused church, and gutting the insides in order to make a sacred space appropriate for the installation of images and conducting of Hindu rituals. Appropriation of other buildings is of course primarily a matter of expediency. From the outside, there are few architectural signifiers to indicate that appropriated buildings are sacred spaces. However, once you cross the threshold, it is immediately apparent that one has crossed into a Hindu space with installed images and ritual paraphernalia.

At the other end of the scale are traditional temples built according to the injunctions of Sanskrit texts called the *Śilpa Śāstras*, such as the Swaminaryan Mandir in London. Building a temple, such as the Swaminarayan Mandir, according to the precise formulae detailed in the *śāstras* is a hugely ambitious and costly project. External features of a building act as architectural signifiers of their inherent purpose. This is doubly important for religious buildings, which signify sacred space, regarded by believers as being ontologically distinct from profane space. Mircea Eliade (1959, p. 25) suggests that 'for a believer, the church shares in a different space from the street in which it stands'. For many believers, it is important that religious buildings have some architectural features that are visible from outside, signifying the distinctive nature of sacred space. Consequently, a building that has been appropriated after previously performing some other function cannot clearly signify the distinctive nature of sacred space.

This has led to an accommodative strategy whereby a vernacular form of temple architecture has developed that clearly identifies a building as sacred space, yet is more appropriate to the cultural, economic and climatic context of contemporary Britain. A prime example of this is the Shree Krishan Mandir near the centre of Wolverhampton. This square red-brick building is clearly a temple. The entrance facing the main road has a small portico topped by a white pyramid-shaped finial with a gold orb on top. There is a large symbol 'OM' in red picked out against a white background in mosaic near the top of the portico. The finial is the highest point on the building, and clearly makes reference to the form of many temples in India. However, unlike temples in India, the highest point is situated above the entrance and not above the central shrine.

The South Indian Community involved in the design and construction of the Venkateswara (Balaji) Temple just outside of Wolverhampton[18] adopted a quite different strategy in order to construct a temple that was more in accord with the prescriptions of the *śāstras*.

At least initially, the South Indian community, unlike Hindus from the Punjab and Gujarat, did not follow patterns of chain migration. Many of the first wave of the South Indian community were professionals, and therefore employment opportunities were available across the country, and consequently the South Indian community was rather more dispersed than the other Hindu communities.

The Shree Krishan Mandir in Wolverhampton.

In 1984, a group of South Indians, many of whom were involved in the group that met at the Shree Geeta Bhavan, began to look for a piece of land to build a temple dedicated to Shree Venkateswara. There were three criteria: the land had to be affordable, accessible, and have planning permission. It took almost eight years to find a suitable site. In 1992, the Black Country Development Corporation offered them twelve and a half acres of old industrial wasteland. Outline planning was granted in 1994 and full planning permission in 1995.

The trustees employed temple architects (*sthapati*) in India, who were experts in the specifications for temples as outlined in the sacred texts (*śāstras*), but knew nothing about building regulations in Britain, or indeed anything about the very different weather conditions. The trustees were also required to employ a registered architect in Britain, who did not know anything about temple architecture. They also hired a consultant academic who was an expert on Indian temple architecture. The three did not necessarily agree. However, a good compromise was found that met the stipulations of the *śāstras* while also satisfying the requirements of building regulations and allowing for weather conditions in Britain. The temple itself was constructed according to the *śāstras,* built on its own foundations and raised up. An extended ground floor was added underneath, which contained amenities such as a reception area, toilets, shoe racks and offices. This made it possible for devotees to enter at the ground floor, leave their shoes, and climb an internal staircase up to the temple itself. As one of the people involved in the design commented, 'the central bit is comfortable to God, and the rest is comfortable for us'.

Temple rituals are performed by priests; there is no need for any one else to be present. The temples are there as resources for any devotees who wish for the sacred sight (*darśan*) of the installed images of deities. In other words, temple rituals are not primarily congregational in character. In Britain, the priests will perform the daily rituals irrespective of attendance, and devotees often simply drop into temples to perform a quick bow (*pranām*) in front of an image. However, temples in Britain also often arrange a more congregational form of worship, one evening a week and/or at weekends. For example, every Tuesday evening the Shree Krishan Mandir near the centre of Wolverhampton arranges collective food, and most Tuesday evenings between fifty to a hundred people gather for the *āratī*, to sing *bhajans* and to eat. This is as much a social as a religious occasion. Consequently, the temple becomes an important institution for the maintenance of tradition and formation of a sense of collective identity. It performs a social and cultural function that is different to the function it performs in the Indian context.

The temple is also an important arena for the transmission of tradition to the next generation. This is not to underestimate the importance of the domestic setting in passing on tradition. Nesbitt (2006) observes that most Hindu houses in Britain have a shrine, or shelf with images of deities, or at the very least some brightly coloured posters of deities as the focus for domestic rituals. These might simply involve offering incense, or be a more involved performance of *pūjā*.

Furthermore, the temple in diaspora has acquired a more formal pedagogical role. The Shree Venkateswara Temple, for instance, has a Balaji Youth Group which organizes events such as the colour throwing for the Holi celebration. It also puts on a number of cultural activities in the community hall next to the temple. These have included acting out the story of Holi in a manner somewhat reminiscent of nativity plays put on by schools. Every year, the temple organizes a youth camp, which in 2008 was attended by about seventy children. This is a week-long residential event at a nearby school. A range of activities is organized including: singing *bhajans*, yoga and meditation, how to conduct *pūjā*, and formal lectures on various aspects of Hindu culture. In the words of the report on the 2008 camp:

> The youths who come to camp are raised in a system where they may find themselves unsure of their identity and role in the world. They may find themselves alienated by the culture they find in their everyday lives, or lack thereof. It is thus imperative, now more than ever, that we ensure that the thousands of years of philosophy, traditions and cultural ideals the Hindu people have developed are passed on to the next generation. (Shree Venkateswara Balaji Temple UK, n.d.)

The vast majority of young Hindus in Britain were born here and have far less connection with India than their parents' or grandparents' generation, and arguably far more interaction with the wider British society. Clearly, this, as the quote above indicates, is a concern for some Hindus. Early commentators, such as James Watson (1977) suggested that second-generation Hindus were caught between two cultures. This implies that there are two relatively homogeneous cultures, and that there is some sort of liminal space between them. It also suggests a fundamental conflict between these cultures. However, as already indicated, the sending community, receiving community, and indeed the diaspora community are not homogeneous. More nuanced commentators such as Roger Ballard (1994, p. 31) claim that second and subsequent generations are 'skilled cultural navigators'; Robert Jackson and Eleanor Nesbitt (1993, p. 178) argue that Hindus born in Britain exhibit 'multiple cultural competence'.

In other words, for second- and third-generation Hindus there is no problem with being both British and Hindu. The sense of subjectivity is determined by context, and individuals navigate between different discourses of self, depending upon location. For example, Jackson and Nesbitt (1993, pp. 176–7) describe how 12-year-old Anita, one of their research participants, adopted the style of her predominantly non-Hindu peer group at school, but was equally comfortable talking about Sathya Sai Baba and singing *bhajans* in the home environment. One of Dhooleka Raj's (2003, p. 152) elderly interviewees, describing the younger British-born generation, indicated, 'they are very Indian at home; once they are out they are English. They are like coconuts, isn't it?[*sic*] Brown on the outside and white inside.'

The discussion of diaspora communities is often linked with the concept of hybridity. In other words, do strategies of accommodation lead to distinctive new cultural forms? The idea that Hindus born in Britain are competent in multiple cultural arenas raises the question of whether a new form of Hinduism is developing in diaspora. Put a different way: is there a transformation from being both British *and* Hindu (multiple cultural competence), to a sense of being British Hindu (cultural hybridization)? There clearly are some hybrid cultural forms. For example, there is a distinctly British South Asian style of music, sometimes referred to as Asian Underground, with artists such as Talvin Singh and Nitin Sawhney drawing on both Indian and Western forms of music to create a new musical form. However, whether it is possible to identify a hybrid form of Hinduism in the British context is far more equivocal. What is unequivocal is that Hindus have found a wide range of ways of adapting to cultural milieus outside of India.

Chapter 6

The Future

Hinduism remains a rich and vibrant religious tradition, which flourishes not only in India, but also in other parts of the world. It is clear that it will continue to do so into the future. However, it is also apparent that Hinduism is a dynamic tradition that has, over the course of its development, responded to changes in context. Hinduism today is not the same as the religion of the Vedic period, the medieval period, or even the Hinduism espoused by the reformers of the late nineteenth and early twentieth century. At the same time, elements from all of these historical periods continue to have a place in the Hindu tradition. I have used the term tradition deliberately because there is in Hinduism a deep sense of a connection with the past. However, as I have indicated, I do not mean by tradition something that is static and unchanging and antithetical to modernity (or even postmodernity). Hinduism is a tradition that is constantly being reinvented, yet at the same time maintaining continuity with the past.[1] This reinvention of tradition is not a conscious and deliberate strategy, but is produced by the various ways in which people naturally respond to changing circumstances.

While it is not the place of the academic to predict the future, even if s/he had a crystal ball, some of the trends that can be identified in the reinvention of tradition might give some indication of the current trajectories.

What's in a Name?

Many Hindus, with some justification, have argued that the term Hinduism is falsely conceived. They claim that the term was imposed by outsiders; that it was used as part of the colonial project; and that its continued use not only misrepresents the tradition, but also perpetuates relations of power. A senior *swāmi* at Sivananda Ashram told me:

> Hinduism is a misnomer: there is no such thing as Hinduism; it was coined by Westerners because they want to distinguish this from that, so they called it Hinduism. It comes from the word Indus, those people living on the Eastern side of the Indus River. Spirituality, when put into practice, is called religion. The spirituality which is practised here is called *Sanātana Dharma*. It has existed from time immemorial. It is not like other religions [which] somebody established, it is the eternal dharma.

Consequently, from this *swāmi's* point of view, the very title of this book is misconceived. Should I persuade the publisher to call it instead *Sanātana Dharma Today*? Are we as teachers and academics simply perpetuating a false perception of the religion by using the term Hinduism in our classes and publications? This is a vexed issue. It could be said that, in the terms of the *swāmi*, we are too concerned with 'distinguishing this from that'. To put it another way, is this book, and in particular the use of the term Hinduism, simply an extension of the Orientalist project, identified by the Palestinian scholar Edward Said? Said argues that a discourse, which he termed Orientalism, divides the world between the Occident (the developed West) and the Orient. This imaginative geography enabled Europe not only to manage 'but also to produce the Orient politically, sociologically, militarily, ideologically, scientifically and imaginatively' (Said, 1991, p. 2). We could also add 'religiously' to Said's list.

There is certainly a recognizable trend, not confined to erudite *swāmis*, that suggests the term *Sanātana Dharma* is a far more appropriate designation than Hinduism. Looking forward, the question arises of whether the term Hinduism will cease to be meaningful in the future. We know that, as the *swāmi* cited above indicated, the origins of the term had no religious connotation. We also know that it was first used in the nineteenth century, by both insiders and outsiders, to designate a religious tradition, and that, for all sorts of complex political and cultural reasons, it swiftly found a resonance with both insiders and outsiders. I am not convinced that, as yet, the use of the term *Sanātana Dharma* has acquired sufficient momentum, across a sufficiently wide constituency, to gain universal currency in the immediate future. However, the discussion about the most appropriate designation is a useful reminder of how problematic the term Hinduism is.

Convergence and Divergence in Modern Forms of Hinduism

There are two apparently contradictory trends in Hinduism: convergence and divergence. There is a trajectory that fuses distinctive elements under the umbrella term Hinduism. It can be argued that this term subsumes such a radical diversity that it cannot be understood as a single religious tradition. The differences within Hinduism are so extreme that they cannot simply be understood in terms of sectarian divides. Von Stietencron argues (2001, p. 41) that 'we cannot avoid concluding that there are a number of different "religions" existing side by side within "Hinduism"'. Should I have convinced the publishers of this book that three titles were needed: *Vaiṣṇavism Today*, *Śaivism Today* and *Śāktism Today*? While this might have been beneficial for me, most Hindus do not relate to these terms, and there is more interaction between the *Vaiṣṇava Śaiva* and *Śākta* traditions than von Stietencron supposes. Furthermore, the mere idea that there is a religion called Hinduism has bought these distinctive forms closer together.

There is evidence of a more ecumenical form of Hinduism which fuses disparate elements into a new syncretic style that can be labelled modern Sanātanism. Modern Sanātanists tend not to be affiliated to any particular sectarian group (*sampradāya*), and tend to prefer the use of the term *Sanātana Dharma*, as opposed to Hinduism. Modern Sanātanists assert that the various different gods and goddesses of the Hindu pantheon are actually just manifestations, forms or powers of a single God. *Advaita Vedānta*, or more precisely Swami Vivekananda's reinterpretation of *Vedānta*, provides the philosophical foundation for the assertion that there is only one Absolute deity that manifests in many different forms. The ethos of modern Sanātanism is encapsulated in statements such as:

> Though He can be called by many names and approached by different people in different ways, the Indian believes that there is only One God. "*Ekam sat vipra bahudha vadanti*", declare the Vedas. "Truth is one, sages express it in different ways." (Swami Venkatesananda, 2003)

This perspective is validated by referring to the Vedic source of the idea.[2] The idea of one absolute truth that is expressed in many different ways also facilitates the discourse that Hinduism is inherently inclusive and tolerant of other worldviews. Swami Venkatesananda continues: 'Some call Him Krishna or a thousand other names and the religion, Hinduism. Some call Him Christ and the religion Christianity.'

Modern Sanātanism interprets caste (*varṇa*) in terms of a meritocracy, rather than any inherent characteristics determined by birth. This interpretation is validated by referring to the Vedic past. It is claimed that, in origin, *varṇa* was a social system that recognized that society is an organic whole and that different individuals within society have to perform different roles according to attitude and aptitude. Consequently, Sanātanism suggests that it is necessary to return to the authentic Vedic origins of Indian culture. This discourse provides a deep connection to the past, and at the same time makes it possible to suggest that Hinduism is entirely compatible with the modern world. These ideas have an incredible appeal.

The question for the future is whether modern Sanātanism has sufficient momentum to subsume all other forms of Hinduism. Modern Sanātanism is a very important form of Hinduism, both in India and in diaspora communities, and the major themes of modern Sanātanism look set to be found in an increasingly wide range of arenas. However, it is not the only force at play, and although Sanātanism looks very likely to become a dominant form of Hinduism, it is unlikely that it will ever become the only form. Hinduism remains a very diverse tradition, and it is possible to identify trajectories of divergence.

Global Networks and Sacred Centres

One of the trends that commentators have observed is that globalization is not a simple process of homogenization, whereby eventually everything will look the same. Globalization creates pressures on various groups to differentiate themselves from others. There is a tendency towards a homogenized Sanātanist form of Hinduism which is broadly ecumenical. On the other hand, more particular senses of identity are also significant. Many Hindus still identify with a particular sect (*sampradāya*). These *sampradāyas* now often form global networks, with a central hub in India. For example, Tirupati, in India, is the nucleus for a network of Venkateswara temples that can be found in other parts of India, as well as in North America, Australia and Britain.

The continuing significance of particular *sampradāyas*, with their own particular traditions, narratives, beliefs and ritual practices, indicates not only that Hinduism will continue to maintain a rich diversity, but that India will continue to have a symbolic place for Hindus. The narratives of most *sampradāyas* are linked to specific places in India. These might be the birth place of the founding *guru* or, as with Venkateswara, the place where a particular deity is believed to have manifested.

The importance of these sacred centres and pilgrimage to them is likely to continue. On an average day, over 50,000 pilgrims visit the Venkateswara Mandir at Tirupati, and this can increase tenfold on special festival days. As modern modes of transport make travelling across India easier, more and more pilgrims make their way to pilgrimage places like Neelkanth and/or one of the *cār dhāms* in the hills above Rishikesh. Pilgrimage is well integrated into the religious lives of Hindus in India today. However, as we have seen, the rationale for these journeys is not always simply religious but now often includes a leisure dimension. This leisure aspect is increasing, as religious tourism has become a significant part of the discourse about visiting sacred places. Both local and state governments, and religious institutions themselves, are developing the infrastructure and amenities to make journeys to sacred places a more comfortable, and even luxurious, experience.

Hindus in diaspora maintain links to the sacred centres in India in a variety of ways. The concept of family is very important for most South Asians, and many have family connections in India. A visit to relatives will often include a visit to a particular sacred place. The priests (*pūjārī*) who perform the rituals in most temples in diaspora have been trained in India, and almost invariably belong to the *jāti* that traditionally performs the rituals at the sacred centre. Priests outside India who are associated with a particular tradition often maintain their authority and legitimacy through their links to sacred centres. In this way, the person of the priest acts as a conduit between congregations in diaspora and the sacred centre in India. This is often reinforced by devotees donating money to the sacred centre via the priest, and the priest returning with various sacred items from the centre. This is clearly evident with the priest at the Baba Balaknath temple in Walsall, on the outskirts of Wolverhampton, who maintains very close links with the centre of the Baba Balaknath tradition in Shahtalai in Himachel Pradesh.[3] This priest also organizes special *darśan* tours for the devotees at the Walsall temple to various pilgrimage places, culminating at Shahtalai (see Geaves, 2007).

Although Hindus born and educated outside of India may not necessarily ever visit the sacred places associated with their particular tradition, these sacred places retain a highly symbolic significance. For example, there are seven hills at the main Venkateswara temple in Tirupati, and the designers of the Venkateswara temple just outside Birmingham in Britain have created seven small mounds which replicate the landscape of the sacred centre of Tirupati.[4] The temple, while not precisely replicating the temple at Tirupati, is clearly based on a similar design. Furthermore, as with the Swaminaryan Mandir in London, the intricate stonework was carved in India, before being shipped to Britain and assembled.

There are two related questions that the relationship between diaspora communities and the sacred geography of India raises. Will the significance of the sacred centres in India become increasingly attenuated for future generations in diaspora? Will sacred centres emerge outside India? If the answer to these questions is yes, then we will have to understand Hinduism as a truly global religion, and not simply as an Indian religion that has spread to other parts of the world. At the moment, the evidence is that the sacred centres are likely to remain important, at least symbolically. Sacred centres maintain their significance, not only through physical and symbolic links throughout the globe, but also through the virtual links of the Internet. In particular, online *pūjā* services, discussed in Chapter 4, enable distant devotees to maintain links with sacred centres. It is possible to suggest that those temples and sacred places, which are not only centres of mythic narratives but also centres of a global communication nexus, will become increasingly significant. Places like the Venkateswara temple in Tirupati are rapidly developing into global hubs.

There is a variety of different types of temples developing in diaspora. Some serve the immediate need of a local population, others now have a wider appeal. Hindus congregate at centres outside India because they identify with the particular *sampradāya*. However, it is clear that there are also centres that attract Hindus who do not identify with the particular tradition. Centres in the United Kingdom, such as Bhaktivedanta Manor, the Swaminaryan Mandir in Neasden and the Venkateswara temple in Tividale attract Hindus from beyond their immediate locale and tradition. These centres have an appeal beyond their normal constituency because Hindus are impressed by the quality of the ritual, the knowledge of the priests, and/or the architectural style of the temple. They cannot be regarded as sacred centres though, because they have not yet developed the mythic narrative that would make them symbolically important in the same way as temples in *tīrthas* such as Tirupati.

However, there is tentative evidence that some places outside of India are developing symbolic importance. Ron Geaves (2007) suggests that Skanda Vale, a monastic community founded by a Sri Lankan *guru* in South Wales, has become a place of pilgrimage and 'is regarded as a *Sakti Petam*, or seat of power where the energy of the god is concentrated into a single place' (Geaves, 2007, p. 218). This does suggest at least the possibility that the sacred geography may eventually extend beyond the boundaries of Bhārat Mātā (Mother India).

Diverging Styles

As well as the maintenance and globalization of specific traditions, the socio-economic conditions of the modern world have created a context for a divergence of styles. The first style is that of the decorous middle-class disposition. This style manifests in phenomena such as: the growing popularity of religious tourism (as opposed to pilgrimage); *satsangs* in modern ashrams; the salience of charitable work (*seva*); the performance and reception of *bhajans* as quasi-concerts; the genteel possession of *brāhmin* women in the urban contexts; and organized colour throwing in the celebration of Holi at a diaspora temple. The second style might be characterized as an exuberant popular disposition. This style manifests in phenomena such as: *darśan* tours; ecstatic possession; the unrestrained throwing of colours during Holi celebrations in northern India; and the excitement of having *darśan* of Lord Venkateswara at Tirupati.

The middle-class religious disposition is the dominant style of Hinduism, and tends towards Sanātanism. However, exuberant popularism is the most popular style. This divergence seems to be exacerbated by the growing economic success of India. This economic success has not been evenly spread, but has provided approximately 10 per cent of India's billion-plus population with a good disposable income. Since the liberalization of the Indian economy in the 1990s, Western consumer goods have been readily available, and the so-called middle classes have been able to buy into a new consumer culture that is characterized not only by Western products, but also by specific Indian cultural products.

Maya Warrier (2005, p. 10) suggests 'consumer culture is evident equally in less tangible spheres of middle-class life, most notably that of religious preference'. Open up the pages of the lifestyle sections of any of the popular Indian newspapers, and it is difficult to distinguish these from any lifestyle section in a Western newspaper; there are the usual articles about health, diet, fashion and celebrity. Many of the products advertised will be familiar to people in North America and Europe. In almost all editions, the reader will also find articles that are reinterpretations of aspects of Hindu traditions; these often pertain to various aspects of yoga and meditation. However, these are presented simply as another lifestyle choice and are indicated as panaceas for the stresses of modern life. For example, in a column entitled 'Mind Body

Soul' in the *Hindu Times Sunday Magazine*, the columnist suggests, 'chanting mantras brings many health benefits. It relieves stress, makes you positive and helps you concentrate' (Sharma, 2008).

An exuberant popular disposition, like the middle-class disposition, tends to be focused on worldly goals. However, these tend to be focused in turn less on general health benefits and alleviating stress than on more specifically defined goals, such as the cure for a particular ailment. The exuberant popular disposition tends to be perceived as integral to life, and not simply as a lifestyle choice. A popular disposition tends to be less individualistic and more embedded in a collective identity. A typical example of this popular religious disposition is described by Lynn Foulston (2002, pp. 145–8), where devotees seek the alleviation of various specific problems from a woman who is believed to be possessed by the Goddess Santoṣī Mā.

The question for the future is whether or not these styles will diverge to such an extent that they will develop into two distinct forms of Hinduism. This question was raised for me when stepping out of the calm and ordered context of Sivananda Ashram, into a noisy excited and colourful crowd of pilgrims surging, like a river in spate, onto Neelkanth. I wondered what the connection was between these two styles, beyond simply being subsumed under the umbrella term Hinduism. While there is a tendency for those who have a reasonable disposable income and a relatively good education to be disposed towards a decorous style of religiousness, and for those from less privileged backgrounds to be more disposed to an exuberant style of religiousness, this is not an absolute. An individual is not necessarily confined to a particular disposition, but in different circumstances might find themselves being in an exuberant or a decorous frame of mind. These dispositions are diverse phenomena, which interact with each other in complex ways, and must be thought of as ends of a spectrum, rather than a binary opposition.

While I am rather wary of metaphors – and commentators on Hinduism have used a variety of them, such as a sponge and banyan tree – I would like to propose one here.[5] One way to think about the complex interaction between the various facets of Hinduism is to imagine a rope that is composed of a wide variety of threads, which are in turn composed of finer filaments. These filaments and threads are not static but are in a process of weaving in and out of each other. Sometimes new filaments are woven in, and sometimes filaments spin out, or even come to an end. For example, the decorous middle-class disposition and exuberant popular disposition can be considered as fairly substantial threads that are loosely interwoven: these draw on both new and old filaments, some of which they share in common. There is no way to predict what the shape and constitution of this 'rope' will be like in the future. However, in the foreseeable future, decorous middle-class dispositions and the exuberant popular disposition look set to continue as broad threads in the rope.

The Future of Caste

Nothing illustrates the dual processes of divergence and convergence more clearly than caste (*jāti*). On one level the significance of caste, especially in diaspora, has become increasingly attenuated. However, the consolidation of *jātis* into modern associations has in many ways assured the continuation of caste as an important signifier of identity. In the context of the modern political system in India, caste identity has become an increasingly political phenomenon. What this might mean for the future is that there may well be fewer castes, and that these more extensive caste affiliations, like the Yadavs discussed in Chapter 3, will subsume more parochial senses of identity and emerge as global networks. Such networks have the potential to perceive themselves as being in direct political and economic competition with one another, and this could exacerbate divisions between them. Substantial caste associations will have to develop narratives that legitimize collective senses of identity. These narratives, as we have seen with the Yadavs, may be articulated in terms of shared culture and/or ethnicity. They will also have to draw upon and rework familiar narratives and symbols. One of the reasons why the Yadavs have been so successful in drawing in a range of previously distinct *jātis* is that they were able to mobilize these groups around the familiar narratives of Kṛṣṇa.

The marginalization and discrimination against individuals because of their caste (*jāti*) identity is a vexed issue. Not only is discrimination on the basis of caste outlawed, but the Indian Constitution has a policy of positive discrimination legally inscribed. While lower castes are legally and politically protected, the issue of casteism has not been resolved at a social and cultural level. Indeed, the strategy of reserving for *dalits*, tribal groups (*ādivāsīs*) and Other Backward Classes a percentage of places in legislative assemblies, higher education and government posts might be said to have exacerbated caste divides. There is a degree of resentment from higher-caste groups of this policy, which on occasions has led to violence. The question for the future is: will this policy eventually lead to the bifurcation of society into two broad groups, *dalits*, tribals and OBCs on one side, opposed to all other castes on the other, or will the policy of positive discrimination eventually manage to redress the balance of power to the extent that these divisions lose their significance?

The Indian census of 2001 suggested that Scheduled Castes constituted 16.2 per cent of the population, and that Scheduled Tribes made up 8.2 per cent. Most estimates suggest that Other Backward Classes (OBCs) constitute around 50 per cent of the population.[6] This is potentially a very significant force in Indian politics. The Bahujan Samaj Party (BSP), under the leadership of Kumari Mayawati, aims to represent all Scheduled Castes and Tribes as well as OBCs. It had hoped to be in a position of balancing power between the two main political parties, Congress and the Bharat Janata Party (BJP), after the election in 2009, with Mayawati at one point claiming that she might even be able to garner enough support to form the government. However, this was not to be and the BSP, while strong in Uttar Pradesh, has not proved to be so successful elsewhere.[7] It is clear that there are limits to horizontal mobility, and while all those *jātis* identified as SC, ST and OBC may share common social and economic disadvantage, Mayawati and the BSP have yet to articulate a common symbolic reference point which will override more specific senses of identity.

The experience of shared oppression, discrimination and marginalization is rarely enough to produce a genuinely unified sense of collective identity. *Dalits*, tribals and OBCs have so far not been successful in articulating a narrative that crosses caste divides. The term *dalit* was itself intended to act as a symbolic point of reference for all groups that can be classified as untouchable. However, as this term was not familiar, it has failed in this aim. Similarly, on the other side of the equation, there is no common narrative or symbolic reference point that unifies all twice-born castes into a single imagined community. Consequently, it seems unlikely that Hindus (or, more broadly, Indians) will bifurcate into two large groups. However, for the foreseeable future, particular caste identities, such as Yadav, look likely to continue to be significant for both insiders and outsiders. This is because the Yadavs both have a narrative that has underpinned a sense of community, and effectively utilize modern communication technologies in the formulation of a global network.

It could be argued that caste as a hierarchical social organization is primarily a rural phenomenon. In small-scale village societies it is relatively easy to maintain very clearly demarcated religio-cultural divisions. However with urbanization, modernization and globalization, these divides become less easy to sustain. Writing in 1984, R. S. Khare

(p. ix) suggested, 'The clear traditional notions of dominance and privilege are becoming blurred as democratic law, politics, and economics release new forces in India.' For example, the opening up of education to those traditionally regarded as low down in the hierarchical structures of caste has entailed an increasing divergence between caste and class. There is now a growing sector of individuals who are classified as low caste but who might be considered to be middle class.[8] Professor Alte, who is the principal of a college and a Mahar,[9] traditionally regarded as an untouchable caste, informed the journalist Edward Luce that, in the city, he was treated with respect, as no one knew his caste. However, when he returned to his village, high-caste people, some of whom were unable to read and write, would not allow him into their home or to share a cup of tea (Luce, 2006, p. 111). However, even the village is not immune to the new forces indicated by Khare.

The current trajectories for caste (*jāti*) suggest that it is unlikely to disappear as such, but that it is gradually being transformed. Horizontal mobility and the sophisticated uses of media technologies mean that there will probably be fewer *jātis* in the future. *Jātis* will increasingly be represented as cultural, rather than quasi-biological, categories. There are signs, particularly in the urban contexts and amongst diaspora Hindus, that the hierarchical evaluation between different castes is becoming less significant. While I think it will be many generations before the notion of untouchability disappears totally, it is becoming harder to sustain as more Untouchables manage to improve their lot, and there is an increasing hiatus between caste and class. Untouchables will continue to find a variety of strategies and resources to challenge their stigmatization and exploitation.

There are two important provisos to the above predictions. First, the pace of change is not even. As I have indicated, the hierarchical nature of caste seems less prevalent in urban and diaspora contexts. Secondly, there is no such thing as a totally egalitarian society, and relationships of power exist in all societies. If, as I suspect, *jāti* remains a significant signifier of collective identity, the hierarchical distinction may well be less severe, but it is unlikely to vanish entirely.

So what about the concept of *varṇa*? While the *jāti* system actually structures Indian society, *varṇa* is more of an ideal. The origin of *varṇa*, as I indicated in Chapter 3, can be traced back to the hymn in the *Ṛg Veda* which suggests that different *varṇas* are produced from the various parts of the cosmic man. Consequently, as there seems to be a Vedic source for the idea of *varṇa*, it has to be acknowledged as authoritative.

However, it tends to be interpreted as an indication that a society is an organic whole, and that different individuals have to perform different roles in order for the organic whole to be maintained. The roles of people in society are not determined by birth, but by their attitudes and aptitudes. This seems a reasonable interpretation, and one that is commensurate with both the Vedic source and modernity. While in the near future this conceptualization of *varṇa* is unlikely to make many Hindus classify, say, a *chamar* who is a high-ranking government minister as really being a *kṣatriya*, this discourse may contribute to the attenuation of hierarchical distinctions.

Relations with Other Religious Traditions

The relationship between Hinduism and other religious traditions tends towards three different attitudes. The first perceives other religious worldviews as simply irrelevant; the second seeks dialogue with other religious worldviews; the third represents other religions as a potential or actual threat.

The notion that other religions are simply irrelevant has a long antecedent. Wilhelm Halbfass observes that during the Vedic period there was no interest in other cultures. In the *Brāhmana* period, the concept of the *mleccha*, the outsider who was not part of the ritual world, became prominent (Halbfass, 1988, p. 175). There is no way that the *mleccha* in their radical otherness could have any influence on Hindu *dharma*. This attitude can still be found today. In ashrams like the Kailash Ashram in Rishikesh, the religious practice (*sādhana*) is purely focused on exegesis of the Sanskrit texts (*śāstras*). Anything other than the interpretation of the *śāstras* is regarded as absolutely extraneous, and all outside worldviews are so alien that they can bring nothing to the project. There is no doubt that in small relatively isolated pockets this attitude will survive.

However, many Hindus, both in India and in diaspora, seek an active dialogue with individuals and groups with different religious perspectives. Through this interaction, Hinduism itself has become transformed. It is possible to suggest that Hinduism as a religion, which can be compared and contrasted with other religions, was itself constructed through this very dialogue with other religions. Swami Vivekananda, particularly through his speech at the World Parliament of Religions in Chicago in 1893, exemplifies in many ways both the impetus and the consequences of inter-religious dialogue. Sister Nivedita (in Swami Vivekananda, 1984, Vol. I, p. x) suggests: 'Of the Swami's address before the Parliament of Religion, it may be said that when he began it was 'of "the religious ideas of Hindus", but when he ended Hinduism had been created'. This is clearly hyperbole; nonetheless there is at least a sort of symbolic truth to her claim.

The conception that *Vedānta* recognizes that all religions represent a partial expression of an absolute Truth suggests that *Vedānta* has a privileged perspective. In the words of Sarvepalli Radhakrishnan (1980, p. 18), 'The Vedanta is not a religion, but religion itself in its most universal and deepest significance.' This enables individuals like Swami Venkatesananda, cited above, to refer to Christ and Kṛṣṇa in the same sentence, and to suggest that there is little more to distinguish the Christian and Hindu traditions than nomenclature. On the one hand, this facilitates interfaith dialogue, as it creates a willingness for those who hold this view to communicate in a positive way with individuals and groups from other faith communities. On the other hand, it has the potential to cause resentment, as it suggests that all religions are only relative and partial expressions of an Absolute Truth. Many Christians, while not necessarily suggesting that Hinduism is mere superstition, would be uncomfortable with the notion that their worldview is best understood as a partial expression of *Vedānta*. On balance though, this all-inclusive perspective bodes well for a continuing and constructive dialogue with other religious traditions.

However, there are certain groups and individuals who perceive other religious traditions as a direct threat. These groups and individuals are mostly affiliated with the Sangh Parivar, discussed in Chapter 3. There is currently a great deal of tension in states like Orissa. The Sangh Parivar, for example, accuse 'Christian terrorists' of murdering Swami Laxmanananda in 2008, and suggest on their website that Christian missionaries are '*harvesting the souls*' of impoverished and uneducated tribals by exploiting their vulnerability and innocence. This belief has led to attacks on Christians in the state. The perceived secularism and Westernization of Indian culture is also often represented as a direct threat to the authentic Hindu culture of India. Certain extreme groups such as the Sri Ram Sena (Lord Ram's Army) have recently attacked various fashionable bars, where young men and women have the opportunity to drink and dance.

The Bharat Janata Party (BJP), which is affiliated to the Sangh Parivar and campaigns on a platform of Hindu nationalism, seemed to have fairly substantial support in the late 1980s to early 2000s. The BJP formed the government between 1998 and 2004, when it was defeated by the coalition led by the Congress Party. When the BJP formed the incumbent government, it instated a policy of what could be called the saffronization of Indian culture. For example, it introduced school textbooks that gave an account of history underpinned by Hindutva ideology. Although the reasons for the political success of the BJP in this period are complex, and cannot be reduced to a single factor, it is clear that the controversy over the Babri Masjid in Ayodhya, coupled with the coincidental broadcasting of the television series of the *Rāmāyaṇa*, contributed to the success of their campaign. The BJP still remains the second largest national political party.[10]

Hindutva does clearly retain some appeal, and the RSS and its affiliates are still active. However, the election in 2009 demonstrated that the BJP had not managed to mobilize as much support as anticipated. Exit polls suggested that it would be a very close election, similar to that in 1994, but the India National Congress was far more successful than was predicted. The Sangh Parivar is likely to remain a significant, albeit minority, force in many aspects of Indian society, culture and politics. Its success or otherwise will be influenced by a large range of complex factors. Even if the BJP manages to win a future election, given the complexities of Indian politics and the necessity for forming coalitions it will never have the capacity to impose Hindutva. When he founded the RSS in 1925, and instituted the *shakha* as the basic unit, Hedgewar realized that Hindutva has to grow from below and not be imposed from above. However, even at the local level, Hindutva only has, and only ever will have, a limited appeal. Nonetheless, Hindutva ideology will continue to have some support. The extent of this will be contingent on a wide range of complex economic and political factors, at both a local and national level.

The Allure of Hinduism

Aspects of Hinduism have had an appeal beyond the Indian constituency. During the height of the colonial period, Hinduism tended to be dismissed as polytheistic, irrational and superstitious. On the other hand, some Westerners, many of whom were disillusioned with the ethos of both Christianity and the scientific paradigm, found something in India that held a deep appeal. This appeal could be simply dismissed as the allure of the exotic. However, those Westerners who were attracted to aspects of Hindu culture have had a major impact, way beyond their actual numbers, on Western societies. The first really significant group of Westerners to see something positive in Indian culture were the Theosophists. The Theosophical Society was founded by Madame Blavatsky and Colonel Olcott in 1875. Blavatsky, in her extensive writings that blended Western esotericism and a reinterpretation of Hindu philosophy, perceived India to be the home of enlightened masters and a perennial wisdom. J. J. Clarke (1997, p. 89) suggests that the Theosophists were largely responsible for introducing terms such as *māyā* and *karma* into European languages. In many ways, the Theosophical Society can be considered as the origin of the New Age Movement. While the New Age is a very amorphous movement, which encompasses individuals and groups with diverse beliefs and practices, Hindu ideas and practices are prevalent.

Awareness of Hinduism was further raised by the counter-culture movement of the 1960s and early 70s, a time when many young people in America and Europe were disillusioned with the mores of their parents' generation. Many looked to India for a worldview that made sense, and that could be utilized in a critique of the perceived empty materialism of Western culture. This period was epitomized by the Beatles, the most renowned pop group of the time, meeting Maharishi Mahesh Yogi in Rishikesh in 1968. Maharishi Mahesh Yogi was the founder of a technique known as Transcendental Meditation (TM). It is equivocal whether TM can be considered a form of Hinduism, as it makes no claims to be: its literature abounds with terms such as 'scientific', and TM makes no use of Sanskrit terminology. Nonetheless, the Beatles' interest in TM did bring an awareness of India and meditation to a much wider audience. It would be fair to suggest that, prior to this symbolic meeting, hardly anyone would have had any conception at all of what is meant by the term meditation, a term now well incorporated into the English language.

During this period, Swami Prabhupada, the founder of the International Society of Krishna Consciousness (ISKCON) travelled to the USA and Britain, introducing a form of devotional Hinduism, with its texts, iconography and chanting. The meeting between the Beatles and Mahesh Yogi, and the exotic appearance of chanting ISKCON monks handing out strange books, inspired many young people to travel to India to seek answers to their existential questions. These travellers to various places like Rishikesh, although comparatively few, brought back many new ideas, and Rishikesh is now a centre of yoga and meditation that attracts seekers from all over the globe.

In particular, the counter-culture seekers of the 1960s and 70s brought back various ideas on yoga and meditation. It is now possible to find yoga and meditation groups and classes, of various different types and styles, throughout the non-Indian world. However, yoga and meditation are often articulated in terms of health and well-being, and their practice is frequently divorced from ascetic lifestyles, metaphysical speculation and soteriology. They are now simply other products that can be purchased in the alternative health and well-being marketplace.

There is a burgeoning literature on yoga and meditation, as well as CDs, DVDs and online instructions. This commercialization has perhaps reached its peak (or perhaps plummeted to its depths) with the sale of meditation machines that promise the purchaser they can achieve a state of deep meditation more easily and simply by listening to sounds through headphones and looking at pulsating lights while wearing glasses equipped with LEDs.[11] This is not to say that the appropriation of Hindu ideas by Western seekers is always, or inevitably, commercialized and divorced from a metaphysical worldview and the quest for liberation.[12]

Finally, of course, many Westerners are drawn to Hindu *gurus* like Mata Amritanandamayi Ma, Sathya Sai Baba and Sri Sri Ravi Shankar. There are always a small number of Western devotees who stay for varying lengths of time at places such as Sivananda Ashram. While Hinduism is not a proselytizing tradition, it will, for a variety of complex reasons, have an allure beyond those who are Indian. This not only manifests in the appeal of yoga, meditation and various *gurus*, but also in the fact that terms such as *karma* and *guru* have been incorporated into the English language, and most people have some understanding of what they mean. Hinduism, albeit a contested term, is truly a global tradition that will continue to impact upon the world in diverse ways. Perhaps the most telling illustration of the globalization of Hinduism is that during the festival of Kṛṣṇa's birthday (*Janmāṣṭamī*) in 2008, in the Kṛṣṇa temple just outside Rishikesh, a Western monk from ISKCON gave a discourse to the jubilant crowd celebrating the event.

It is clear that Hinduism retains a relevance for both Indians and non-Indians. It looks set to continue as a rich, vibrant, colourful and diverse tradition. Writing in 1985, the renowned historian Romila Thapar identified what she calls a syndicated Hinduism, which is largely Brahminical, and primarily makes reference to the *Bhagavad Gītā* and *Vedānta* philosophy. This syndicated form of Hinduism, Thapar warns, is a juggernaut with the potential to crush the rich diversity of Hinduism. Almost twenty-five years later, I am not convinced that her fears have been realized. Hinduism has a vast reservoir of symbolic resources, which includes a variety of philosophical ideas, an extensive body of texts, an array of ritual practices, and an abundant iconography. These are not, and are unlikely to become, a homogeneous entity. Hindus will continue to draw upon these symbolic resources: selecting, transforming and reinterpreting them in different ways that provide renewed relevance to the particular contexts of time and place.

Notes

Chapter 1

1 The convention used throughout this book will be BCE (Before the Common Era), and CE (the Common Era). These are the preferred terms for what in the past have been identified as BC (Before Christ) and AD (Anno Domini).

2 Mohenjo-Daro and Harappa are not the original names of these settlements. What these settlements were originally called is now lost.

3 There is some debate about Rammohun Roy's actual date of birth, and some suggest that he was born in 1774.

4 Other important figures include: Dayānanda Saraswati (1824–83), who founded the Arya Samaj; Keshub Chunder Sen (1838–84), who became the leader of the Brahmo Samaj; the famous Bengali poet Rabrindranath Tagore (1861–1941); Mohandās Karamchand (Mahatma) Gandhi (1869–1948); Aurobindo Ghose (1872–1950); Sri Ramana Maharishi (1879–1950); Paramhansa Yogananda (1893–1952); and Swami Sivananda (1887–1963).

5 For a completed version of this chart see Killingley, 2008, p. 942.

6 There are six orthodox schools of Hindu philosophy (*darśanas*). They are referred to as orthodox, as their philosophical speculation is based on ideas found in the Vedas. Buddhism and Jainism are regarded as unorthodox, as their ideas do not refer to the Vedas. The six *darśanas* are: *Vaiśeṣika*, *Nyāya*, *Yoga*, *Sāṃkhya*, *Mīmāmsā* and *Vedānta* (see Flood, 1996 and Hamilton, 2001).

7 The other important schools of *Vedānta* are the dualistic school (*Dvaita*) and the qualified non-dualistic school (*Viśiṣṭādvaita*).

8 Śankara is also referred to as Śankarācārya. *Ācārya* is an honorific,

more or less meaning 'enlightened teacher'. Śankara founded four monastic centres at the cardinal points of the subcontinent. The head of these institutions has the title Śankarācārya, and consequently the historic Śankara is also referred to as Adi Śankarācārya – 'The First Śankarācārya'.

9 The term *māyā* is sometimes translated as 'illusion', but the term misperception better captures the connotations of this metaphysical concept.

10 See Gokhale, 2001, pp. 3–5, for an evocation of 108 names of Śiva.

11 See Daniélou, 1991, pp. 214–21, for details on the symbolic significance of these various aspects of Śiva's iconography.

12 Sometimes simply referred to as the Hare Krishnas.

Chapter 2

1 The term *cār dhām* is often used in relation to the four pilgrimage places at the cardinal points of the subcontinent: Badrinath in the north; Puri in the east; Rameswaram in the south; and Dwarka in the west. It can also be used in relation to four special sites of sacredness in a more localized setting – see Grodzin Gold, 1988, p. 34.

2 Mahatma literally means 'Great Soul'. This was an epithet applied to Gandhi, but it is a term used to describe anyone intensively involved in religious practices.

3 The term derives from the root *tṛ*, which is the same root for the term *avatār*.

4 See also Shinde's (2007) study of religious tourism in Vrindavan.

5 Hinduism utilizes a lunar calendar.

6 See Anne Grodzin Gold, 1988, especially chapter 5 where she describes her experience of accompanying a *darśan* tour with some Rajasthani pilgrims.

7 The thirteenth day after death is the most commonly accepted point for the performance of *śrāddha*; however, some Hindu traditions suggest the twelfth day, and for *swāmis* a different post-funerary rite is generally performed on the sixteenth day after death.

8 Note that *kāma* must not be confused with *karma*; these are two very different concepts.

9 It is very difficult to obtain reliable figures for the number of Divine Life Society branches. One informant suggested there are now 500 branches.

10 This derives from Swami Vivekananda's division of yoga into four main branches: *karma yoga*, the yoga of selfless action; *bhakti yoga*, the yoga of devotion; *raja yoga*, which is derived from classical yoga outlined by Patañjali; and *jñāna yoga*, the yoga of knowledge.

11 This is associated with the myth of the Churning of the Ocean, as, when Śiva swallows the poison, it is said that he became overheated.

12 Those who participate in the *abhiṣekam* receive a much more substantial *prasād* – including a box of sweets, some fruit and some flowers.

13 The terms *havan*, *homa* and *yajña* are often used interchangeably, although technically *homa* and *havan* are types of *yajña*.

14 Patañjali was responsible for systematizing yoga, in the seminal work known as *The Yoga Sūtras*, which was probably composed between the third and fifth centuries CE.

Chapter 3

1 The *āśrama* system suggests there are four stages of life: the stage of the celibate student (*brahmacarya*); the householder stage (*gṛhastha*); the stage of the forest dweller (*vānaprastha*); and finally the stage of renunciation (*sannyāsa*).

2 These are the groups that in popular parlance are referred to as Untouchables.

3 Scheduled Tribes are groups that are determined to be tribal. These groups live in particular designated areas. The classification of particular groups as scheduled is determined by parliament. These groups are sometimes referred to as *Ādivāsīs* – literally 'original or old inhabitant'.

4 OBCs consists of *jātis* who cannot be classified as either Scheduled Castes or Scheduled Tribes but who are still regarded as socially and economically deprived.

5 The term *Sant* derives from the Sankrit *sat*, meaning truth. The implication is that a *Sant* is one who has understood the truth, and as Schomer (in Schomer and McLeod, 1987, p. 3) warns us it is both conceptually and etymologically distinct from the English word saint.

6 Lalu Yadav had to resign as the Chief Minister of Bihar in 1997 because of an accusation that he had been involved in a massive

fraud that was known as the 'Fodder Scam'. This involved embezzling from the state government vast sums for fictitious herds of cattle.

7 The term *sati* refers to both the act itself and the woman who performs the act.

8 See Weinberger-Thomas, 1999 and Hawley, 1994. For more journalistic accounts of *sati* see Sen, 2002 and the chapter entitled 'The Deorala Sati' in Tully (1992).

9 A quick search of the Internet revealed reports of only three suspected cases of *sati* since that of Roop Kanwar.

10 *Tantra* is a vast and complex phenomenon, which can be found in Jainism, Buddhism and Hinduism. The tantric tradition is so called after a body of texts that are often referred to as the *Tantras*. There are *Śaiva*, *Vaiṣṇava* and *Śākta Tantras*. While the *Tantras* are very diverse, they are primarily concerned with religious practice (*sādhana*), which normally entails some form of initiation and the performance of ritual; see Flood, 1996, pp. 158–60, and Feuerstein, 1998.

11 *Pardā* is a practice frequently associated with higher castes. In the process of Sanskritization, low-status *jātis* who have achieved a degree of financial success and are attempting to articulate a higher status sometimes adopt the institution of *pardā*.

12 Hindu nationalists' preferred term for India.

13 A group of historians from the Jawaharlal Nehru University in Delhi specifically refute the claim that there is any historical or archaeological evidence to support this claim; see Gopal and Thapar (1989).

Chapter 4

1 See Eleanor Nesbitt (1999) for a fascinating account of how young British Hindus perceived Morari Babu's *katha* in Coventry in 1993.

2 See, for example, Paula Richman's (2001) account of a *Rāmlīla* in Southall, London.

3 Agarwal and other renowned singers of *bhajans* do, of course, also perform in temples and ashrams.

4 See http://www.youtube.com/watch?v=urdadPmpl6U&feature=related.

5 Personal correspondence with the author.

6 Inglis, 1995, p. 66, indicates that the larger companies produce in the region of ten million images a year, and popular images can have a print run in the region of 100,000.
7 See http://jaisantoshimaa.com.
8 Sai Baba of Shirdi must not be confused with the popular transnational *guru* Sathya Sai Baba.
9 Http://www.hindunet.org/.
10 The *Guru* is God Himself: http://sivanandaonline.org/html/dls/multimedia/sivanandavideo.shtm.
11 See http://www.geocities.com/kaalighat.
12 This is one of the most popular *mantras*. It is an invocation to the sun, and it is most commonly recited at dawn. It is also imparted to twice-born boys when they are initiated with the sacred thread.
13 The New Age is notoriously problematic to define. It is a generic term that is applied to a range of different groups who tend to:

a. be disillusioned with institutional forms of religiousness;
b. place an emphasis on personal experience; and
c. be eclectic in nature, often appropriating ideas and concepts from other religions, and in particular Indian traditions.

(See Chryssides, 1999, pp. 315ff.)

14 Not to be confused with Ravi Shankar, the famous sitar player.

Chapter 5

1 The Adherents.com website suggests a figure of 900,000,000 Hindus worldwide and the Indian Census of 2001 indicates 827,578,880 Hindus in India.
2 Http://www.hinducounciluk.org.
3 Paramahansa Yogananda is most famous for his book *Autobiography of a Yogi*. In 1925 he founded a group called the Self Realization Fellowship, which has its headquarters in Los Angeles.
4 In October 2008 the Hindu Council UK wrote to Newcastle City Council asserting that, in general, crematoria failed to take into account Hindu beliefs and practices about death. They suggested a compromise, which seems to suggest the possibility of having a small fire lit inside the coffin prior to the actual cremation. The full letter can be found at <http://www.hinducounciluk.org/newsite/

articledet.asp?rec=235>. In May 2009 the British High Court refused an appeal by a Hindu to be allowed an open funeral pyre.

5 See the official temple website: http://www.mandir.org.

6 Guru Nanak and Guru Gobind Singh are regarded as the first and last of the human *gurus* of Sikhism.

7 For an excellent account of Ek Niwas and an account of how this blurring of boundaries created controversy, see Geaves, 2007.

8 See, for example, http://www.jeevansathi.com/matrimonials/uk-matrimonial/.

9 It is very difficult to obtain numbers of Valmikis in the UK. Eleanor Nesbitt, 1994, suggests that there are around 1,000 Valmikis in the Coventry area.

10 This is a French term that is used by the anthropologist Claude Lévi-Strauss. *Bricolage* refers to 'the creation of symbolic structure from a variety of culturally available symbols' (Bowie, 2000, p. 79).

11 In Punjabi the equivalent term is *zat*.

12 The term Indians is used, as the survey included both Hindu and Sikh organizations, as well as Ambhedkarites (Buddhist) and Ravidasis etc.

13 Lohanas are traditionally regarded as being *kṣatriya*.

14 See Chryssides, 1999, pp. 167–78, for a good overview.

15 Malory Nye, 2001, p. 25, indicates that there were 9,000 visitors to Diwali in 1974. ISKCON reckons that in 2008 this had increased to over 15,000 celebrants.

16 Gauḍiya Vaiṣṇavism is a devotional movement that can be traced back to the sixteenth-century mystic Caitanya, who is himself now regarded as a manifestation of Kṛṣṇa.

17 The dispute was centred on the fact that Bhaktivedanta Manor had permission to be a theological college, but not a place of worship. See Nye, 2001, especially chapters 3 and 4, for a detailed account.

18 See http://www.venkateswara.org.uk.

Chapter 6

1 This differs from Eric Hobsbawm's notion of an invented tradition, in which he suggests that insofar as there is such reference to a historic past, the peculiarity of 'invented' traditions is that the continuity with it is largely factitious (Hobsbawm and Ranger, 1992, p. 2).

2 The verse cited by Swami Venkatesananda – 'Truth is one, sages express it in different ways' – is a free translation from the *Ṛg Veda* 1:64:46.

3 My thanks to Ron Geaves for this information, given in a personal conversation about his ethnographic work. Also see Geaves' 2007 publication *Saivism in the Diaspora*.

4 The temple intends to dedicate each of these mounds to a different religious tradition. Currently, a large carving of Buddha stands on one. In November 2008, Rowan Williams, the current Archbishop of Canterbury, dedicated another mound to friendship between Christian and Hindu communities.

5 See Ronald Inden, 1992, for a critique of metaphors used to describe Indian culture.

6 The census does not collect information about castes other than SCs and STs. The Mandal Commission report in 1980 suggests that 52 per cent of the population could be classified as OBCs.

7 The BSP has 21 seats in the Lok Sabha (the lower elected house of the Indian Government). All but one of their members represent constituencies in Uttar Pradesh.

8 While there is considerable debate about what constitutes the middle classes in India, I am using the term simply to indicate a sufficient income to enable an individual to make certain lifestyle choices, particularly in regard to the burgeoning consumer culture. Members of the middle classes also tend to have an undergraduate degree.

9 The Mahars are the *jāti* to which Ambedkar belonged, many of whom followed Ambedkar in converting to Buddhism.

10 In the current Lok Sabha (People's House), which is not dissimilar to the House of Commons, India National Congress has 206 MPs, the BJP has 116 MPs and the Samajwadi Party has 22 MPs. There are 552 seats in the Lok Sabha, and there are 38 different political parties with MPs.

11 See http://www.meditations-uk.com/index.html.

12 I have personally met many very serious Western spiritual practitioners (*sādhakas*) who have dedicated their lives to their spiritual practice (*sādhana*), some of whom have also taken *sannyāsa*. Also see Khandelwal, 2007.

Glossary

Abhiṣeka	The ritual anointing of an image (*mūrti*).
Ācārya	A teacher, someone who is versed in the *śāstras*. *Ācārya* is sometimes added as a suffix in titles. For example, there are four centres associated with *Advaita Vedānta*, and the head of each centre is referred to as the Śankarācarya.
Ādivāsī	Literally 'first inhabitant' – this is a generic term that applies to a wide variety of tribal groups. More officially these are referred to as Scheduled Tribes.
Āratī	The waving of an oil lamp or burning camphor before an image of the deity. This is a shortened form of *pūjā*, and is often performed at dawn and dusk.
Āśram	Often anglicized as ashram, an *āśram* normally refers to a place to undertake spiritual practice. See *sādhana*. The term is also used to indicate the four stages of life: the celibate student (*brahmacarya*), the householder (*gṛastha*), the forest dweller (*vānaprastha*) and the renunciate (*sannyāsa*).
Asura	Demon. Traditionally the enemies of the *devas, asuras* represent *adharma*.
Ātman	The true Self. The substratum of the individual, which according to *Advaita Vedānta* is identical to the substratum of all existence (*Brahman*).
Avatār	Literally 'to cross down'. This term refers to divine descents and is most commonly associated with the ten *avatārs* of Viṣṇu. It is often suggested that Viṣṇu descends to earth to restore *dharma*.

Bhajan Devotional song.

Bhakta A devotee: someone whose primary religious orientation is loving devotion.

Bhakti Loving devotion to God. There are two main forms – devotion to the sacred with form/attributes (*saguna bhakti*) and devotion to the sacred without form/attributes (*nirguṇa bhakti*). *Bhakti Yoga* is one of the three traditional paths (*mārgas*) to liberation (*mokṣa*).

Brahmā The creator deity. NOT to be confused with Brahman. In *Purāṇic* cosmology, the cyclical manifestation and dissolution of the universe is described in terms of days and nights of Brahmā. Iconographically, Brahmā is most often depicted as seated in a lotus that emerges from the navel of the reclining Viṣṇu.

Brahmacarya The first stage of life (*āśrama*), that of the celibate student. The term is now often used to identify anyone who leads a celibate life, and/or a novice monk. *Brahmacaryas* tend to wear either white or yellow clothing, rather than the saffron of the *sannyāsin*.

Brahman The impersonal Absolute. *Brahman* is considered as being beyond qualities, and is the all-pervading invisible and uncreated essence of the universe, without beginning or end.

Brāhmin A member of the priest caste (see *varṇa*).

Cakra Literally 'wheel', this refers to the spiritual centres located in the subtle body. In most yogic schools it is commonly accepted that there are seven of these centres. See *Kuṇḍalinī.*

Dalit Literally 'oppressed one'. The preferred self-designation used by many untouchable groups and individuals. The official term for these groups is Scheduled Castes.

Darśan Literally 'sight', '*darśan* refers to the belief that the devotee not only sees the sacred in the form of an image (*mūrti*) or *guru*, but is also within the sacred vision of the deity. The term *darśana* is also used to refer to the six orthodox schools of Hindu philosophy. These are the schools of thought that base their speculations on the Vedas.

Deva — Literally 'shining', this term is generally used to refer to the deities of the Vedic pantheon, but is also used as generic term for any deity. *Devas* are often associated with *dharma* (see *asura*). *Iṣṭa devatā* refers to the concept that Hindus choose a particular deity as the main focus for their devotional practice.

Devi — The goddess.

Dharma — A universal norm or law that is applicable to all aspects of existence; cosmic and individual, social and moral. *Dharma* has a wide range of meanings including: truth, duty, law, religion etc. *Dharma* is often associated with the duty determined by caste. *Sanātana Dharma*, 'the eternal truth', is often the preferred term used by many Hindus to refer to their religious tradition.

Dvija — Twice born. This refers to the three highest castes and indicates that the boys of these castes undergo a rite of initiation at about the age of 11. See *varṇa*.

Ghāt — Step. This term is used primarily to refer to the steps made at pilgrimage places alongside rivers, especially Gangā, to allow pilgrims easy access to take a ritual bath.

Guru — A spiritual preceptor. Many *gurus* are often referred to as *Sat Guru*, or 'True *Guru*', suggesting that they are liberated from the wheel of transmigration.

Hindutva — 'Hinduness'. The core of Hindu nationalist ideology, which suggests that a Hindu is anyone who believes that India is both homeland and holy land. This is the ideology of groups such as the Rashtriya Swayamsevak Sangh (RSS).

Japa — Repetition of a *mantra* for meditational or ritual purposes.

Jāti — An endogamous group, originally determined by occupation and locality. Sometimes translated as caste.

Jñāna — Knowledge. In *Advaita Vedānta* this refers to the knowedge that the Self (*ātman*) is identical with the Absolute (*Brahman*). *Jñāna yoga* is considered as one of the three paths (*mārgas*) to liberation (*mokṣa*).

Karma — The concept of *karma* originally indicated ritual activity, but now signifies any action. The law of cause and effect states that one's present life is determined by *karma* accumulated in previous lives, and action in this life will determine future rebirth. *Karma* is the driving force of *saṃsāra*. *Karma yoga*, or renouncing the fruits of one's actions, is one of the three traditional *mārgas* or paths to liberation (*mokṣa*).

Kathā — Recitation, most often recitation of the *Rāmāyaṇa* (*Rāmkathā*). Listening to the recitation is regarded as a devotional practice.

Kīrtan — A form of devotional practice that normally involves congregational singing and chanting.

Kumkum — A red powder made from turmeric, which is used to place an auspicious mark between the eyebrows of devotees at the end of ritual performances such as *āratī*.

Kuṇḍalinī — Yogic power, which is often represented in the form of a coiled snake that resides in the lowest centre of spiritual energy (*cakra*).

Līlā — Literally 'play' or 'sport', this denotes the idea that creation is like a game that has no purpose beyond itself. The concept of joyful creation is often described in terms of a child who builds a sandcastle and then knocks it down. The term *līlā* is also often used in describing many of the mischievous acts that are detailed in narratives of the young Kṛṣṇa, especially his sport with the milkmaids (*gopīs*). It is also the term used for dramatic performances of sacred narratives – for example *Rāmlīlā* is the acting out of the *Rāmāyaṇa* as a devotional practice.

Liṅga — Literally 'form'. This is the aniconic representation of Śiva. It is a smooth rounded column, normally made from stone, which sits on a plinth called a *yoni*.

Mahāvākya — The great sayings found in the *Upaniṣads*, which encapsulate Vedānta. There are generally accepted to be four: (1) *Tat tvam asi* – 'Thou art that', found in the *Chāndogya Upaniṣad;* (2) *Aham brahmāsi* –

'I am the Absolute', found in the *Bṛhadāraṇyaka Upaniṣad;* (3) *Ayam ātmā brahma* – 'this self is the Absolute', found in the *Māṇḍukya Upaniṣad;* (4) *Prajñānam brahman* – 'Brahman is supreme knowledge', found in the *Aitareya Upaniṣad.*

Mālā — A rosary of beads used for keeping count of the number of repetitions of a *mantra*. These most commonly have 108 beads.

Mandir — Literally 'dwelling', the term means a place where the sacred abides. In other words, a temple.

Mantra — A word or short phrase, often derived from the Vedas, which is repeated, and which is believed to have a special power. *Mantras* can be used in both ritual activity and in meditation. Many of the popular *mantras*, used in meditation and ritual, are associated with a particular deity and are not derived from the Vedas. For example the six-syllable Śiva *mantra*: '*Om Namah Śivayā*'.

Māyā — The misperception of the non-dual Reality (*Brahman*) as the phenomenal world of multiple and transient phenomena. The analogy often used is that just as we might misperceive a rope to be a snake, we misperceive *Brahman* and believe that the phenomenal world of names and forms has a real existence.

Mokṣa — Liberation from the wheel of transmigration (*saṃsāra*).

Mūrti — An image of the deity. Usually used to refer to an image that has been ritually installed in a temple.

Other Backward Classes — The official designation for economic and socially deprived groups who are not classified as Untouchables (Scheduled Castes) or tribal (*Ādivāsī*).

Paramparā — A *guru* lineage.

Pranām — A bow of respect, normally made with the palms of the hands held together in front of the chest. This is often a gesture used by Hindus before an image of a deity (*mūrti*).

Prasād — Literally 'grace'. This primarily refers to sweets and food that have been offered to the image of the deity (*mūrti*), and are then distributed to devotees at the end of *pūjā*.

Pūjā	The core ritual of devotional Hinduism. This involves the sequenced offering of various offerings, such as incense and flowers, to an image (*mūrti*) of the deity.
Purāṇas	'Ancient Tales'. A collection of texts that contain many of the narratives of the deities such as Śiva and Viṣṇu.
Puṣṭi Mārga	'Path of Grace', an important *sampradāya* that focuses on devotion to Kṛṣṇa. This sect is very popular in western India, and in particular the states of Gujarat and Rajasthan.
Ṛṣi	A sage. This term is primarily used to refer to the seers to whom the Vedas were revealed.
Sādhana	Spiritual practice. Any activity that is intended to help the aspirant on the path to liberation (*mokṣa*).
Sādhu	An ascetic, normally one who adopts a wandering, as opposed to a monastic, lifestyle (see *swāmi*).
Śaivism	A generic term for devotional movements focused on Śiva. See *Śākta* and *Vaiṣṇavism*.
Śākta (*Śāktism*)	A generic term for goddess worship – one of the three main strands of Hindu devotionalism. See *Śaivism* and *Vaiṣṇavism*.
Śakti	The power associated with goddesses and women. The female animating principle of creation.
Samādhi	The deepest meditational state in which all distinctions such as that between the meditator and the object of meditation cease to exist. *Mahā samādhi* is the state of existence that liberated souls enter after they have left the physical body.
Sampradāya	Tradition. This refers to sectarian divisions within the Hindu communities, with distinctive forms of teachings that have been handed down from a founding *guru*.
Saṃsāra	The wheel of transmigration – birth, life, death and rebirth. Phenomenal existence.
Sannyāsin	Someone who has renounced the world and actively seeks liberation. The fourth stage (*āśrama*) of life.
Sangh Parivar	The Family of the Association. A generic name for all the various affiliates of the Hindu nationalist group the Rashtriya Swayamsevak Sangh (RSS), including the political party the Bharat Janata Party (BJP).

Sant	A generic term used to describe a group of *bhaktas* from the fourteenth century onwards, who are believed to have had direct knowledge of the sacred. The *Sants* were not *sannyāsins*, nor associated with any particular *sampradāya*. They were mostly from the lower strata of society, and extremely critical of the Brahminical tradition. The poetry of the *Sants* has become very popular.
Śāstra	A generic term for sacred texts, usually used in a restricted sense to refer to texts composed in Sanskrit.
Satsang	'Good company'. A *satsang* refers to being in the company of an enlightened *guru* and/or the company of other devotees. The term is now used widely for congregational gatherings on modern ashrams that normally involve *kīrtan* and a discourse.
Seva	Selfless service. The idea that an action should be performed for its own sake, and not for the sake of reward. The concept has been extended to mean any charitable activity.
Smṛti	Literally 'that which is remembered'. This is used as a generic term to refer to texts which are regarded as elucidations of the primary revealed texts (*śruti*), and are of human, rather than divine, origin.
Śruti	Literally 'that which is heard'. This generally is the term used to refer to the Vedas, and indicates that these texts are eternal, and were revealed to the ancient *ṛṣis* (see *smṛti*).
Swāmi	A renunciate and a term of respect for those who have dedicated their lives to the pursuit of liberation (*mokṣa*). Normally used to refer to those who lead a monastic rather than a wandering lifestyle (see *sādhu*).
Swaminarayan	A Hindu reformer and founder of an eponymous *sampradāya* that is particularly popular amongst Gujuratis.
Tantra	A collection of texts and a variety of traditions that base their spiritual practices on these texts. There are *Śaiva*, *Vaiṣṇava* and *Śākta Tantras*.
Tapas	Ascetic practices.
Tīlak	A sacred mark made between the eyebrows. This can be simply a spot of *kumkum* given to devotees at

the end of a ritual, or elaborate sectarian designs adopted by some *sādhus*.

Tīrtha — Literally 'to cross over', the term implies a ford. It is the term used to indicate a place of pilgrimage: a place where it is particularly easy to cross from mundane to sacred space. *Tīrthayātrā* denotes a journey to a sacred place, a pilgrimage.

Upaniṣad — The final part of the Vedic corpus. The term literally means 'to sit near', suggesting that the *Upaniṣads* were originally considered to be esoteric knowledge. Much of the material in the *Upaniṣads* is concerned with philosophical speculation. See *Vedānta*.

Vaiṣṇavism — A generic term for devotional movements focused on various forms of the deity Viṣṇu. See *Śākta* and *Śaivism*.

Varṇa — Sometimes translated as caste. The idea that society is divided into four distinct groups: priests (*brāhmins*); rulers/warriors (*kṣatriyas*); traders (*vaiśya*); and servants (*śūdras*).

Veda — The revealed scriptures. There are four Vedas; *Ṛg*, *Sāma*, *Yajur* and *Atharva*. This extensive body of compositions is often regarded as the foundational texts of Hinduism.

Vedānta — Literally 'the end of the Vedas'. This refers to the *Upaniṣads*, which are not only the last part of the Vedas but are also regarded as the culmination of all preceding thought. One of the six orthodox schools of Hindu philosophy (*darśanas*), whose speculation is based on the ideas found in the *Upaniṣads*. *Advaita Vedānta* refers to the monistic school of philosophy whose main exponent was Śankara (8th–9th century CE).

Vrat — A vow. This is most commonly associated with women's religious practice. A *vrat* normally involves some abstinence, like fasting or going without particular types of food for a specified period. The vow is normally undertaken in order to achieve a particular end.

Yajña — The Vedic fire ritual. However the term is still used to refer to contemporary rituals that are focused on a fire, rather than an image (*mūrti*).

Yoga Derived from the root *yuj*, 'to yoke'. *Yoga* implies the union of the individual with the sacred. There are a number of different spiritual disciplines that are referred to as yoga. These include *haṭha yoga* (the yoga of force), *bhakti yoga* (the yoga of devotion, *karma yoga* (the yoga of action) and *jñāna yoga* (the yoga of knowledge). Generally, yoga is regarded as the techniques for achieving liberation. One of the six schools of Hindu philosophy, yoga as a philosophy was systematized by Patañjali in the *Yoga Sūtras* and is sometimes referred to as *Rāja Yoga* (Kingly Yoga) or *Aṣṭanga Yoga* (Eight Limbed Yoga).

Bibliography

ACK Media (n.d.), *Amra Chitra Katha*, < http://www.ack-media.com/> (accessed 28/05/09).

Adherents.com (n.d.), http://www.adherents.com/Na/Na_305.html (accessed 20/06/08).

Alper, Harvey (1991), *Understanding Mantras*, Delhi: Motilal Banarsidass.

Ama Amritapuri (2008), http://www.amritapuri.org/> (accessed 21/12/08).

Ananthanarayanan, N. (1987), *From Man to God-Man: The Inspiring Life Story of Swami Sivananda*, Erode: Ananthanarayanan.

Andersen, Walter and Damle, Shridhar (2005), 'RSS: Ideology, Organisation and Training', in C. Jaffrelot (ed.), *The Sangh Parivar: A Reader*, New Delhi: Oxford University Press.

Art of Living Foundation (2007–8), *Sudarshan Kriya*, http://www.artofliving.org> (accessed 24/06/09).

Babb, Lawrence (1991), *Redemptive Encounters: Three Modern Styles in the Hindu Tradition*, Berkeley: University of California Press.

Bacchetta, Paola (2005), 'Hindu Nationalist Women as Ideologues', in C. Jaffrelot (ed.), *The Sangh Parivar: A Reader*, New Delhi: Oxford University Press.

BAPS Swaminarayan Sanstha (n.d.), *London Mandir*, http://www.swaminarayan.org (accessed 12/11/08).

Ballard, Roger (ed.) (1994), *Desh Pardesh: The South Asian Presence in Britain*, London: Hurst and Company.

Ballard, Roger (1996), 'Panth, Kismet, Dharm te Qaum: Continuity and Change in Four Dimensions of Punjabi Religion', originally published in P. Singh and S. Thadi (eds), *Punjabi Identity in a*

Global Context. Delhi: Oxford University Press, available online at http://www.arts.manchester.ac.uk/casas/papers/pdfpapers/pkdq.pdf>.

Baumann, Martin (2004), 'Becoming a Colour of the Rainbow: The Social Integration of Indian Hindus in Trinidad, Analysed Along a Phase Model of Diaspora', in K. Jacobsen and P. Kumar (eds), *South Asians in the Diaspora: Histories and Religious Traditions*, Leiden: Brill.

Beckerlegge, Gwilym (1996), 'Iconographic Representations of Sri Ramakrishna and Swami Vivekananda', *Journal of Contemporary Religion*, 11 (3), pp. 319–35.

Beckerlegge, Gwilym (2006), *Swami Vivekananda's Legacy of Service: A Study of the Ramakrishna Math and Mission*, New Delhi: Oxford University Press.

Benjamin, Walter (2005), 'The Work of Art in the Age of Mechanical Reproduction', in Raiford Guins and Omayra Cruz (eds), *Popular Culture: A Reader*, London: Sage.

Bharati, Agehananda (1963), 'Pilgrimage in the Indian Tradition', *History of Religions*, Vol. III, pp. 135–67.

Bharati, Agehananda (1970), 'The Hindu Renaissance and Its Apologetic Patterns', *Journal of Asian Studies*, 29, pp. 267–87.

Bharat Mata Mandir (n.d.), http://www.bharatmatamandir.org/html/mandir.html> (accessed 18/05/09).

Bhardwaj, Surinder (1973), *Hindu Places of Pilgrimage in India*, Berkeley: University of California Press.

Biardeau, Madeleine (1994), *Hinduism: The Anthropology of a Civilization*, Delhi: Oxford University Press.

Birmingham Valmiki Sabha (n.d.), 'Bhagvan Valmiki Ji: Our Path Finder', *Monthly Valmiki Community News Letter*, available at http://www.bhagwanvalmiki.com/service.htm> (accessed 6/04/09).

Borbas, Gina (2006), 'No Escape: Caste Discrimination in the UK', *Dalit Solidarity Network UK Report*, available from http://www.dsnuk.org> (accessed 6/04/09).

Bowie, Fiona (2000), *The Anthropology of Religion*, Oxford: Blackwell.

Brockington, John (1997), 'The Bhagavadgītā: Text and Context', in J. Lipner (ed.), *The Fruits of Our Desiring: An Enquiry into the Ethics of the Bhagavadgītā for our Times*, Calgary: Bayeux Arts.

Bryant, Edwin (2004), *Quest for the Origins of Vedic Culture: The Indo-Aryan Migration Debate*, New York: Oxford University Press.

Burghart, Richard (ed.) (1997), *Hinduism in Great Britain*, London: Tavistock.

CasteWatch UK (n.d.), 'Frequently Asked Questions', http://www.castewatchuk.org/faq.htm> (accessed 3/04/09).

Caplan, Anita (1997), 'The Role of Pilgrimage Priests in Perpetuating Spatial Organization within Hinduism', in R. Stoddard and A. Morinis (eds), *Sacred Places: Sacred Spaces: The Geography of Pilgrimage*, Baton Rouge: Geoscience Publications.

Carrette, Jeremy and King, Richard (2005), *Selling Spirituality: The Silent Takeover of Religion*, London: Routledge.

Chakraborty, Chandrima (2007), 'The Hindu Ascetic as Fitness Instructor: Reviving Faith in Yoga', *The International Journal of the History of Sport*, 24 (9), pp. 1172–86.

Chatterji, Bankimcandra (2005), *Ānandamaṭh, or The Sacred Brotherhood*, trans. J. Lipner, Oxford: Oxford University Press.

Chitkara, M. S. (2004), *Rashtriya Swayamsevak Sangh: National Upsurge*, New Delhi, APH Publishing.

Chryssides, George D. (1994), 'Britain's Changing Faiths: Adaptation in a New Environment', in G. Parsons (ed.), *The Growth of Religious Diversity – Volume Two: Issues*, London: Routledge in association with The Open University Press.

Chryssides, George D. (1999), *Exploring New Religions*, London: Cassell.

Clarke, J. J. (1997), *Oriental Enlightenment: The Encounter between Asian and Western Thought*, London: Routledge.

Cohen, Robin (1997), *Global Diasporas: An Introduction*, London: UCL Press.

Coney, Judith (1999), *Sahaja Yoga*, London: Routledge.

Courtright, P. (1994), 'The Iconographies of Sati', in J. Hawley (ed.), *Sati – The Blessing and the Curse: The Burning of Wives in India*, Oxford: Oxford University Press.

Daniélou, Alain (1991), *The Myths and Gods of India*, Rochester: Inner Traditions.

Davis, Richard H. (1991), *Ritual in an Oscillating Universe: Worshipping Śiva in Medieval India*, Princeton, NJ: Princeton University Press.

Davis, Richard H. (1997), *Lives of Indian Images*, Princeton, NJ: Princeton University Press.

Dawson, Lorne and Cowan, Douglas (2004), *Religion Online: Finding Faith on the Internet*, London: Routledge.
De Michelis, Elizabeth (2004), *A History of Modern Yoga*, London: Continuum.
Deadwyler III, William (1996), 'The Devotee and the Deity: Living a Personalistic Theology', in J. Waghorne and N. Cutler (eds), *Gods of Flesh, Gods of Stone: The Embodiment of Divinity in India*, New York: Columbia University Press.
Deliége, Robert (2001), *The Untouchables of India*, Oxford: Berg.
Dhanda, Meena (2009), 'Punjabi *Dalit* Youth: Social Dynamics of Transition in Identity', *Contemporary South Asia*, 7 (1), pp. 47–64.
DLSHQ (2005), 'The Divine Life Society: What it is and How it Works', http://www.dlshq.org/aims.htm#aims> (accessed 22/12/08).
Doniger, Wendy with Brian K. Smith (1991), *The Laws of Manu*, London: Penguin.
Dumont, Louis (1970), *Homo Hierarchicus: The Caste System and Its Implications*, Chicago: University of Chicago Press.
Dwyer, Rachel (1994), 'Caste, Religion and Sect in Gujurat', in R. Ballard (ed.), *Desh Pardesh: The South Asian Presence in Britain*, London: Hurst and Company.
Dwyer, Rachel (2006), *Filming the Gods: Religion and Indian Cinema*, Oxon: Routledge.
Eck, Diana (1983), *Banaras: City of Light*, Princeton, NJ: Princeton University Press.
Eck, Diana (1985), *Darśan: Seeing the Divine Image in India*, Chambersburg: Anima Books.
Eck, Diana (1996), 'The Goddess Ganges in Hindu Sacred Geography', in G. Hawley and D. Wulff (eds), *Devi: Goddesses of India*, Berkeley: University of California Press.
Eck, Diana (2000), 'Negotiating Hindu Identities in America', in H. Coward, J. Hinnels and R. Williams (eds), *The South Asian Religious Diaspora in Britain, Canada, and the United States*, Albany: State University of New York Press.
Eliade, Mircea (1959), *The Sacred and the Profane: The Nature of Religion*, New York: Harcourt, Brace & World.
Eliade, Mircea (1989), *Yoga: Immortality and Freedom*, London, Arkana.
Erndl, Kathleen (2000), 'Is Shakti Empowering for Women̩ Reflections on Feminism and the Hindu Goddess', in A. Hiltebeitel and K.

Erndl (eds), *Is the Goddess a Feminist: The Politics of South Asian Goddesses*, Sheffield: Sheffield Academic Press.
Eisenstein, Elizabeth (1979), *The Printing Press as an Agent of Change*, Cambridge, UK: Cambridge University Press.
Feuerstein, Georg (1998), *Tantra: The Path of Ecstasy*, London: Shambala Press.
Fisher, Michael (2006), *Counterflows to Colonialism*, Hyderabad: Orient Blackswan.
Flood, Gavin (1996), *An Introduction to Hinduism*, Cambridge, UK: Cambridge University Press.
Flood, Gavin (1997), 'The Meaning and Context of the Puruṣārthas', in J. Lipner (ed.), *The Fruits of Our Desiring: An Enquiry into the Ethics of the Bhagavadgītā for our Times*, Calgary: Bayeux Arts.
Flood, Gavin (ed.) (2005), *The Blackwell Companion to Hinduism*, Malden, MA: Blackwell.
Flueckiger, Joyce (2007), 'Wandering from "Hills to Valleys" with the Goddess: Protection and Freedom in the Matamma Tradition of Andhra', in T. Pintchman (ed.), *Women's Lives, Women's Rituals in the Hindu Tradition*, Oxford: Oxford University Press.
Foulston, Lynn (2002), *At the Feet of the Goddess: The Divine Feminine in Local Hindu Religion*, Brighton: Sussex Academic Press.
Frykenberg, Robert (2001), 'The Emergence of Modern 'Hinduism' as a Concept and as an Institution: A Reappraisal with Special Reference to South India', in G. Sontheimer and H. Kulke (eds), *Hinduism Reconsidered*, New Delhi: Manohar, pp. 82–107.
Fuller, C. J. (1992), *The Camphor Flame: Popular Hinduism and Society in India*, Princeton, NJ: Princeton University Press.
Gandhi, M. K. (1982), *An Autobiography: The Story of My Experiments with Truth*, Harmondsworth: Penguin.
Gautier, François (2007), *The Guru of Joy: Sri Sri Ravi Shankar and the Art of Living*, London: Hay House.
Geaves, Ron (2007), *Saivism in the Diaspora: Contemporary Forms of Skanda Worship*, London: Equinox.
Geaves, Ron (2008a), 'Bhakti Movement', in D. Cush, C. Robinson and M.York (eds), *Encyclopedia of Hinduism*, London: Routledge.
Geaves, Ron (2008b), 'Satsang', in D. Cush, C. Robinson and M. York (eds), *Encyclopedia of Hinduism*, London: Routledge.

Gita Press (n.d.), 'Gita Press: An Introduction', http://www.gitapress.org/intro.htm> (accessed 26/05/09).

Gokhale, Namita (2001), *The Book of Shiva*, New Delhi: Penguin Books.

Gold, Ann Grodzins (1988), *Fruitful Journeys: The Ways of Rajasthani Pilgrims*, Berkeley: University of California Press.

Gopal, Sarvepalli and Thapar, Romilla (1989), 'The Political Abuse of History: The Babri Masjid-Ramjanmabhumi Dispute – an Analysis by Twenty-five Historians', in A. G. Noorani (ed.), *The Babri Masjid Question*, Vol. I (2003), Delhi: Tulika Books.

Grewal, Royina (2001), *The Book of Ganesh*, New Delhi: Penguin.

Grimes, John (1996), *A Concise Dictionary of Indian Philosophy: Sanskrit Terms Defined in English*, Albany: State University of New York Press.

Gyanshruti, Sannyasi and Srividyananda, Sannyasi (2006), *Yajna: A Comprehensive Survey*, Bihar: Yoga Publications Trust.

Hacker, Paul (1995), 'Aspects of Neo-Hinduism as Contrasted with Surviving Traditional Hinduism', in Wilhelm Halbfass (ed.), *Philology and Confrontation: Paul Hacker on Traditional and Modern Vedanta*, Albany: State University of New York Press.

Halbfass, Wilhelm (1988), *India and Europe: An Essay in Understanding*, Albany: State University of New York Press.

Halbfass, Wilhelm (1991), *Tradition and Reflection: Explorations in Indian Thought*, Albany: State University of New York Press.

Hallstrom, Lisa (1999), *Mother of Bliss: Ānandamayī Mā*, Oxford: Oxford University Press.

Hamilton, Sue (2001), *Indian Philosophy: A Very Short Introduction*, Oxford: Oxford University Press.

Hancock, Mary (1995), 'The Dilemmas of Domesticity: Possession and Devotional Experience among Urban Smārta Women', in L. Harlan and P. Courtright (eds), *From the Margins of Hindu Marriage: Essays on Gender, Religion and Culture*, New York: Oxford University Press.

Hartsuiker, Dolf (1993), *Sādhus: Holy Men of India*, London: Thames and Hudson.

Hawley, John (ed.) (1994), *Sati: The Blessing and the Curse*, Oxford: Oxford University Press.

Hawley, John (1995), 'The Saints Subdued: Domestic Virtue and National Integration in Amar Chitra Katha', in L. Babb and S. Wadley (eds), *Media and the Transformation of Religion in South Asia*, Philadelphia: University of Pennsylvania Press.

Heelas, Paul, Lash, Scott and Morris, Paul (eds) (1996), *Detraditionalization: Critical Reflections on Authority and Identity*, Oxford: Blackwell.

Hess, Linda and Singh, Shukdev (trans.) (1986), *The Bījak of Kabir*, Delhi: Motilal Banarsidass.

Hobsbawm, Eric and Ranger, Terence (eds) (1992), *The Invention of Tradition*, Cambridge, UK: Cambridge University Press.

Horstmann, Monika (1995), 'Towards a Universal Dharma: Kalyāṇ and the Tracts of the Gītā Press', in V. Dalmia and H. von Stietencron (eds), *Representing Hinduism: The Construction of Religious Traditions and National Identity*, New Delhi: Sage Publications.

Inden, Ronald (1992), *Imagining India*, Oxford: Blackwell.

Inglis, Stephen (1995), 'Suitable for Framing: The Work of a Modern Master', in L. Babb and S. Wadley (eds), *Media and the Transformation of Religion in South Asia*, Philadelphia: University of Pennsylvania Press.

Jackson, Robert (1977), 'Holi in North India and in an English City: Some Adaptations and Anomalies', *New Community*, V, pp. 203–10.

Jackson, Robert and Nesbitt, Eleanor (1993), *Hindu Children in Britain*, Stoke-on-Trent: Trentham Books.

Jacobs, Stephen (1999), 'Hindu Identity, Nationalism and Globalisation', unpublished PhD thesis, University of Wales, Lampeter.

Jacobs, Stephen (2007), 'Virtually Sacred: The Performance of Asynchronous Cyber Rituals in Online Spaces', *The Journal of Computer Mediated Communication*, 12 (3), available at http://jcmc.indiana.edu/vol12/issue3>.

Jacobs, Stephen (2008), 'Ayodhya', in D. Cush, C. Robinson and M. York (eds), *Encyclopedia of Hinduism*, London: Routledge.

Johnson, W. J. (trans.) (1994), *The Bhagavad Gita*, Oxford: Oxford University Press.

Jones, Kenneth (1998), 'Two *Sanātan Dharma* Leaders and Swami Vivekananda: A Comparison', in W. Radice (ed.), *Swami Vivekananda and the Modernization of Hinduism*, Delhi: Oxford University Press.

Joshi, Barbara (ed.) (1986), *Untouchable! Voices of the Dalit Liberation Movement*, London: Zed Books.

Justice, Christopher (1997), *Dying the Good Death: The Pilgrimage to Die in India's Holy City*, Albany: State University of New York Press.

Kaalighat (n.d.), 'Online Puja', http://www.geocities.com/kaalighat/> (accessed 12/06/09).

Kallidai, Ramesh (2008), *Caste in the UK: Report for the Hindu Forum of Britain*, available at http://www.hfb.org.uk/> (accessed 2/04/09).

Kapur, Anuradha (1993), 'Deity to Crusader: The Changing Iconography of Ram', in G. Pandey (ed.), *Hindus and Others: The Question of Identity in India Today*, New Delhi: Viking.

Keemattam, Augusthy (1997), *The Hermits of Rishikesh: A Sociological Study*, New Delhi: Intercultural Publications.

Keer, Dhananjay (1966), *Veer Savarkar*, Bombay: Popular Prakashan.

Khandelwal, Meena (2007), 'Foreign Swamis at Home: Transmigration to the Birthplace of Spirituality', *Identities: Global Studies in Culture and Power*, 14, pp. 313–40.

Khare, R. S. (1984), *The Untouchable as Himself: Ideology, Identity and Pragmatism among the Lucknow Chamars*, Cambridge, UK: Cambridge University Press.

Killingley, Dermot (2005), 'Modernity, Reform and Revival', in G. Flood (ed.), *The Blackwell Companion to Hinduism*, Oxford: Blackwell.

Killingley, Dermot (2008), 'The Vedas', in D. Cush, C. Robinson and M. York (eds), *Encyclopedia of Hinduism*, London: Routledge.

Kinsley, David (1977), *The Sword and the Flute: Dark Visions of the Terrible and the Sublime in Hindu Mythology*, Berkeley: University of California Press.

Kinsley, David (1987), *Hindu Goddesses: Visions of the Divine Feminine in the Hindu Religious Tradition*, Delhi: Motilal Banarsidass.

Kinsley, David (1998), *The Ten Mahāvidyās: Tantric Visions of the Divine Feminine*, Delhi: Motilal Banarsidass.

Kishwar, Madhu (2001), 'Yes to Sita, No to Ram: The Continuing Hold of Sita on Popular Imagination in India', in P. Richman (ed.), *Questioning Ramayanas: A South Asian Tradition*, Berkeley: University of California Press.

Klostermaier, K. (1999), 'Questioning the Aryan Invasion Theory and Revising Ancient Indian History, *ISKCON Communication Journal*, 6 (1).

Knott, Kim (1986), *Hinduism in Leeds: A Study of Religious Practice in the Indian Hindu Community and in Hindu Related Groups*, Leeds: Community Religions Project.

Knott, Kim (1996), 'Hindu Women, Destiny and *Stridharma*', *Religion*, 26, pp. 15–35.

Kramrisch, Stella (1992), *The Presence of Śiva*, Princeton, NJ: Princeton University Press.
Lipner, Julius (1994), *Hindus: Their Religious Beliefs and Practices*, London: Routledge.
Lorenzen, David (1995), *Bhakti Religion in North India*, Albany: State University of New York Press.
Lorenzen, David (2005), 'Who Invented Hinduism', in J. E. Llewellyn (ed.), *Defining Hinduism: A Reader*, London: Equinox.
Lothspeich, Pamela (2009), 'The Mahabharata's Imprint on Contemporary Literature and Film', in K. M. Gokulsing and W. Dissanayake (eds), *Popular Culture in a Globalised India*, London: Routledge.
Luce, Edward (2006), *In Spite of the Gods: The Strange Rise of Modern India*, London: Abacus.
Lutgendorf, Philip (1995), 'All in the (Raghu) Family: A Video Epic in Cultural Context', in L. Babb and S. Wadley (eds), *Media and the Transformation of Religion in South Asia*, Philadelphia: University of Pennsylvania Press.
Lutgendorf, Philip (2002), 'Evolving a Monkey: Hanuman Poster Art and Postcolonial Anxiety', *Contributions to Indian Sociology*, 36 (1–2), pp. 71–112.
Mādhavānanda, Swāmi (trans.) (1978), *Vivekacūdāmani of Śri Śankarācārya*, Delhi: Advaita Ashram.
Mannekar, Purnima (1999), *Screening Culture, Viewing Politics*, Durham: Duke University Press.
Matchett, Freda (2005), 'The Purāṇas', in G. Flood (ed.), *The Blackwell Companion to Hinduism*, Malden, MA: Blackwell Publishing.
McDaniel, June (2007), 'Does Tantric Ritual Empower Women̤ Renunciation and Domesticity among Female Bengali Tantrikas', in T. Pintchman (ed.), *Women's Lives, Women's Rituals in the Hindu Tradition*, Oxford: Oxford University Press.
McGee, Mary (1991), 'Desired Fruits: Motive and Intention in the Votive Rites of Hindu Women', in J. Lesley (ed.), *Roles and Rituals for Hindu Women*, London: Pinter Publishers.
McKean, Lise (1996), 'Bhārat Mātā: Mother India and her Militant Matriots', in J. Hawley and D. Wulff (eds), *Devi: Goddesses of India*, Berkeley: University of California Press.
McCluhan, Marshall (2002), *Understanding Media*, London: Routledge.

Melwani, Lavina (n.d.), 'The Story of Hinduism Today', available at http://www.hinduismtoday.com/about_us.shtml#lavina-story> (accessed 29/05/09).

Michaelson, Maureen (1987), 'Domestic Hinduism in a Gujurati Trading Caste', in Richard Burghart (ed.), *Hinduism in Great Britain*, London: Tavistock.

Michell, George (1988), *The Hindu Temple: An Introduction to Its Meaning and Forms*, Chicago: University of Chicago Press.

Michelutti, Lucia (2004), 'We (Yadavs) are a Caste of Politicians: Caste and Modern Politics in a North Indian Town', *Contributions to Indian Sociology*, 38 (1 & 2), pp. 43–71.

Morinis, Alan (1984), *Pilgrimage in the Hindu Tradition: A Case Study of West Bengal*, Delhi: Oxford University Press.

Narayanan, Vasudha (1996a), 'Arcāvatāra: On Earth as He is in Heaven', in J. Waghorne and N. Cutler (eds), *Gods of Flesh, Gods of Stone: The Embodiment of Divinity in India*, New York: Columbia University Press.

Narayanan, Vasudha (1996b), 'Śri', in J. Hawley and D. Wulff (eds), *Devi: Goddesses of India*, Berkeley: University of California Press.

Narayanan, Vasudha (2007), 'Performing Arts, Reforming Rituals: Women and Social Change in South India', in T. Pintchman (ed.), *Women's Lives, Women's Rituals in the Hindu Tradition*, Oxford: Oxford University Press.

Nesbitt, Eleanor (1994), 'Valmikis in Coventry: The Revival and Reconstruction of a Community', in R. Ballard (ed.), *Desh Pardesh: The South Asian Presence in Britain*, London: Hurst and Company.

Nesbitt, Eleanor (1999), 'The Impact of Morari Bapu's *Kathas* on Young British Hindus', *Scottish Journal of Religious Studies*, 20 (2), pp. 177–91.

Nesbitt, Eleanor (2006), 'Locating British Hindus' Sacred Space', *Contemporary South Asia*, 15 (2), pp. 195–208.

Noorani, A.G. (2003), *The Babri Masjid Question: A Matter of National Honour 1528–2003*, Vols 1 and 2, Delhi: Tulika Books.

Nye, Malory (2001), *Multiculturalism and Minority Religions in Britain*, Richmond: Curzon.

Oberoi, Harjot (1997), *The Construction of Religious Boundaries: Culture, Identity and Diversity in the Sikh Tradition*, New Delhi: Oxford University Press.

Obeyesekere, Gananath (1984), *Medusa's Hair: An Essay on Personal Symbols and Religious Experience*, Chicago: University of Chicago Press.

Office of His Holiness Sri Sri Ravi Shankar (2009), 'Official Web Site of His Holiness Sri Sri Ravi Shankar, http://www.srisri.org/~fortune1/biography/timeline (accessed 17/06/09).

Office of the Registrar General and Census Commissioner India (2007), 'Scheduled Castes and Scheduled Tribes Population', http://www.censusindia.net/ (accessed 16/04/09).

Office for National Statistics (2003), 'Census 2001', http://www.statistics.gov.uk/census2001> (accessed 19/03/09).

O' Flaherty, Wendy Doniger (1973), *Śiva: The Erotic Ascetic*, Oxford: Oxford University Press.

O'Flaherty, Wendy Doniger (1980), *Women, Androgynes and Other Mythical Beasts*, Chicago: University of Chicago Press.

O'Flaherty, Wendy Doniger (trans.) (1981), *The Rig Veda: An Anthology*, London: Penguin Books.

Olivelle, Patrick (1993), *The Āśrama System: The History and Hermeneutics of a Religious Institution*, New York: Oxford University Press.

Parry, Jonathan (1994), *Death in Banaras*, Cambridge, UK: Cambridge University Press.

Puri, Naresh (2003), 'The Caste Divide', Radio Four, transcript available from CasteWatch UK, http://www.castewatchuk.org>.

Radhakrishnan, Sarvepalli (1980), *The Hindu View of Life*, London: Unwin Paperbacks.

Raj, Dhooleka (2003), *Where Are You From? Middle Class Migrants in the Modern World*, Berkeley: University of California Press.

Ramanujan, A. K. (1994), 'Three Hundred Rāmāyaṇas: Five Examples and Three Thoughts on Translation', in P. Richman (ed.), *Many Rāmāyaṇas: The Diversity of a Narrative Tradition in South Asia*, Delhi: Oxford University Press.

Ramji, Hasmita (2006), 'British Indians Returning Home: An Exploration of Transnational Belongings', *Sociology*, 40 (4), pp. 645–60.

Roy, Rammohun and Ghose, Jogendra (1978), *The English Works of Rammohun Roy*, New York: AMS Press.

Richards, Glyn (ed.) (1985), *A Sourcebook of Modern Hinduism*, London: Curzon.

Richman, Paula (2001), 'The Ramlila Migrates to Southall', in P. Richman (ed.), *Questioning Ramayanas: A South Asian Tradition*, Berkeley: University of California Press.

Rocher, Ludo (2005), 'The Dharmaśāstras', in G. Flood (ed.), *The Blackwell Companion to Hinduism*, Malden, MA: Blackwell Publishing.

Rojek, Chris (2007), *Brit-myth: Who do the British Think They Are?*, London: Reaktion Books.

RSS (n.d.), 'RSS 2009 Report', available at http://rssonnet.org/index.php> (accessed 18/05/09).

Rudolph, Lloyd and Rudolph, Susanne (1984), *The Modernity of Tradition: Political Development in India*, London: University of Chicago, Midway Reprint.

Sagar Arts (n.d.), 'Sagar Arts: Serials', available at http://www.sagartv.com/Serials.asp?serialid=18> (accessed 6/06/09).

Sahaja Yoga (n.d.), 'About Sahaja Yoga', available at http://www.sahajayoga.org/whatissy/default.asp> (accessed 15/06/09).

Said, Edward (1991), *Orientalism: Western Conceptions of the Orient*, London: Penguin Books.

Sangh Parivar (n.d.), 'Violent Missionaries and Beleaguered Hindus of Orissa', available at http://www.sanghparivar.org/violent-missionaries-and-beleaguered-hindus-of-orissa> (accessed 20/07/09).

Savarkar, V. D. (1942), *Hindutva*, Poona: S. R. Date.

Schaller, Joseph (1995), 'Sankritisation, Caste Uplift and Social Dissidence in the Sant Ravidās Panth', in D. Lorenzen (ed.), *Bhakti Religion in North India*, Albany: State University of New York Press.

Schechner, Richard (1998), 'Crossing the Water: Pilgrimage, Movement, and Environmental Scenography of the Ramlila of Ramnagar', in B. Hertel and C. Humes (eds), *Living Banaras: Hindu Religion in Cultural Context*, New Delhi: Manohar.

Scheifinger, Heinz (2008), 'Hinduism and Cyberspace', *Religion* 38, pp. 233–49.

Schomer, Karine and McLeod, W. H. (eds) (1987), *The Sants: Studies in a Devotional Tradition of India*, Delhi: Motilal Banarsidass.

Sen, Mala (2002), *Death by Fire*, London: Phoenix.

Sharma, Shikha (2008), 'Mantra Magic', in the *Hindu Times Sunday Magazine*, 7 September, p. 25.

Sharpe, Eric (1985), *The Universal Gītā: Western Images of the Bhagavadgītā*, London: Duckworth.
Sherma, Rita DasGupta (2000), 'SA HAM – I am She: Woman as Goddess', in A. Hiltebeital and K. Erndl (eds), *Is The Goddess a Feminist: The Politics of South Asian Goddesses*, Sheffield: Sheffield Academic Press.
Shinde, K. (2007), 'Visiting Sacred Sites in India: Religious Tourism or Pilgrimage?', in R. Raj and N. Morpeth (eds), *Religious Tourism and Pilgrimage Management: An International Perspective*, Wallingford: CABI Publishing, pp. 184–97.
Shree Venkateswara (Balaji) Temple UK (n.d.), 'Balaji Youth Camp', available at http://www.venkateswara.org.uk> (accessed 14/04/09).
Sivananda Ashram (2005), 'The Lord Visvanath Temple', available at http://sivanandaonline.org/html/dls/ashram/viswanath-mandir.shtm> (accessed 30/12/08).
Sivananda, Swami (1984), *Lectures on Yoga and Vedanta*, Shivanandanagar: The Divine Life Society.
Sivananda, Swami (1994), *Japa Yoga: A Comprehensive Treatise on Mantra Sastra*, Shivanandanagar: The Divine Life Society.
Sivananda, Swami (1995), *Autobiography of Swami Sivananda*, Shivanandanagar: The Divine Life Society.
Sivananda, Swami (2007), *All About Hinduism*, Shivanandanagar: The Divine Life Society.
Smith, Brian, K. (2003), 'Hinduism', in J. Neusner (ed.), *God's Rules: The Politics of World Religions*, Georgetown: Georgetown University Press.
Smith, H. Daniel (1995). 'Impact of "God Posters" on Hindus and their Devotional Traditions', in L. Babb and S. Wadley (eds), *Media and the Transformation of Religion in South Asia*, Philadelphia: University of Pennsylvania Press.
Smith, Travis (2008), 'Śiva', in D. Cush, C. Robinson and M. York (eds), *Encyclopedia of Hinduism*, London: Routledge.
Spiro, Melford E. (1982), *Buddhism and Society: A Great Tradition and Its Burmese Vicissitudes*, Berkeley: University of California Press.
Srinivas, M. N. (1972), *Social Change in Modern India*, New Delhi: Orient Longman.
Strauss, Sarah (2005), *Positioning Yoga: Balancing Acts across Cultures*, Oxford: Berg.

Subrat (2008), 'New Ramayana Serial on NDTV Imagine', *Hindu Blog*. http://www.hindu-blog.com/2008/01/new-ramayan-serial-on-ndtv-imagine.html> (accessed 6/06/09).

Thapar, Romila (1985), 'Syndicated Moksha?', *Seminar*, 313, pp. 14–22.

Thapar, Romila (1992), 'The Ramayana Syndrome', *Seminar*, 353, pp. 71–5.

Tully, Mark (1992), *No Full Stops in India*, London: Penguin.

Turner, Victor (1995), *The Ritual Process: Structure and Anti-Structure*, New York: Aldine De Gruyter.

Venkatesananda, Swami (2003), 'One Experience, Many Expressions: The Eternal Religion', available at http://www.dlshq.org/discourse/nov2003.htm> (accessed 17/07/09).

Vertovec, Steven (2000), *The Hindu Diaspora: Comparative Patterns*, London: Routledge.

VHP (n.d.), 'Vishva Hindu Parishad', available at http://www.vhp. org> (accessed 21/05/09).

VHP (1990), *Evidence for the Ram Janmabhoomi Mandir: Presented to the Government of India on 23 December 1990 by the Vishva Hindu Parishad*.

Vivekananda, Swami (1974), *Practical Vedanta*, Calcutta: Advaita Ashram.

Vivekananda, Swami (1978), *Raja Yoga*, Calcutta: Advaita Ashram.

Vivekananda, Swami (1984), *The Complete Works of Swami Vivekananda*, Calcutta: Advaita Ashram.

von Stietencron, Heinrich (2001), 'Hinduism: On the Proper Use of a Deceptive Term', in G. Sontheimer and H. Kulke (eds), *Hinduism Reconsidered*, New Delhi: Manohar.

Wadley, Susan (1995). 'No Longer a Wife: Widows in Rural North India', in L. Harlan and P. Courtright (eds), *From the Margins of Hindu Marriage: Essays on Gender, Religion and Culture*, Oxford: Oxford University Press.

Waghorne, Joanne (2004), *Diaspora of the Gods: Modern Hindu Temples in an Urban Middle Class World*, Oxford: Oxford University Press.

Warrier, Maya (2005), *Hindu Selves in a Modern World: Guru Faith in the Mata Amritanadamayi Mission*, London: Routledge.

Watson, James. L. (ed.) (1977), *Between Two Cultures: Migrants and Minorities in Britain*, Oxford: Blackwell.

Waughray, Annapurna (2009), 'Caste Discrimination: A Twenty-first Century Challenge for UK Discrimination Laws', *Modern Law Review*, 72 (2), pp. 182–219.

Weller, Paul (ed.) (2007), *Religions in the UK: Directory 2007–2010*, Derby: Multifaith Centre.

Weinberger-Thomas, Catherine (1999), *Ashes of Immortality: Widow Burning in India*, London: University of Chicago Press.

Williams, R. (1980), *The Long Revolution*, Harmondsworth: Penguin.

Williams, R. (1988), *Keywords: A Vocabulary of Culture and Society*, London: Fontana Press.

Zavos, John (2008), 'Stamp it Out! Disciplining the Image of Hinduism in a Multicultural Milieu', *Contemporary South Asia*, 16 (3), pp. 323–37.

Zelliot, Eleanor (2001), *From Untouchable to Dalit: Essays on the Ambedkar Movement*, New Delhi: Manohar.

Index